The
World Book
of

Study **P**ower
Activities

2

World Book, Inc.
Chicago London Sydney Toronto

P-C A
W896
1995
v. 2

Staff

Publisher Emeritus
William H. Nault

President
John E. Frere

Editorial

Vice President,
Editor in Chief
Dick Dell

Managing Editor
Maureen Mostyn Liebenson

Associate Editor
Karen Zack Ingebretsen

Editor
Mary Feely

Permissions Editor
Janet T. Peterson

Writer
Juliette Underwood

Art

Executive Director
Roberta Dimmer

Art Director
Wilma Stevens

Senior Designer
Melanie Lawson

Designer
Deirdre Wroblewski

Illustrator
Steven Mach

Product Production

Vice President,
Production and Technology
Daniel N. Bach

Director, Manufacturing/Pre-
Press
Sandra Van den Broucke

Manager, Manufacturing
Carma Fazio

Manufacturing Staff
Assistant
Trisha Ripp

Senior Production Manager
Randi Park

Assistant Production
Manager
Audrey Palese

Proofreaders
Anne Dillon
Daniel J. Marotta

Direct Marketing

Managing Editor
Amy Moses

World Book, Inc.
525 W. Monroe
Chicago, IL 60661

ISBN: 0-7166-3596-8
ISBN: 0-7166-3597-6 (set)
LC: 94-61379

Printed in the United States of America

1 2 3 4 5 6 7 8 9 10 99 98 97 96 95

Contents

Express **Y**ourself

Suppose a reporter from a magazine called *Eye on You* wanted to do a feature story about you. What special things would you want the reporter to know about you? How would you show or tell the reporter those things? How would you describe what's happened in your life—from the day you were born until now?

Preview

Pages 5 to 14 contain ideas that will help you gather and organize information about yourself. Skim these pages. Look at the titles, the pictures, and the kinds of activities they describe. Then choose the projects that sound good to you and get started! If you want to, you can change the projects slightly to suit your special needs and interests.

The House That You Built

YOU NEED
★ Plain paper or graph paper ★ Colored pencils or markers ★ A ruler ★ Scissors
★ A board or piece of cardboard for each level ★ Glue ★ "Building" materials, such as
a cardboard box, toothpicks, scraps of fabric, and dollhouse furniture ★ A tape measure
★ Old magazines (optional)

Imagine a house that would be just right for you. What would it be like? How many rooms would it have? What colors would they be? Would there be special rooms set aside for your hobbies or interests?

This activity will show you how to build your dream house—from the rough floor-plan sketch to the finished 3-D model. You also will learn how you can display your house and share it with others.

Part 1: Gaining Perspective— A "Giant's-Eye" View

Have you ever wondered what a giant would see if he walked through your neighborhood? To get an idea, first imagine that *you* are walking through your neighborhood. As you look around, you probably see a variety of things, such as cars, buildings, trees, and people. Because you are looking at most objects and people straight on— from your own eye level—you can see how tall they are and how they are shaped. (This is called seeing things in 3-D, or three-dimensionally.) If you saw a car in 3-D, for instance, it would look like this:

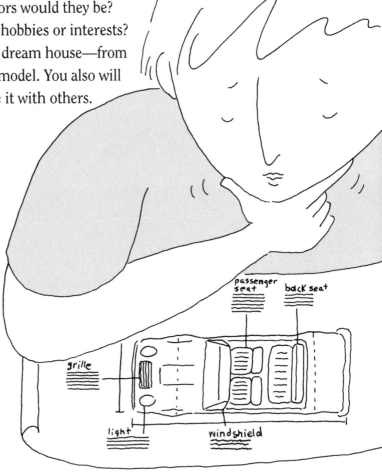

Now imagine that the giant is walking through your neighborhood. He looks straight down at things, so he sees only the tops of them. He might see how some things are shaped, but he can't see how tall they are. To him, things look 2-D, or two-dimensional. So if the giant saw that same car, it would look like the one above.

Now imagine that the giant is looking down at someone's dream house before the roof has been put on. Here's what he might see:

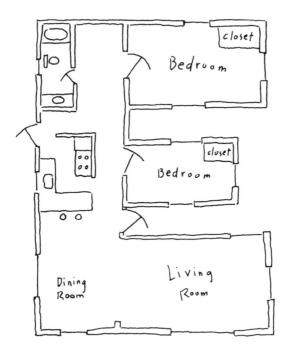

Part 2: Sketching Your Dream House

Before you sketch the floor plan for your house, you need to look at it from a "giant's-eye" view. You also will need to figure out what scale to draw the house in. *Scale* means the size of a drawing compared with the size of an actual thing. The easiest way is to use graph paper. Make each square stand for a certain unit of measurement, such as 1 foot. So if you had a couch in your living room that was 8 feet long and 3 feet wide, you would count 8 squares by 3 squares on the paper and draw as shown below.

Now you can begin sketching. If your dream house has an unusual shape, as Ellen's does, sketch the outline first. Then you can divide the house into rooms and sketch one room at a time. As you add various pieces of furniture, you may find it helpful to take a tape measure and actually measure things in your real house to get an idea of what size they are. Also, if your dream house has several levels, sketch each level on a separate sheet of paper.

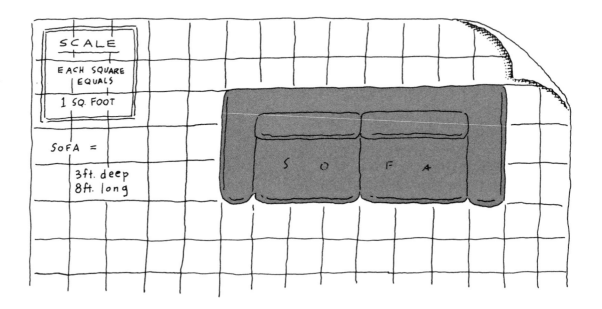

SCALE
EACH SQUARE EQUALS
1 SQ. FOOT

SOFA =
3ft. deep
8ft. long

S O F A

Building Your Dream House in 3-D

Now that you have sketched out your house, you are ready to build it. Begin by finding a space where you can spread out your materials. Pick a spot where they will not be disturbed. Build your house on the board or cardboard. (If it has several levels, use a separate board for each level.)

Build your house out of any materials available. You may want to furnish parts of it with the dollhouse furniture or pictures cut from old magazines.

You can make your house the same size as your scale drawing, or you can enlarge or reduce it. If you want to enlarge it, multiply your scale by 2 to make it twice as big. (The couch that was 8 squares by 3 squares would now be 16 squares by 6 squares.) If you want to reduce the size of your house, divide your scale by 2 to make it half as big. (The couch then would be 4 squares by 1-1/2 squares.)

Just as you drew your floor plans one level at a time, you should build your house one level at a time. Then, when you are all finished, carefully stack the levels on top of each other. (You'll probably want some help with this.)

7

Word Map

YOU NEED
★ Plain writing paper ★ A ruler ★ A pencil or pen

Your dream house tells a lot about you! But there's so much more. Suppose that reporter from *Eye on You* magazine said, "Tell me all about yourself." What would you say? Where would you begin?

You could start by making a word map about yourself. A word map helps you organize things and ideas into different categories, or groups. For example, if you were to make a word map for an object, some of the categories might be "What it looks like," "What it feels like," and "What it is used for."

Think of some categories you'd like to use to tell about yourself and then make a word map. Copy a blank word map like the one on page 9 onto a piece of paper.

If some of your categories are already on the word map shown on page 9, keep them. If they are not on the sample, add or substitute your own categories.

STUDY STRATEGY:

Categorizing

★ When you put things or ideas in a certain order, make sure they are all related in the same way.

★ Sometimes a thing or an idea fits into more than one category. That's fine—you can put it in both places. Here's an example:

Has a tail	Moves on two legs
kangaroo	kangaroo
fish	person

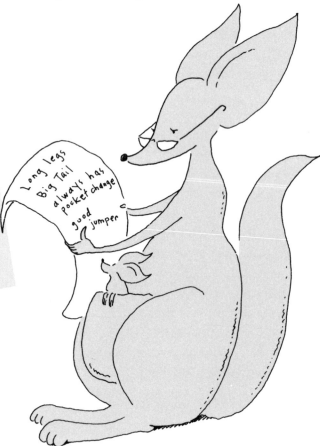

Long legs
Big Tail
always has
pocket change
good jumper

What I Like to Do

What I Look Like

My Favorite Things

Your name goes here

My Favorite Places

You fill in this one

My Favorite People

Your Personal Glossary

YOU NEED
★ Plain or lined paper or note cards ★ Colored pencils, crayons, or markers ★ Scissors
★ Glue ★ Old photographs (optional—get permission to use these.)

Do any of the following words describe you?

intelligent *Charming* **STRONG** Unique
skillful outrageous athletic *witty*

What other words describe you? Think of some that you—or people you know—use to describe you. (Look back at your word map if you need ideas.) Write each word on a separate sheet of paper or note card. After the word, write a brief "glossary" entry that defines or tells the meaning of the word. Draw pictures or add photographs to illustrate some of your entries if you'd like. Then alphabetize your entries and put them together to make your personal glossary. Here are two sample entries to help you get started:

athletic: Christa loves sports and she's good at them. She is an extremely athletic person. She has been swimming for five years. Last year she made it to the Junior Olympics. Besides swimming, Christa likes riding bikes, jogging, and playing soccer.

Dolph: swims as quickly and gracefully as a dolphin (and loves the water as much!), so her friends gave her this nickname.

STUDY STRATEGY:

Alphabetizing

★ Just like dictionary and encyclopedia entries, glossary entries are always listed in alphabetical order.

★ Do you remember what to do if two words begin with the same letter—like the words *strong* and *skillful?* (Look at the second letter in each word. The letter *k* comes before *t,* so *skillful* comes before *strong.)*

★ What letters would you look at to alphabetize *witty* and *wise?* (Look at the third letters, *t* and *s.)*

A Walk Through Your Life

YOU NEED
★ Plain or lined paper ★ A pencil ★ A ruler ★ A tape recorder and cassettes (optional) ★ A video camera and videotape (optional) ★ Cardboard boxes, orange crates, or other household items to use as display cases ★ Things to put into the display cases

Why do people go to museums? Most of us like to look at exhibits of important, rare, or ancient things. Museums help people learn by explaining what things are and how they work.

You can set up a kind of "museum exhibit" that tells all about you and your life. Invite your friends and family to come and walk through it.

Before you begin setting up the exhibit, you may want to sketch it on paper. If you need a little help, the next two pages contain ideas for how you might organize your exhibit.

Begin by deciding what to include in your exhibit. It helps to think about the following:
★ What kinds of things are in museum exhibits?
★ Why were those items and artifacts chosen for display? What is their value and interest?
★ How do people learn about the exhibits that they are viewing?

Set up your exhibit by categories.

You may want to make a word map like the one on page 9 and then set up your exhibit according to your categories. Let's say that two of your categories are "Favorite Things" and "Favorite Places." You could display all your favorite things (or pictures of them) in one display case. You could display pictures or post cards of your favorite places in another case. You may want to include your dream house.

In the cases, you might also want to display such things as drawings, photographs, journals, awards or trophies, your baby shoes, books, letters, or souvenirs.

As part of your exhibit, you might want to set up audiotape or videotape displays. These would work well if your favorite hobbies include things like dancing, singing, or playing hockey. If you can't capture these activities on tape, photograph or draw them—or include a live performance or demonstration in your exhibit.

Set up your exhibit like a three-dimensional time line.

If you don't want to set up your exhibit according to categories, you could set it up *chronologically* (according to time order). Then, as people walk through your exhibit, they would be looking at your life one year at a time—from the year you were born until now. You could use display cases, each representing a different year.

You might want to display some of the projects from pages 5 to 10 in your time-line exhibit. Also consider including live or taped performances or demonstrations.

Your **F**eature **S**tory

YOU NEED
★ Plain or lined writing paper ★ Colored pencils, crayons, or markers ★ Scissors ★ Glue
★ A ruler ★ A camera and film or a video camera (optional—get permission to use these)

The big day has finally arrived! The issue of *Eye on You* containing your feature story has just hit the newsstands. What does the article say? Is it illustrated with pictures of you and your dream house?

Write the article you would like to see in *Eye on You* magazine. Look back at all the work you have done on pages 5 to 13 and decide what to include in the article. Of course, some of the things you created—such as the exhibit or the model of your house—are hard to describe in words. For those things, you may want to use pictures. Get permission to photograph them. Then you can put the photos in the article and write some captions to go with them. (If you can't photograph them, consider drawing them.)

Once you have finished the article, publish it. Make copies for your friends and family. You might want to help other friends or family members write their own articles. Then you could put them all together and make your own magazine. Maybe you could call it . . . *Eye on You!* (And if your idea really takes off, you might even want to turn *Eye on You* into a TV show by videotaping your stories instead of writing them.)

What **D**o **Y**ou **T**hink?

About Yourself
★ What new things did you discover about yourself while you did the activities on the previous pages?
★ Which activity did you like best? Why?
★ Which activity did you like least? Why?
★ If you could add another activity, what would it be? Why?

About Your Work Habits
★ Which activity was easiest for you to do? Why?
★ Which activity stretched you most? Why?
★ If you could change anything about the way you planned or worked on any of the projects, what would you do differently? Why?

Communication

Speaking and writing are two of the most common ways in which people communicate with one another, but there are many other ways. On pages 4 to 15 of this book, you communicated by "expressing yourself" in several ways. You used writing, drawing, building, speaking, and moving to communicate information about yourself.

Preview

On pages 16 to 32, you will explore some of the other ways in which people communicate. The web below shows some of them. Does it include ways of communicating that you already know about? Can you add other ways to the web?

When you have finished looking at the web, skim pages 16 to 32. As you read the titles and look at the pictures, you may want to put a check or a star next to the ideas or activities that look especially interesting to you. Then, you can go back and read those things first.

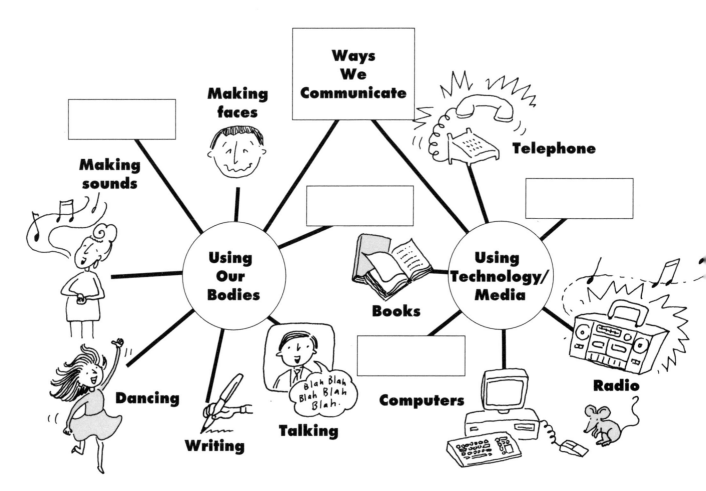

Make a **S**tatement

Have you ever heard the expression, "Make a statement without saying a word"? Well, long before people had languages and alphabets and written words, they communicated, or made statements, without words. Instead, they made sounds or gestures.

Today, many people who are deaf or hard of hearing use gestures—known as sign language—to communicate. One gesture in sign language may stand for a word or whole phrase. Here are the gestures for "I love you," "good night," "tree," and "moon."

I love you

Good Night

Tree

Moon

...**W**ithout...

Sometimes, however, there is no gesture for a particular idea or concept. Then people can use the finger alphabet to spell specific words. Here is what the finger alphabet looks like. Can you use it to finger-spell a message to a friend or family member?

A Fingers down; thumb up.

B Fingers up; thumb down.

C Fingers and thumb bent into a "C."

D First finger up; other fingers down; thumb touches second finger.

STUDY STRATEGY:

Getting Information from Words and Pictures

Sometimes the best way to give or get information is to use a combination of words and pictures. Here's an example: Either orally or in writing, try to define the words *round, big,* and *bumpy.* Is it almost impossible for you not to use your hands to make pictures as you speak or draw pictures to go along with what you write?

Now look at the finger alphabet. How difficult would it be for you to finger-spell if you didn't have the pictures? How difficult would it be if you didn't have the words?

...**S**aying...

E Fingers down; thumb touches fingers.

F First finger and thumb form a circle; last three fingers up and apart.

G Hand closed; first finger and thumb apart and pointing sideways (horizontally).

H Hand closed; first two fingers together and pointing sideways; thumb curls down.

I Little finger up; thumb across other fingers.

J Same as "I," only little finger moves to form a "J."

K First two fingers up (second finger forward); thumb up, touching second finger; other fingers down.

. . . a **W**ord!

L   First finger up; thumb out to form an "L"; last three fingers down.

M   Hand closed; thumb up between last two fingers.

N   Hand closed; thumb up between middle and "ring" fingers.

O   Fingers and thumb bend to form an "O"; thumb touches first finger.

P   First finger points out; second finger points down; thumb touches second finger; other fingers closed.

Q   Thumb and first finger apart and pointing down; other fingers closed.

R   First two fingers crossed; thumb over last two fingers.

S Hand closed in fist; thumb over fingers.

T Hand closed; thumb up between first two fingers.

U First two fingers up and together; thumb touches little finger.

V First two fingers up and apart; thumb touches last two fingers.

W First three fingers up and apart; thumb touches little finger.

X First finger up and bent; thumb across last three fingers.

Y Thumb and little finger up; other fingers down.

Z Last three fingers down; thumb touches middle finger; first finger up and moves to form the letter "Z."

Pictographs

YOU NEED
★ Plain paper ★ Colored pencils, crayons, or markers ★ Audiotape recorder and cassette (optional)

Early people used gestures to make statements without saying words. And sometimes they made pictographs. *Pictographs* are pictures or symbols that stand for people, things, and ideas. When several pictographs are put together, they tell a story.

Through pictographs, early people often told stories about things that had happened in their lives, such as celebrations or storms or hunting trips. They drew pictographs on the walls of caves, on monuments, and in tombs.

To get a sense of how pictographs worked, think of an event or a celebration in your life that you would like to tell about. (If you need an idea, try skimming through a magazine or a newspaper, or listening to the news.) Tell your story in pictographs. Draw as many pictures as you need to communicate your story as clearly as possible to your friends and family.

As in early times, some of your pictographs might stand for things or people.

And some of your pictographs might stand for ideas, such as those below.

When you have finished your pictograph story, share it with others. See if they can tell you what your pictographs say. If you have a tape recorder, record everyone's story.

Don't be surprised if some people can't read your story easily, or if different people give you different versions of it. Sometimes, forms of communication can be unclear or confusing. This is especially true when the form of communication has no words.

When you have finished recording everyone's version of your story, record your own version. Play back the different versions and compare them. See which versions came closest to the story you were trying to communicate, and which versions missed the point completely.

Compare and contrast the different versions. Are there any similarities in the retellings? Which pictographs were clear to the reader most often? Which were clear least often? You may want to consider keeping the pictographs that worked and revising those that didn't communicate well.

Modern **P**ictographs

YOU NEED
★ A pad of paper, or sheets of unlined paper stapled together ★ Colored pencils, crayons, or markers ★ Old magazines, scissors, and glue (optional)

When we think of pictographs, we often think of them as a prehistoric way of communicating. But let's think again. If pictographs are pictures that stand for things, people, and ideas, don't we see lots of modern pictographs all around us? For example, what does each of these pictures communicate to you?

Here's something to try: Have a pad of paper and a pencil handy the next time you watch TV or walk through your neighborhood. Whenever you see a modern pictograph, sketch it. Include signs, flags, and product symbols.

On the back of your paper—or on another sheet—write down what each pictograph stands for. How many pictographs did you collect? Do you know what each one stands for? If you don't, ask a friend or family member to help.

NOTE: If you don't think you can draw some of the pictographs you see, cut them out of old magazines and glue them onto your paper. Just be sure to get permission before you start cutting!

Create an Ad Campaign

YOU NEED

★ Plain paper ★ A pencil ★ An eraser ★ Colored pencils, crayons, or markers ★ A ruler ★ Magazines for brainstorming ★ A tape recorder and an audiotape (optional) ★ A video camera and videotape (optional)

Look again at your modern pictographs. How many are product symbols? Manufacturers hope that consumers (buyers) will notice and remember those symbols as they shop.

What Is a Logo?

As we know, a pictograph is a picture that stands for a person, thing, or idea. Well, a logo is a kind of pictograph. In advertising, logos can stand for products, services, companies, or ideas.

As far back as ancient Greece, artists stamped logos on their works of art to let people know who made them. In advertising today, logos serve a similar purpose. Companies put logos on their products to let consumers know who made them. They also hope that when shoppers see a company's logo, they will immediately think of the product using some of the following words:

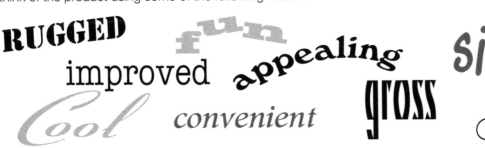

RUGGED fun improved appealing NEW silly gross Cool convenient easy

Before you can begin designing the logo for your advertising campaign, stop and think about what you want to advertise. Use your imagination—will you create a new computer game, athletic shoe, or toy? Will you start your own pet-sitting or lawn-care service? Will you run your own store? Or would you rather start your own comic-book company? Whatever you decide, be sure to keep your product, service, or company firmly in mind as you work on your campaign.

Design Your Own Logo

Look through some magazines and study the logos in their ads. When you have an idea of how logos work, begin sketching some designs of your own. Sketch several designs—you may end up combining the best parts of different ones. As you sketch, ask yourself the following questions:

★ What would be the strongest "identifying symbol" of my product, service, or company?

★ Do I want my logo to be just a picture, or do I want it to have words, too?

★ How will my logo help me create a good first impression?

★ How will my logo help me tell people about myself, my product, or my service?

★ How will my logo help me "stand out from the crowd"?

★ How will my logo help people remember me when they need my product or service again?

Design Your Business Card

Now that you have finished your logo, it's time to design your business card. Of course you'll want to include your logo somewhere on your business card, but you also might like to include a slogan. A slogan is a short sentence or a phrase that advertisers repeat in all of their ads. Many slogans contain buzz words that help people remember particular products, services, or companies.

Take a look at these slogans and see if you can complete them:

"_____ _____. Don't leave home without it."

"_____ paper towels, the quicker picker-upper!"

"At _____ _____ _____, we do chicken right!"

"We're _____ Airlines, doing what we do best."

Janet Jones
Pet-sitter
call 987-6543

STUDY STRATEGY:

Brainstorming

Did you know that brainstorming is a powerful tool? You've probably already brainstormed to come up with a creative solution to a problem or an assignment. When we brainstorm, we allow our thoughts to flow freely. We think and think until ideas that started out being fuzzy and "way out" finally become clear. (Did you ever see the light bulb that turns on over a cartoon character's head when he or she has a good idea? That's the result of some good brainstorming!)

Here are some brainstorming rules to remember:

1. No criticizing allowed! Brainstorming means getting out your ideas quickly and not worrying about how they sound. The time for criticizing and picking out the best ideas is later.

2. There are no bad, dumb, or wrong ideas when you brainstorm. Every idea should be considered. Sometimes the best and most logical solutions come from the wildest ideas!

3. The more ideas, the better, especially when you brainstorm with other people. You'll probably find that the more suggestions you have to choose from, the easier it is to come up with ideas. And that just goes to show that two heads—or three or four or more—really are better than one.

When you're happy with your slogan, you can begin designing your business card. Again, you may want to try several versions until you've got just the design you want. Although most business cards are a standard size (2 inches by 3-1/2 inches), don't be afraid to experiment. As you design your card, here are some things to keep in mind:

★ Business cards are small, so don't make your card too crowded. Include only the most important information, such as your name, phone number, company and product name, and—if you have a store—your business hours.

★ Think again about the first impression you want to make. Your business card, along with your logo and slogan, should be helping you make that impression.

★ People tend to keep business cards and use them when they need a particular product or service. So your business card should not only make a good first impression, but also a lasting one. If someone is looking through a stack of business cards, will yours stand out from the rest?

★ Experiment with different colors as you work on your business card. (Like buzz words, colors often help people make stronger associations with products and services.) For example, you might use a green card or green lettering to advertise a lawn-care service, or neon-colored cards or lettering to advertise a tropical-fish store.

★ If you design an unusually shaped card, be sure that the shape sends a strong message to potential customers. To advertise a tropical-fish store, for example, a card could be shaped like the one on the left.

What products, companies, or services might these cards be advertising?

Compose a Jingle

Think about some of the slogans you see and hear every day. How many are set to music?

Musical slogans, called *jingles,* are just one more way to make sure that a product, service, or company stays in the consumer's mind. Think about it: How many times have you heard a jingle on the radio or TV and then walked around singing it afterward? That's the work of advertisers, doing what they do best!

Now that you've got the slogan for your product, service, or company, why not try setting it to music? You don't have to compose the music yourself. Many of the jingles you hear today are set to the tunes of popular songs written by other people. Some jingles even use the original song *lyrics* (words).

You can compose your jingle in one of two ways. You either can write the words first and then think of a song you'd like to set them to. Or you can choose the song first and write your words to match the melody—unless the words of the original song work for you, of course. If anyone you know plays an instrument, you might consider asking him or her to help you make a tape recording of your jingle.

29

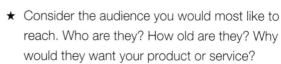

At Pete's Pet Palace, we positively pamper your persian and put your pomeranian on a pedestal.

★ Consider the audience you would most like to reach. Who are they? How old are they? Why would they want your product or service?

★ What is the most important information you want to give your audience about your product or service? (You may want to brainstorm this information on a piece of scrap paper.)

★ What would be the best way to communicate the information to your audience?

★ If you're advertising a product, will you show it? Will you show how to use it? Will you show how much people need or enjoy it?

★ If you're advertising a company or a service, will you talk about the benefits of using that company or service? Will you have others talk about those benefits?

★ Will you flash your logo on the screen? If so, when and how often?

★ Will you play your jingle? If so, when and how often? How loudly or softly?

★ Will you use any buzz words in the commercial? If so, which ones—and why?

★ Will you use gestures or sign language in your commercial? (For example, how could a person show that she really loves her new "Thingamajig"?)

★ How else might you communicate with your audience?

Write and Perform a TV Commercial

Imagine that your new advertising campaign is working, and your business is growing by leaps and bounds! You've decided to advertise it on TV. You've got a 60-second time slot for your commercial. What will you include in that minute to communicate the most complete and important information possible? As you write your commercial, here are some things to think about:

STUDY STRATEGY:

Using a Storyboard Frame

As you write your TV commercial, you will be planning to communicate with your audience in not just one way, but in three ways. You will communicate through actions, pictures, and sound (both words and music). A good way to keep these in mind as you write your commercial is to use a storyboard frame. Below is part of a storyboard frame for a commercial for Aquarium Maintenance Services.

Once you've written your commercial, ask others to help you perform it. Practice several times before your final performance, and try to get the music and sound effects timed just right with the dialogue. (If you recorded your jingle earlier, be sure to use it now.) If you have a video camera, you may want to tape your commercial. Then you can put it together with your logo, your business card, and your jingle and make yourself a "portfolio" of your advertising campaign.

ACTION	PICTURES	SOUND
Scene: Jeff's dining room. Two 10-year-old boys, Jeff and Scott, are doing their homework at Jeff's dining room table. Zoom into a fish tank next to the table.	murky fish tank; fish barely visible; hardly any plants or ornaments in the tank	"Aquarium Maintenance" jingle music plays softly in the background. The music fades out as Scott begins to speak. Scott: What's wrong with your fish tank, Jeff? I can barely see the fish!
Camera sweeps to Jeff and Scott sitting at the table.	View of Jeff and Scott from the shoulders up. Jeff looks sad and a little confused.	Jeff: I know. I wish I knew someone who could help me take care of it. It really needs a lot of work. "Aquarium Maintenance" jingle music begins softly.
Zoom into a close-up of Scott's face.	Close-up of Scott's face. He has an excited expression.	Scott: Hey, I know! The Aquarium Maintenance man! He worked miracles with Mr. Fletcher's tank!

What **D**o **Y**ou **T**hink?

About Yourself

★ Go back to the web on page 16. Can you now add any other kinds of communication to it?

★ What are some of the most important things you learned about communication?

★ How will those things help you be a better communicator?

★ Can you think of three different ways to communicate the words "I love you"?

About This Book

★ Complete these sentences:

1. My favorite activities in this book so far are _____.

2. Three words I would use to describe this book are _____,
_____, and _____.

3. On a scale of 1 to 10 (10 being the highest), I would rate this book a _____.

About Your Work Habits

★ Which completed activity are you most proud of? Why?

★ Which activity stretched you the most? Why?

★ If you could change anything about the way you planned or worked on any of the projects, what would you do differently? Why?

Books, **B**ooks, and **M**ore **B**ooks!

You know many different ways to give information. You probably also know many different ways to get information. One of the best ways is by reading books. There are books on almost every topic in the world—from aardvarks to zeppelins!

Preview

Pages 34 to 47 are full of information on books—where to find them, how to use them, how to read them, how to write them, and how to make them. Preview these pages. If you are working on a project at school, would any of these pages help you complete your project? If so, you may want to read those pages first. Then go back and read the others.

Using the Card Catalog

Suppose you're in the library, working on a report for school. You've just started researching tropical rain forests, and you decide that you want to zero in on the Amazon rain forest in South America. Where can you look for information? You might start with the card catalog. Today many card catalogs are computerized, but some consist of a set of drawers. The card catalog contains a title card, an author card, and a subject card for every book in the library. All the cards are in alphabetical order and are identified with numbers called *call numbers.* Here are the title, author, and subject cards for a book on the Amazon rain forest.

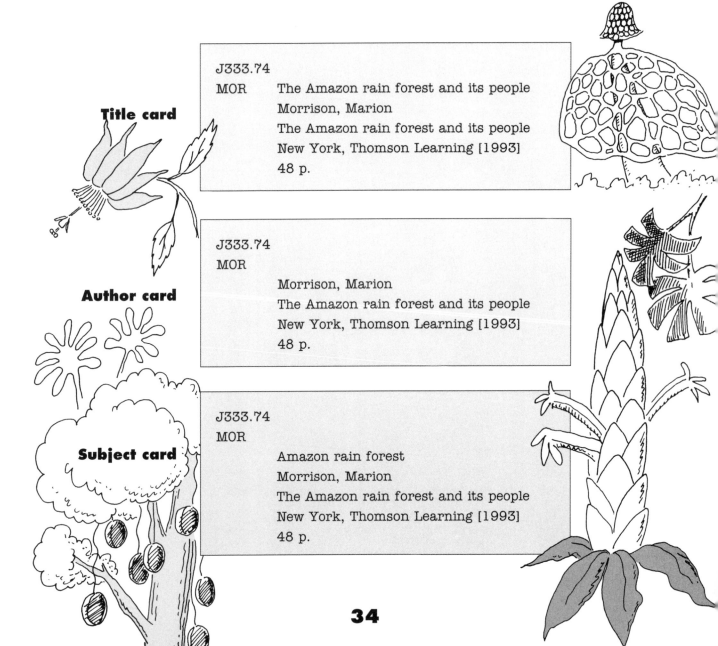

Title card

J333.74
MOR   The Amazon rain forest and its people
        Morrison, Marion
        The Amazon rain forest and its people
        New York, Thomson Learning [1993]
        48 p.

Author card

J333.74
MOR

        Morrison, Marion
        The Amazon rain forest and its people
        New York, Thomson Learning [1993]
        48 p.

Subject card

J333.74
MOR

        Amazon rain forest
        Morrison, Marion
        The Amazon rain forest and its people
        New York, Thomson Learning [1993]
        48 p.

Using the Dewey Decimal System

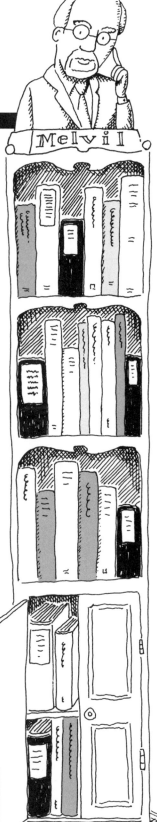

The call numbers that you see in the card catalog and on books are part of a classification system called the Dewey Decimal Classification. The Dewey Decimal Classification—sometimes called the Dewey Decimal System—is named for Melvil Dewey, the man who developed it in 1876. Not all libraries use Dewey's system, but most do. Here is the way the system works:

The Dewey Decimal System classifies books into 10 main categories, numbered from 000 to 999. Each of the main categories is broken up into smaller ones. For example, under 700—The Arts—you would find books on such topics as architecture, sculpture, painting, music, sports, and photography.

The next two pages give you the classifications of the Dewey Decimal System. Look them over carefully. Why do you think the book on the Amazon rain forest (described on page 34) has been classified in the 300 category?

000   Generalities
This section contains general information books. It includes atlases, dictionaries, and encyclopedias. It also has reference books that list all the books, magazines, and newspapers in print today.

100   Philosophy and Related Disciplines
This section has books about philosophy, psychology, and logic.

200   Religion
This section offers information about different religions and churches.

300   Social Sciences
Among other things, this section includes information about politics, law, education, economics, and social problems and services.

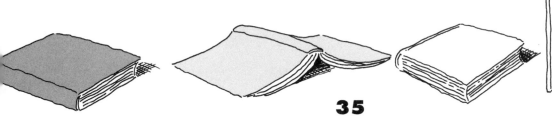

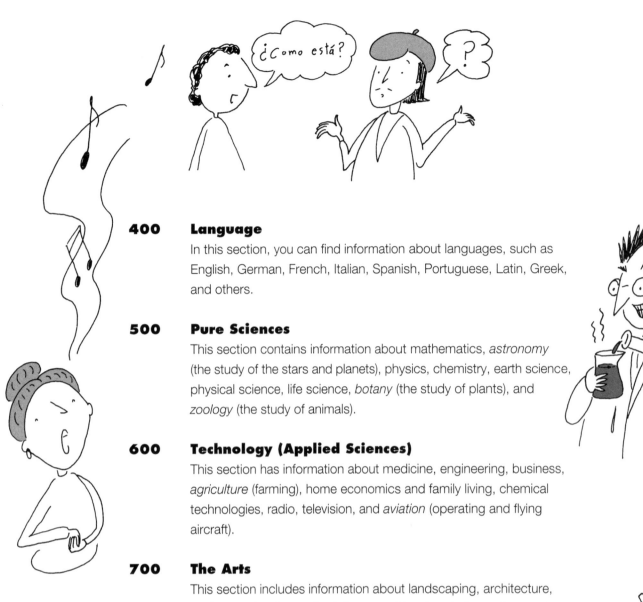

400 Language

In this section, you can find information about languages, such as English, German, French, Italian, Spanish, Portuguese, Latin, Greek, and others.

500 Pure Sciences

This section contains information about mathematics, *astronomy* (the study of the stars and planets), physics, chemistry, earth science, physical science, life science, *botany* (the study of plants), and *zoology* (the study of animals).

600 Technology (Applied Sciences)

This section has information about medicine, engineering, business, *agriculture* (farming), home economics and family living, chemical technologies, radio, television, and *aviation* (operating and flying aircraft).

700 The Arts

This section includes information about landscaping, architecture, sculpture, drawing and painting, graphic arts, photography, music, sports, and the *performing arts* (such as singing, acting, and dancing).

800 Literature

This section covers *literature* (novels, poetry, and plays) in many different languages and from different cultures, including American, English, German, Italian, Spanish, Portuguese, Latin, and Greek.

900 Geography and History

This section has information about biography and *genealogy* (family histories and "family tree" information). It also contains information on travel and the geography and history of Europe, Asia, Africa, North America, South America, and other parts of the world.

Make Your Own Books

YOU NEED

★ Writing paper (or a computer) ★ A pencil or pen ★ Paint or other materials to illustrate your books ★ Two sheets of heavy paper, hole punch, a large needle, and yarn to bind your books

Now that you know something about how books are organized in the library, why not create your own library? It doesn't matter if you don't have many books—you can always make your own! The suggestions on the next several pages will tell you how to write, illustrate, and bind your own books. You will also learn how you can start your own library.

Writing Your Book

Have you ever heard the expression "practice makes perfect"? It is especially true when it comes to writing. Few people can sit down and write something perfect in just one try. For example, a writer might be really satisfied with the beginning of a piece but may feel that the middle or the ending isn't quite right. So the writer will work on that part until the whole piece comes out just right.

Writers often follow a process like the one on page 38. When you begin your own book, you can follow the same steps.

STUDY STRATEGY:

Following the Steps in the Writing Process

STEP 1. Writing a Rough Draft

Before you begin:

★ Decide what your subject or topic will be.
★ Decide what you want to communicate.
★ Decide who your audience will be.
★ Decide on the structure of your piece (short story, essay, play, poem).

As you write your rough draft, don't worry too much about spelling, punctuation or grammar, neatness, or organization. Just get your ideas down. You'll have plenty of time to revise what you've written when you get to *step 2*.

STEP 2. Revising Your Writing

Revise your rough draft by asking yourself some of the following questions:

★ Have I said everything I wanted to say?

★ Have I said too much?
★ Have I chosen my words well?
★ Have I explained my ideas clearly?
★ Is my writing interesting?
★ Is it well organized?
★ Will my readers understand and enjoy it?

STEP 3. Proofreading and Editing

Proofread and edit your writing by correcting any errors in grammar, spelling, and punctuation. After you have finished writing:

★ Check any spellings you're unsure of.
★ Make sure you capitalized correctly.
★ Make sure your punctuation is correct.
★ Make sure you used quotation marks correctly.
★ Check for consistent verb tense.
★ Make sure your subjects and verbs agree.
★ Make sure you used descriptive words.

Copying Your Book

When you get to the final draft of your book, you'll probably want to make a new copy that is as neat and clean as possible. (If you've been working on a computer, you'll probably want to make a final printout.) As you make your final copy, be sure to leave plenty of room on each page for borders or illustrations.

If you're going to copy your book by hand, why not try using other writing tools instead of just a pen or pencil? For example, if you have written a story about a bird, you could use a feather or a quill pen. (For added color and effect, you could dip the end of the feather in paint and brush it lightly across your paper. Be sure to let the paint dry before you write.)

This page and the next show a few examples of writing tools you could try. If none of them seems quite right for the kind of book you are writing, use your imagination. Come up with some ideas of your own. You don't have to write your whole book with your special writing tool. You might use it only for special words or for a section of the book you want to stand out.

Illustrating Your Book

Illustrating your book means putting pictures—such as drawings, photos, or painted symbols—in it. You can use illustrations in many different ways. For example, if you own a rubber stamp in the shape of a star, you could use it to sprinkle colored stars across the pages.

Or, you could make your own stamp. Ask an adult to help you cut a potato in half. With the adult's help, carve the potato into a simple shape, such as a star. Dip the potato into ink or paint and stamp the shape wherever you want it. You could do the same thing with a piece of soap.

Using Borders

Illustrators often use borders to illustrate books. Borders create a sort of "picture frame" around the words on a page. Depending on their purpose—and on the piece they are illustrating—borders can be very simple or they can be full of details. Sometimes a border is used simply to provide decoration. It might consist of flowers or leaves, a simple pattern, or a single color. Some borders reflect the tone or mood of a story. If a story is happy, for example, its borders might be done in bright colors, or filled with a rainbow, flowers, and a smiling sun. What do you think the borders might look like for a scary story?

Sometimes borders point out important details in a piece of writing. In a mystery story, for example, the borders might give clues to help readers solve the mystery. In a book that provides information, the borders might serve to illustrate the materials or the steps needed to make something.

Look at the border around this page. What do you think its purpose is?

Using Pictures

Writers use words to tell stories. Illustrators add pictures to make the words more vivid and meaningful. When you illustrate your book, it's important to make sure that your pictures match or explain your text. For example, if your story says that Jack put on his blue jacket, jeans, and sneakers and walked his three dogs, your pictures need to show Jack in the right outfit and walking the right number of dogs.

If your text explains how to make or do a certain thing, your pictures should help explain the process and make it clearer—especially the parts that are more difficult to understand. You may want to use graphs, diagrams, or photographs. (Get permission to cut photos out of magazines.)

Another thing to consider when you illustrate your book is that, in some cases, you need to make sure that your pictures don't tell too much of the story. If your story has some element of mystery or surprise or humor in it, for example, putting too many clues in your illustrations could give things away before your readers get a chance to read about them. It's OK to illustrate the important events—but be sure you don't show them in pictures before your reader has had a chance to read about them in the text.

Putting Your Book Together

There are many different ways to make your own books. The one described below is a method of Japanese bookbinding. Depending on the type of book you have written, you can choose to bind your book using this method, or you may prefer to invent your own method.

Bookbinding
by
Brenda

Japanese Bookbinding

1. To make the front and back covers, cut two pieces of heavy paper the same size as your pages or slightly larger.

2. Lightly draw a straight line about 1/2 inch from the left edge of the front cover. Mark dots every 1/2 inch or so along the line. Put your papers between the covers, and clip everything together on the opposite edge so nothing slips.

3. Use a sharp tool to punch holes through the dots. Make sure your holes go through all the layers. You may want to turn the book so that the spine is at the top and the back cover is facing you.

4. You will need a large needle and a length of yarn that is five times the length of the cover. Don't knot the end or double the yarn. Push the threaded needle from the back cover through the first hole, leaving a 4-inch "tail." (You will use this "tail" to tie your binding in *step 5*.) Wrap the yarn over the spine edge and go back through the same hole. Now pull the needle through the front of the next hole and again wrap the yarn over the spine edge and go back through the same hole. Repeat these steps until you reach the last hole.

5. Wrap the yarn around the uppermost edge. Then sew straight back across the line—in one hole and out the next. All spaces should now be filled. Wrap the yarn around the other edge and tie it in the back to the "tail" you left in *step 4*. Cut off any extra yarn. Crease your cover at the yarn line.

Starting Your Own Library

YOU NEED

★ Books, books, and more books! ★ A pen or pencil

Now that you have made your own book, you're ready to start building your library. Don't worry if you have only a few books, or even just one. Building a library of books that you treasure can be a hobby that lasts a lifetime. In the meantime, here are a few pointers for getting your library started.

★ Some people like to put reading materials of all kinds into their library. In your library, along with your regular books, you may want to include maps, letters, newspapers, magazines, books on videotape, books on audiotape, and even posters.

★ Some people like to have libraries that contain just one particular kind of literature or reading material. You may want to have a library made up entirely of mystery stories, for example, or entirely of comic books. Or you might have a library of books written by the same author or illustrated by the same artist.

★ Some people like to collect books that have been autographed by the writer, or magazines that have been autographed by the people who appear in them. If you have any autographed reading materials, consider giving them a place in your library.

45

Here are several kinds of reading materials and types of literature that you may want to include in your library.

- ★ almanacs
- ★ alphabet (ABC) books
- ★ atlases
- ★ autobiographies
- ★ biographies
- ★ comic books
- ★ cookbooks
- ★ dictionaries
- ★ fairy tales
- ★ folk tales
- ★ historical fiction
- ★ how-to books

- ★ joke and riddle books
- ★ legends
- ★ magazines
- ★ mysteries
- ★ myths
- ★ picture books
- ★ poetry
- ★ science fiction
- ★ short stories
- ★ sports stories
- ★ tall tales
- ★ thesauruses

STUDY STRATEGY:

Creating a Coding System

Now that you've started gathering books for your library, you'll need a way to organize them. A system like the Dewey Decimal Classification is pretty complicated and probably won't suit your needs, so you may want to come up with a system of your own. There are many ways to organize your books. Here are some ideas:

- ★ by *genre* (type of literature, such as science fiction, mystery, sports stories)
- ★ in alphabetical order by author's last name
- ★ in alphabetical order by book title
- ★ easy books/difficult books
- ★ adult books/children's books
- ★ fiction books/nonfiction books
- ★ books with words/books without words
- ★ books with pictures/books without pictures
- ★ books that have been autographed/books that have not been autographed
- ★ books written by you/books written by others

What Do You Think?

About Yourself

★ What do you know about books and libraries that you didn't know before reading pages 33 to 46 of this book?

★ Is there anything about books or libraries that you would like to explore further?

About This Book

★ Complete these sentences:

1. The most important information I've learned in this book so far is

_____.

2. If I could improve one project, it would be _____.

3. If I had to list three projects from my favorite (1) to my least favorite (3), I would number them this way:

_____

_____

_____

About Your Work Habits

★ Which completed activity are you most proud of? Why?

★ Which activity stretched you most? Why?

★ If you could change anything about the way you planned or worked on any of the projects, what would you do differently? Why?

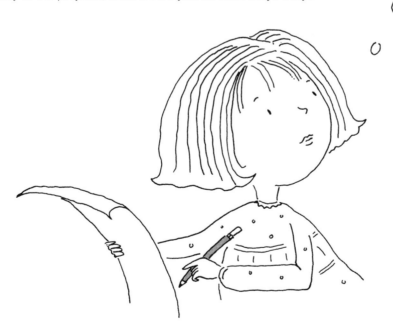

Developing Good Study Habits

When you wake up in the morning, what is the first thing you do? What are the second and third things you do? If you're like most people, you do pretty much the same things every weekday morning. Things you do over and over, and in the same way each time, are your habits. Habits don't happen overnight. They take time to develop. Sometimes they develop after you've done something several different ways and finally decided which way works best.

Developing good study habits takes time, too. Since no one learns the same things in exactly the same ways, it probably will take you some time to figure out which study habits or strategies work best for you. In the meantime, here are some suggestions for you to consider.

Choose a Good Place to Study

Sometimes it's difficult to pay attention when you're studying, especially when you're bored, tired, or distracted—or when the subject isn't one of your favorites. Finding a place that is quiet, comfortable, and well lit will help you concentrate better. Ask others to help by lowering the volume on the TV or the radio, and by taking phone messages if anyone calls for you.

Choose a Good Time to Study

How many times have you intended to do something after school, only to find that it's time for bed and you still haven't done it? Doing something at the same time every day is a good way to make sure it gets done. Set a regular time to begin studying and a regular time to finish. Then, if someone calls and invites you to do something, you'll be able to plan around your study time.

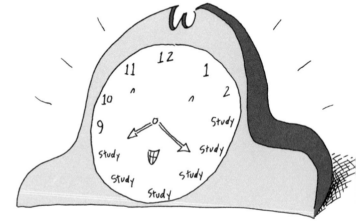

Divide and Conquer

Look at all your assignments. Do they seem overwhelming? If they do, look at everything you have to do and break it down into smaller chunks. Decide which assignments you must do right away and which ones you can put off for a little while. In this way, you will avoid having to do everything at the last minute. To help you remember things, you can make yourself a schedule. Copy the chart on the next page if you need help getting started.

48

Time	Monday	Tuesday	Wednesday	Thursday	Friday	Saturday	Sunday

Pace Yourself

After you've worked out a study schedule, try to stick to it. Look at the clock or your watch occasionally to make sure you aren't spending too much time on any one assignment. Otherwise, you might run out of time before you finish everything.

Sometimes, rearranging your schedule is helpful. For example, if you're having trouble concentrating on a particular homework assignment, you may want to skip to another one that you know you can finish quickly. The sense of accomplishment you get from finishing the "quickie" assignment will help give you confidence that you can complete the other one.

Take Time Out for Breaks

Sometimes the way to improve your concentration is to take a break for a while. Your break doesn't have to last a long time—10 or 15 minutes will do. You'll be amazed at how much more refreshed and focused you'll feel afterward. Here are some things you may want to do during your study breaks:

★ Run around the block.
★ Make a quick phone call.
★ Do one of your favorite exercises.
★ Get something to eat or drink.
★ Dance to a song on the radio.
★ Flip through your favorite magazine.
★ Play with or feed your pet.
★ Take a short nap. (Set your alarm so you don't sleep too long.)
★ Talk to a family member.
★ Draw or doodle.

Using Graphic Organizers to Help You Study

While you study, graphic organizers are a great help in arranging and understanding ideas. Graphic organizers help you make pictures out of ideas, so you can see and remember them better. Graphic organizers also help you see how ideas are related or connected to each other. You could say that graphic organizers "link your thinking."

The next few pages contain explanations of different kinds of graphic organizers and how to use them. Feel free to copy or adapt them when you study or prepare for tests.

Webs (also known as Clusters or Maps)

Do you remember the word map you did on page 9 and the "Ways We Communicate" web you added to on page 16? Well, those graphic organizers are two different kinds of webs. There are many other kinds of webs, but they all serve the same basic purpose. Just as a spider web is made by weaving strands of silk together, a graphic-organizer web weaves strands of ideas together. Webs can be made in many shapes, or configurations, depending on the ideas they represent—and on how those ideas relate to each other. Here is an example of a typical web.

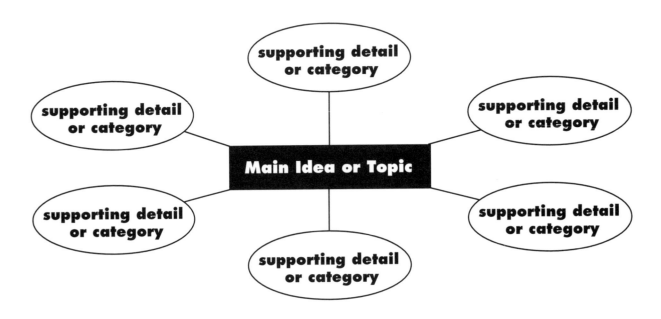

Main Idea Tables

A main idea table is a kind of graphic organizer. It helps you understand the main idea and supporting details in a paragraph or an article. If you picture an actual table in your mind, you can imagine the top of the table as the main idea and the legs as the details that "support" the main idea. Here is what a main idea table looks like:

(THE MAIN IDEA GOES HERE.)
Gorillas are friendly and smart.

(THE FIRST SUPPORTING DETAIL GOES HERE.)	(THE SECOND SUPPORTING DETAIL GOES HERE.)	(THE THIRD SUPPORTING DETAIL GOES HERE.)	(THE FOURTH SUPPORTING DETAIL GOES HERE.)
Gorillas never hurt people unless they are attacked.	The first gorillas kept in zoos may have died of loneliness.	Gorillas play games similar to *Follow the Leader* and *King of the Mountain.*	A female gorilla called Koko learned to communicate in sign language.

Story Maps

Story maps help you pull together the main ideas and events in pieces of fiction. Story maps also help you retell or summarize stories more clearly. Since the story map contains only the main ideas, you won't get carried away telling unimportant details or events.

The next time you read a book, you may want to make a story map bookmark. As you read the book, fill out each part of the story map. When you get to the end of the book, your story map will be completed!

STORY MAP

Title: The Wind in the Willows

Setting: A river in England

Characters: Rat and Mole

Badger

Toad of Toad Hall

Problem: Toad is good-natured but foolish. He is always going from fad to fad.

Event 1: Toad falls in love with cars.

Event 2: Toad crashes car after car.

Event 3: Toad steals a car and goes to jail.

Event 4: Toad escapes but Toad Hall has been invaded by stoats and weasels.

Event 5: Toad, Rat, Mole, and Badger win a battle over Toad Hall.

Solution: Toad learns to value his home and friends.

Sequence Chains

Sequence chains help you keep the order of things straight. They work for fiction as well as nonfiction. With fiction, you can fill in the boxes according to what happened in a story first, second, third, and so on. (**1.** Sam took a walk to the store. **2.** On the way, he found a dog and began to pet it. **3.** The dog said its name was Mike. . . .)

With nonfiction, you can fill in the boxes as you would for fiction—according to what happened first, second, third, and so on. Or you can fill in the boxes according to the order in which something should be done. (**1.** Before you start making your chocolate chip cookies, read through the entire recipe and make sure you understand it. **2.** Gather all the ingredients and materials you will need. **3.** If you have long hair, tie it back. . . .)

SEQUENCE CHAIN FOR | The Life of a Star

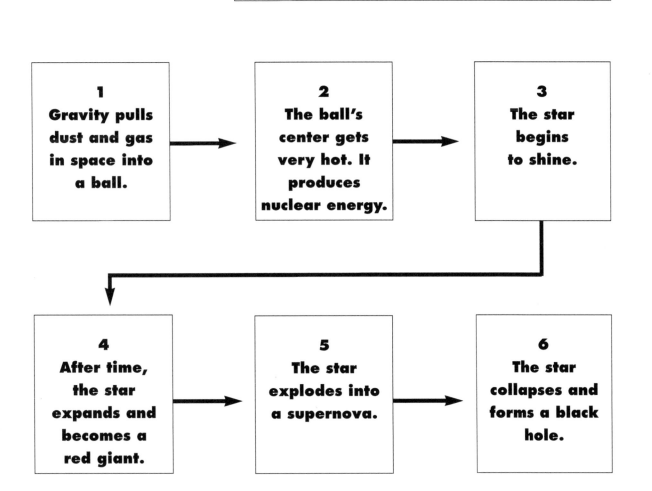

1
Gravity pulls dust and gas in space into a ball.

2
The ball's center gets very hot. It produces nuclear energy.

3
The star begins to shine.

4
After time, the star expands and becomes a red giant.

5
The star explodes into a supernova.

6
The star collapses and forms a black hole.

Venn Diagrams

Venn diagrams use circles to help you understand how two things are alike and how they are different. You write how the two things are different in the outer parts of the circles. Write how the two things are alike in the center—the part where the two circles overlap.

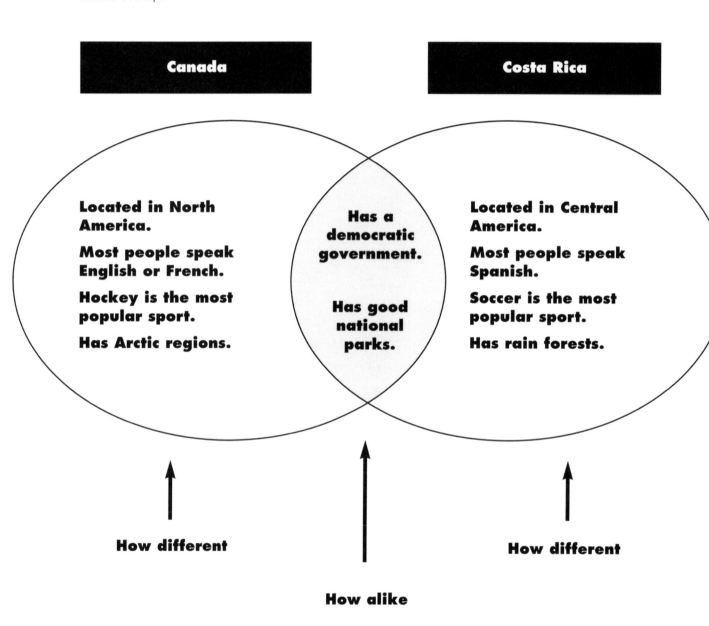

Canada

Costa Rica

Located in North America.

Most people speak English or French.

Hockey is the most popular sport.

Has Arctic regions.

Has a democratic government.

Has good national parks.

Located in Central America.

Most people speak Spanish.

Soccer is the most popular sport.

Has rain forests.

How different

How alike

How different

Feature Analysis Charts

A Venn diagram helps you compare and contrast two things, but when you want to compare and contrast more than two things, you need a feature analysis chart. The chart below compares how several different animals hide, imitate, or bluff to protect themselves from danger. As you can see, most of the animals have the ability to match or blend with their surroundings. However, only a few are able to change their bodies or make themselves look like other animals or objects.

When you set up your own feature analysis chart, be sure to write the names of the things being compared and contrasted along the left-hand side. Then write the ways in which you are comparing them across the top.

Animal	Matches or Blends with Surroundings	Becomes Still When in Danger	Changes Body Color or Shape	Kicks When Attacked	Masquerades as Another Animal or Object	Gives up Body Part When Attacked
fawn	✓	✓				
grasshopper	✓					
butterfly	✓		✓		✓	
chameleon	✓		✓			
tiger	✓					
glass lizard					✓	✓
giraffe	✓			✓		
measuring worm	✓		✓		✓	
lanternfish	✓				✓	
screech owl	✓					
porcupine-fish			✓			

Test-Taking Tips

Pages 56 to 59 offer suggestions on how you can improve your test-taking skills. Being a skilled test taker requires practice. But once you've got a good system down, you should have no trouble making the grade!

Begin Studying Early

Imagine the following situation: It's Friday afternoon. Chad's teacher has just announced that there will be a social studies test in exactly one week. "Plenty of time," Chad thinks to himself. "The test isn't until next Friday, and I have all next week to study." At the moment, all Chad can think about are his great plans for the weekend. "Who wants to be bothered thinking about a boring old test?"

Can you predict the outcome? One possible result, based on the information you've been given, is that Chad will put off studying until right before the test—and then won't do well. Another possible outcome, however, is that Chad will change his mind and start preparing for the test early. He might make a study schedule so he can take his time and really absorb the material. And by doing that, Chad just might breeze through the test.

If you were Chad, which way would you go? Perhaps you'd like to begin studying early, but you're not quite sure where to start. If that's the case, read on. . . .

Make Yourself a Schedule

The most helpful thing you can do before you actually sit down to study is make yourself a schedule. Before you start, think about the information the test will cover. Will it include a certain chapter or chapters in a textbook? Will it cover all or part of a novel? Will you be required to demonstrate something that you've learned, such as how to write a persuasive paragraph or article? Once you've determined what the test will cover, you should have a better idea of how long and how much you will have to study. As you make up your study schedule, here are some things you should consider:

★ the number of days you have until the test
★ the amount of time you have each day to study
★ special circumstances you need to work around (a ballet class, a basketball game, church, or family commitments)
★ the kind of test you will be taking (What subject will the test cover? Will it be multiple-choice, essay, or demonstration?)
★ your knowledge of the subject
★ your strengths and weaknesses as a learner

Since Chad has a week until his social studies test, here's what his study schedule might look like:

DATE OF TEST: Friday, January 20
SUBJECT: Social Studies, Chapter 8

Day	What to do	Study Time
Saturday	Take a break—weekend	
Sunday	Take a break—weekend	
Monday	Reread Chapter 8 Take notes and make graphic organizers	5:30 p.m.–7:30 p.m.
Tuesday	Review class notes	5:30 p.m.–6:30 p.m.
Wednesday	Memorize	7:00 p.m.–8:00 p.m. (after basketball)
Thursday	Review one last time	5:30 p.m.–7:30 p.m.

Gather and Organize Your Study Materials

As you can see from Chad's schedule, he will have several things to look at while he studies: the chapter in his social studies book, the notes and graphic organizers he creates, and the notes he took during class. When you study for a test, you probably will have some of these same things to look at. To keep everything you need right at your fingertips, you may want to make yourself a "portable desk" by putting all your study materials into a three-ring binder or a folder with pockets. You'll find your "desk" very convenient, especially if you can't study in the same place every day.

Here are some other study materials that you may want to have handy:

★ index cards
★ pens (different colors)
★ lead pencils
★ colored pencils
★ pencil sharpener
★ pencil cup
★ erasers
★ correction fluid or tape

★ highlighting markers
★ a ruler
★ folders
★ a calculator
★ a stapler
★ a staple remover
★ a hole punch
★ rubber bands

★ paper clips (different sizes)
★ a planning calendar
★ a wrist watch
★ an encyclopedia
★ an atlas
★ a dictionary
★ a thesaurus

Last-Minute Preparations

It's the night before the test, and you've just finished your final review. You've studied hard all week and you know the material. All that's left to do now is . . . relax! Do you have a favorite hobby or pastime that you can lose yourself in for a while? How about reading a favorite book, comic book, or magazine? Or taking a bubble bath? Depending on the amount of time you have before bed, choose an activity that will take your mind off the test and put you at ease. Don't do anything too exciting or strenuous—a good night's sleep is very important before a test.

On the morning of the test, eat a good breakfast. Your mind and body function better when they are rested and well fed. Try to stay away from sugar and empty calories. Have something nourishing instead, such as eggs, juice, and toast.

Taking the Test

No matter how prepared they are, some people still feel nervous before a test. If that happens to you, here are a few things you can try:

★ Take some deep breaths. If possible, close your eyes and concentrate for a while. Imagine yourself relaxing in one of your favorite places—on a beach, in your room, at the park. As you picture the scene, breathe in and out very slowly.

★ Relax your body. Starting with your head and working down to your toes, feel your body slowly begin to relax. Pretend you are on the moon and your body is weightless. Feel all the tension go away as you continue to breathe deeply.
★ Think positive thoughts. You've worked hard and you're well prepared. Tell yourself that you can do it!

Well, the moment has arrived, and your teacher has handed you the test. You put your name on it, and you're ready to dive in. But wait! Try these things first. They could save you a lot of time and trouble in the long run.

★ Read the directions first. Just because you think you've seen a particular test format before, don't assume that you don't need to read the directions. Sometimes, even when a format is familiar, different responses may be required. For example, on a multiple-choice or fill-in-the-blank test, you may be asked to select the two best answers to a question instead of just one.
★ Preview the entire test. Your test may be made up of different sections, such as a multiple-choice section, a matching section, and an essay section. Knowing in advance what the sections are will help you estimate how much time to spend on each one.
★ Decide which part you want to do first. Who says you have to go through a test from beginning to end? There's nothing wrong with skipping around, especially if you know a particular section well and can do it quickly. Doing the easy parts first will help you in two ways: (1) you'll gain confidence as you go, and (2) you'll have more time to spend on parts that may be difficult or time-consuming.

Taking Different Kinds of Tests

As you go through school, you'll probably take many different kinds of tests. Here are some tips on what to watch for:

True/False

★ Watch for words such as *all, always, none,* and *never.* These words often generalize and tend to make statements false.

★ Beware of opinion statements in true/false tests. Just because you agree with a statement doesn't mean it is necessarily true.

★ Try not to think too much about any one question or read too much into it. The answer you choose first is likely to be the right one, so go with your instincts.

Multiple-Choice

★ In multiple-choice tests, be sure to read the directions carefully. Some directions ask for more than one correct answer. Other directions ask for the best or worst answers.

★ For each item, read all of the choices before you select the best answer (or answers).

★ Once you've read all the choices, rule out those you know are wrong; then choose from among the remaining choices.

Matching

★ In matching tests, be sure to read the directions carefully. Some directions ask you to mark answers with letters or numbers. Other directions ask you to draw lines between matching entries. Still others ask you to use some answers more than once.

★ Matching tests are usually set up in two columns. Read each entry in the first column and try to answer the question without looking at the choices in the second column. If you're sure you know the answer, read down the second column until you find it or one that is similar.

★ Following this procedure, first match all the items you're sure of; then go back and try to match the rest.

Fill-in-the-Blank (Short-Answer)

★ Watch for grammatical clues in fill-in-the-blank formats. Any blank that has the word *an* before it calls for an answer that begins with a vowel. A blank that has the word *a* before it calls for an answer that begins with a consonant.

★ If you don't know the answer to an item, skip it for a while. You may find clues in later items.

★ If the blank you're filling in is at the beginning of a sentence, be sure to capitalize your answer.

Essay

★ Read essay directions carefully. Often they ask you for a specific kind of writing, such as a compare-and-contrast essay or one that is organized by main idea and supporting details.

★ Once you understand what the directions are asking for, take some time to put your thoughts together. Using a graphic organizer is a quick and easy way to organize your ideas. It also tells you whether you are following the directions. (If you need to write a compare-and-contrast essay, for example, you can use a Venn diagram to organize your ideas.)

Quick Tips: Using Quotation Marks

When you are writing a story that has dialogue in it, do you ever have trouble remembering where to put the quotation marks or what they should look like? If you do, here are a few tips:

Pick up a book or a magazine that has some dialogue in it. Now zero in on a sentence of dialogue and look very closely at the quotation marks. If you don't have a book or magazine handy, here is a sentence that you can look at:

" That's a beautiful dog you have, " said Janice.

Do the quotes in the sentence above resemble anything? How about the numbers 6 and 9? Try this: write two number 6's and then fill in the bottom part of each one. Do they look like a set of opening quotation marks? Now try the same thing with two number 9's.

If you remember 6's and 9's the next time you write dialogue—and if you remember that 6 comes before 9 when you count—you should have no trouble remembering how to write opening and closing quotation marks!

Now you know what opening and closing quotation marks should look like, but do you know exactly where to put them in a sentence? If you ever have trouble remembering, here is something you can try:

Imagine that you and a friend are trying to talk in a noisy place. To make it easier for your friend to hear your voice, you cup your hands around your mouth and talk into your friend's ear, like this:

Think about it for a moment. If you were the person speaking in the picture, when would you put your hands up and down during the conversation? Most likely, you would put them up before you began speaking and down after you finished. If you think of quotation marks as being little "hands" around your words, you will always remember where to put them when you write!

If you want to test this idea, decide where the quotation marks should go in the sentences below. (The answers are given below—try not to peek until you've had a try at all three sentences.)

1. Have you finished your homework yet? asked Pat.

2. Yes, why do you want to know? replied Jerry.

3. It's still light outside, Pat answered. I'd like to play catch for a while.

Quick Tips: Multiplying by 9

Here are two fun and easy tips for remembering how to multiply by 9. If you'd like, you can try the method on this page first, and then you can use the method on the next page to check your answers. Are you ready? Here's what to do:

1. First, put your hands up, facing you, like this:

2. Now think of a number from 1 to 10 that you want to multiply by 9. (We'll use the number 4.) Count four fingers over, starting with your left pinkie.

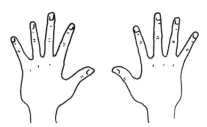

3. Bend that fourth finger down, and count the fingers to the left and right of your bent finger.

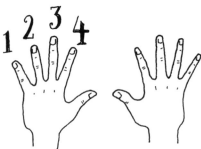

4. You should have come up with 3 fingers to the left of your bent finger and 6 fingers to the right. That means that 9 x 4 = 36! The next page will show you a way to check your answer, but first try experimenting with a few more numbers. What do you get when you try 9 x 6? How about 9 x 2, or 9 x 9?

Here's another way to remember how to multiply by 9. Copy this chart and keep it in your math folder, or make a bookmark out of it and keep it in your math book:

9x1	**=**	**09**
9x2	**=**	**18**
9x3	**=**	**27**
9x4	**=**	**36**
9x5	**=**	**45**
9x6	**=**	**54**
9x7	**=**	**63**
9x8	**=**	**72**
9x9	**=**	**81**
9x10	**=**	**90**

Study the right-hand column of the chart for a moment. Do you notice these patterns?
- ★ The numbers on the left side of the column (the first digits) go from 0 to 9.
- ★ The numbers on the right side (the second digits) go from 9 to 0.
- ★ The digits in each number add up to 9 (0 + 9 = 9; 1 + 8 = 9; 2 + 7 = 9).

Now that you know the patterns, do the following:
1. Think of a number from 1 to 10 that you want to multiply by 9. (For our example, we'll use the number 4 again.)

2. Starting with 0, write the first four numbers in order on a sheet of paper.

3. What is the fourth number you wrote? (It should be 3.) This is the first digit of your answer. (If you were multiplying by 2, for example, you would look at the second number.)

4. Subtract 3 from 9. (You should get 6.) This is the second digit of your answer. Your answer is 36.

5. To check yourself, look back at the chart for the answer to 9 x 4.

What Do You Think?

About Yourself

★ In what ways do you think this book has helped you become a better learner?

★ In what ways do you think you still need to improve?

About This Book

★ In your opinion, what was the most interesting part of this book?

★ Which part did you most enjoy doing?

★ Which part did you least enjoy doing?

★ Think of a favorite study strategy or tip that you could add to this book.

★ Which things will you do or use again?

Mathematics

2

Strategic
Intervention Guide

Macmillan/McGraw-Hill
Glencoe

Image Credits
Cover: Getty Images; all other photographs are by Macmillan/McGraw-Hill.

The McGraw-Hill Companies

**Macmillan
McGraw-Hill**

Send all inquiries to:
Macmillan/McGraw-Hill
8787 Orion Place
Columbus, OH 43240-4027

ISBN: 978-0-02-106155-6
MHID: 0-02-106155-6

Printed in the United States of America.

8 9 10 HSO 10

GRADE 2
Contents

Education Resource Center
University of Delaware
Newark, DE 19716-2940

Strand Assessment

Each strand assessment has a student activity page and a teacher page with instruction and skills chart.

T71546

Skill Builder Lessons and Activities

Number Sense

Patterns

Operations

Place Value

Measurement and Geometry

Data and Probability

To the Teacher

Welcome to the *Macmillan/McGraw-Hill Strategic Intervention Guide.* The goal of these materials is to provide assessment and instruction in the prerequisite skills that some of your students need to be successful in math at this grade level.

For each strand in the student text, there is an inventory test. You will find these inventory tests as blackline masters on the "A" pages in this Guide. The results of these assessments will help you diagnose any gaps in student knowledge. You can then provide students with materials needed to reteach as appropriate.

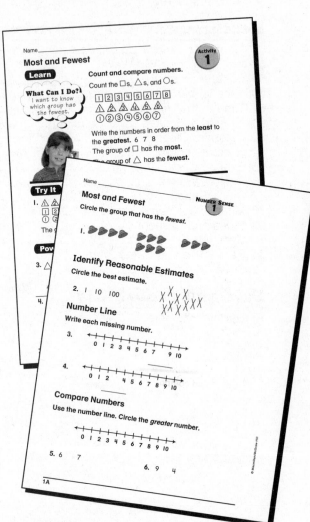

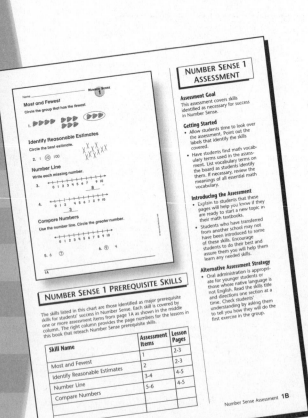

The charts found on the "B" pages following the blackline masters will prescribe a special *Skill Builder* lesson in the handbook for each test item that a student answers incorrectly.

The *Skill Builder* lessons, in blackline format, are presented in language that is simple and direct. The lessons are highly visual and have been designed to keep reading to a minimum. The blackline masters are in the last section of this book, pages 2–113.

The *Learn* section begins with a student asking *What Can I Do?* This section provides stepped-out models and one or more strategies to help bridge any gaps in the student's knowledge. Following this is *Try It*, a section of guided practice, and *Power Practice*, a section containing exercises to ensure that your students acquire the math power they need to be successful in each chapter of their math textbook.

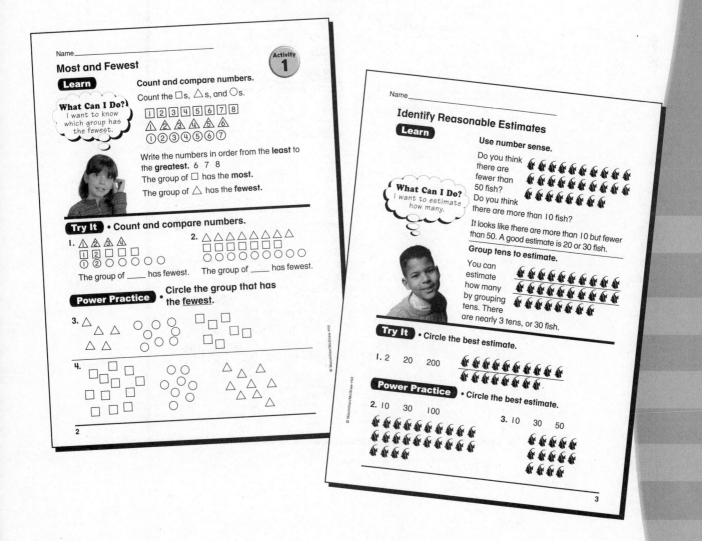

The Teacher Guide, found on the "T" pages, provides a complete lesson plan for each *Skill Builder.* Each *Skill Builder* lesson plan includes a lesson objective, *Getting Started* activities, teaching suggestions, and questions to check the student's understanding. There is also a section called *What If the Student Can't*, which offers additional activities in case a student needs more support in mastering an essential prerequisite skill or lacks the understanding needed to complete the *Skill Builder* exercises successfully.

Many of the *Skill Builder* lesson plans have a feature called *Learn with Partners & Parents.* This activity is intended for students to use at home with parents or siblings or at school with a classmate-partner to practice a math skill in a game-like setting.

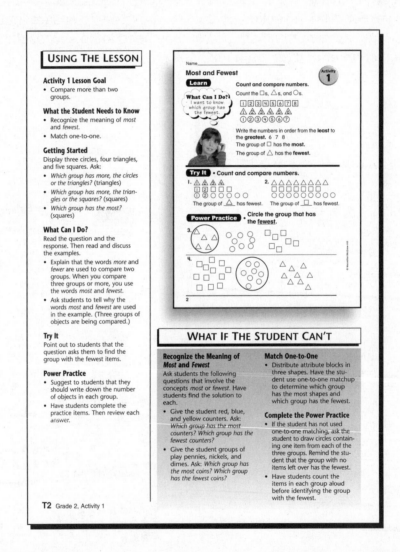

STRAND ASSESSMENT

Name _____

NUMBER SENSE
1

Most and Fewest

Circle the group that has the _fewest_.

1.

Identify Reasonable Estimates

Circle the best estimate.

2. 1   10   100

Number Line

Write each missing number.

3.

0 1 2 3 4 5 6 7   9 10

_____

4.

0 1 2   4 5 6 7 8 9 10

_____

Compare Numbers

Use the number line. Circle the _greater_ number.

0 1 2 3 4 5 6 7 8 9 10

5. 6   7

6. 9   4

© Macmillan/McGraw-Hill

1A

Name _____

Most and Fewest

Circle the group that has the *fewest*.

1.

Identify Reasonable Estimates

Circle the best estimate.

2. 1 (10) 100

X X X X
X X X X X

Number Line

Write each missing number.

3.
0 1 2 3 4 5 6 7 __ 9 10
8

4.
0 1 2 __ 4 5 6 7 8 9 10
3

Compare Numbers

Use the number line. Circle the *greater* number.

0 1 2 3 4 5 6 7 8 9 10

5. 6   (7)

6. (9)   4

© Macmillan/McGraw-Hill

1A

NUMBER SENSE 1 PREREQUISITE SKILLS

The skills listed in this chart are those identified as major prerequisite skills for students' success in Number Sense. Each skill is covered by one or more assessment items from page 1A as shown in the middle column. The right column provides the page numbers for the lessons in this book that reteach Number Sense prerequisite skills.

Skill Name	Assessment Items	Lesson Pages
Most and Fewest	1	T2-T3
Identify Reasonable Estimates	2	T2-T3
Number Line	3-4	T4-T5
Compare Numbers	5-6	T4-T5

NUMBER SENSE 1 ASSESSMENT

Assessment Goal

This assessment covers skills identified as necessary for success in Number Sense.

Getting Started

- Allow students time to look over the assessment. Point out the labels that identify the skills covered.

- Have students find math vocabulary terms used in the assessment. List vocabulary terms on the board as students identify them. If necessary, review the meanings of all essential math vocabulary.

Introducing the Assessment

- Explain to students that these pages will help you know if they are ready to start a new topic in their math textbooks.

- Students who have transferred from another school may not have been introduced to some of these skills. Encourage students to do their best and assure them you will help them learn any needed skills.

Alternative Assessment Strategy

- Oral administration is appropriate for younger students or those whose native language is not English. Read the skills title and directions one section at a time. Check students' understanding by asking them to tell you how they will do the first exercise in the group.

Name _____

More and Fewer

Circle the group that has *more*.

1.

2.    

3.    

Compare Numbers

Compare. Write >, <, or =.

4. 38 _____ 83

5. 26 _____ 25

6. 13 _____ 31

7. 46 _____ 38

8. 52 _____ 67

9. 88 _____ 25

10. 21 _____ 17

11. 62 _____ 25

12. 34 _____ 50

13. 42 _____ 29

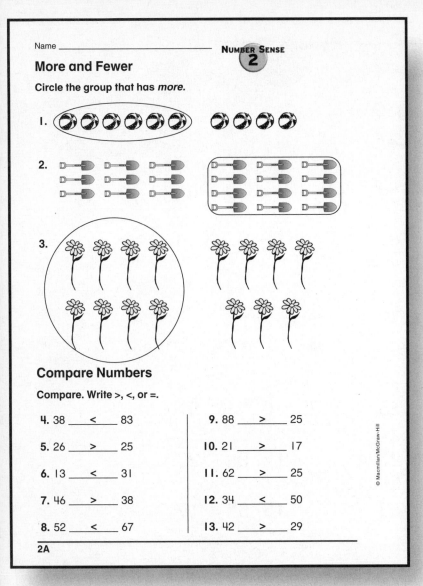

Name _____

More and Fewer

NUMBER SENSE 2

Circle the group that has *more*.

1.

2.

3.

Compare Numbers

Compare. Write >, <, or =.

4. 38 ___<___ 83

5. 26 ___>___ 25

6. 13 ___<___ 31

7. 46 ___>___ 38

8. 52 ___<___ 67

9. 88 ___>___ 25

10. 21 ___>___ 17

11. 62 ___>___ 25

12. 34 ___<___ 50

13. 42 ___>___ 29

© Macmillan/McGraw-Hill

2A

NUMBER SENSE 2 PREREQUISITE SKILLS

The skills listed in this chart are those identified as major prerequisite skills for students' success in Number Sense. Each skill is covered by one or more assessment items from page 2A as shown in the middle column. The right column provides the page numbers for the lessons in this book that reteach the Number Sense prerequisite skills.

Skill Name	Assessment Items	Lesson Pages
More and Fewer	1-3	T6-T7
Compare Numbers	4-13	T8-T13

NUMBER SENSE 2 ASSESSMENT

Assessment Goal

This assessment covers skills identified as necessary for success in Number Sense.

Getting Started

- Allow students time to look over the assessment. Point out the labels that identify the skills covered.

- Have students find math vocabulary terms used in the assessment. List vocabulary terms on the board as students identify them. If necessary, review the meanings of all essential math vocabulary.

Introducing the Assessment

- Explain to students that these pages will help you know if they are ready to start a new topic in their math textbooks.

- Students who have transferred from another school may not have been introduced to some of these skills. Encourage students to do their best and assure them you will help them learn any needed skills.

Alternative Assessment Strategy

- Oral administration is appropriate for younger students or those whose native language is not English. Read the skills title and directions one section at a time. Check students' understanding by asking them to tell you how they will do the first exercise in the group.

Name_____

Greater Than and Less Than

Circle the number that is *greater*.

1. 14   16   2. 27   39   3. 12   43

4. 77   55   5. 10   21   6. 36   18

Compare Whole Numbers

Circle the number that is *less*.

7. 78   87   8. 95   65   9. 96   51

10. 46   45   11. 39   27   12. 34   22

13. 72   86   14. 44   63   15. 54   19

Compare Numbers

Use the number line. Circle the number that is *greater*.

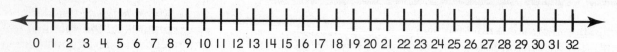

16. 12   22   17. 30   13   18. 10   6

19. 16   18   20. 20   28   21. 8   2

22. 25   31   23. 27   19   24. 30   23

Name_____ NUMBER SENSE **3**

Greater Than and Less Than

Circle the number that is *greater*.

1. 14 (16)   2. 27 (39)   3. 12 (43)

4. (77) 55   5. 10 (21)   6. (36) 18

Compare Whole Numbers

Circle the number that is *less*.

7. (78) 87   8. 95 (65)   9. 96 (51)

10. 46 (45)   11. 39 (27)   12. 34 (22)

13. (72) 86   14. (44) 63   15. 54 (19)

Compare Numbers

Use the number line. Circle the number that is *greater*.

0 1 2 3 4 5 6 7 8 9 10 11 12 13 14 15 16 17 18 19 20 21 22 23 24 25 26 27 28 29 30 31 32

16. 12 (22)   17. (30) 13   18. (10) 6

19. 16 (18)   20. 20 (28)   21. (8) 2

22. 25 (31)   23. (27) 19   24. (30) 23

© Macmillan/McGraw-Hill

3A

Assessment Goal

This assessment covers skills identified as necessary for success in Number Sense.

Getting Started

- Allow students time to look over the assessment. Point out the labels that identify the skills covered.
- Have students find math vocabulary terms used in the assessment. List vocabulary terms on the board as students identify them. If necessary, review the meanings of all essential math vocabulary.

Introducing the Assessment

- Explain to students that these pages will help you know if they are ready to start a new topic in their math textbooks.
- Students who have transferred from another school may not have been introduced to some of these skills. Encourage students to do their best and assure them you will help them learn any needed skills.

Alternative Assessment Strategy

- Oral administration is appropriate for younger students or those whose native language is not English. Read the skills title and directions one section at a time. Check students' understanding by asking them to tell you how they will do the first exercise in the group.

NUMBER SENSE 3 PREREQUISITE SKILLS

The skills listed in this chart are those identified as major prerequisite skills for students' success in Number Sense. Each skill is covered by one or more assessment items from page 3A as shown in the middle column. The right column provides the page numbers for the lessons in this book that reteach Number Sense prerequisite skills.

Skill Name	Assessment Items	Lesson Pages
Greater Than and Less Than	1-6	T6-T7
Compare Whole Numbers	7-15	T10-T13
Compare Numbers	16-24	T8-T9

Number Chart

Fill in the missing numbers.

1.

1	2	3	4	5	6	7	8	9	10
11	12	13	14	15	16	17	18	19	20
21	22	23	24	25	26	27	28	29	
31	32	33	34	35	36	37	38	39	
41	42	43	44	45	46	47	48	49	
51	52	53	54	55	56	57	58	59	

Order Numbers

Write the number that comes just *before*.

2. _____ 76

Write the number that comes *between*.

3. 49 _____ 51

Write the number that comes just *after*.

4. 29 _____

5. 35 _____

Name_____

Number Chart

Fill in the missing numbers.

1.

1	2	3	4	5	6	7	8	9	10
11	12	13	14	15	16	17	18	19	20
21	22	23	24	25	26	27	28	29	30
31	32	33	34	35	36	37	38	39	40
41	42	43	44	45	46	47	48	49	50
51	52	53	54	55	56	57	58	59	60

Order Numbers

Write the number that comes just *before*.

2. __75__ 76

Write the number that comes *between*.

3. 49 __50__ 51

Write the number that comes just *after*.

4. 29 __30__

5. 35 __36__

© Macmillan/McGraw-Hill

4A

NUMBER SENSE 4 PREREQUISITE SKILLS

The skills listed in this chart are those identified as major prerequisite skills for students' success in Number Sense. Each skill is covered by one or more assessment items from page 4A as shown in the middle column. The right column provides the page numbers for the lessons in this book that reteach Number Sense prerequisite skills.

Skill Name	Assessment Items	Lesson Pages
Number Chart	1	T14-T15, T22-T23
Order Numbers	2-5	T14-T15

NUMBER SENSE 4 ASSESSMENT

Assessment Goal

This assessment covers skills identified as necessary for success in Number Sense.

Getting Started

- Allow students time to look over the assessment. Point out the labels that identify the skills covered.
- Have students find math vocabulary terms used in the assessment. List vocabulary terms on the board as students identify them. If necessary, review the meanings of all essential math vocabulary.

Introducing the Assessment

- Explain to students that these pages will help you know if they are ready to start a new topic in their math textbooks.
- Students who have transferred from another school may not have been introduced to some of these skills. Encourage students to do their best and assure them you will help them learn any needed skills.

Alternative Assessment Strategy

- Oral administration is appropriate for younger students or those whose native language is not English. Read the skills title and directions one section at a time. Check students' understanding by asking them to tell you how they will do the first exercise in the group.

Parts of a Group

Write how many.

1. How many As? _____

2. How many Bs? _____

3. How many Cs? _____

4. How many in all? _____

Equal Groups

Write how many groups. Write how many are in each group.

5.

6.

_____ groups of _____   _____ groups of _____

Parts of a Group

Write how many.

A A A A B B B C

1. How many As?   __4__

2. How many Bs?   __3__

3. How many Cs?   __1__

4. How many in all?   __8__

Equal Groups

Write how many groups. Write how many are in each group.

5.

6.

__4__ groups of __2__   __2__ groups of __3__

© Macmillan/McGraw-Hill

5A

NUMBER SENSE 5 PREREQUISITE SKILLS

The skills listed in this chart are those identified as major prerequisite skills for students' success in Number Sense. Each skill is covered by one or more assessment items from page 5A as shown in the middle column. The right column provides the page numbers for the lessons in this book that reteach Number Sense prerequisite skills.

Skill Name	Assessment Items	Lesson Pages
Parts of a Group	1-4	T16-T17
Equal Groups	5-6	T16-T19

NUMBER SENSE 5 ASSESSMENT

Assessment Goal

This assessment covers skills identified as necessary for success in Number Sense.

Getting Started

- Allow students time to look over the assessment. Point out the labels that identify the skills covered.

- Have students find math vocabulary terms used in the assessment. List vocabulary terms on the board as students identify them. If necessary, review the meanings of all essential math vocabulary.

Introducing the Assessment

- Explain to students that these pages will help you know if they are ready to start a new topic in their math textbooks.

- Students who have transferred from another school may not have been introduced to some of these skills. Encourage students to do their best and assure them you will help them learn any needed skills.

Alternative Assessment Strategy

- Oral administration is appropriate for younger students or those whose native language is not English. Read the skills title and directions one section at a time. Check students' understanding by asking them to tell you how they will do the first exercise in the group.

Ordinal Numbers

Follow the directions.

1. Draw a circle around the *third* animal.

2. Make an X on the *sixth* animal.

3. Draw a hat on the *fourth* animal.

4. Give the *ninth* animal a flag.

Skip Counting by 2s

Fill in the missing numbers.

5.

1	2	3	4	5	6	7	8	9	10
11		13		15		17		19	
21		23		25	26	27	28	29	30
31	32	33	34	35	36	37	38	39	40
41	42	43	44	45	46	47	48	49	50
51	52	53	54	55	56	57	58	59	60
61	62	63	64	65	66	67	68	69	70
71	72	73	74	75	76	77	78	79	80
81	82	83	84	85	86	87	88	89	90
91	92	93	94	95	96	97	98	99	100

Name_____

Ordinal Numbers

Follow the directions.

1. Draw a circle around the *third* animal.

2. Make an X on the *sixth* animal.

3. Draw a hat on the *fourth* animal.

4. Give the *ninth* animal a flag.

Skip Counting by 2s

Fill in the missing numbers.

5.

1	2	3	4	5	6	7	8	9	10
11	12	13	14	15	16	17	18	19	20
21	22	23	24	25	26	27	28	29	30
31	32	33	34	35	36	37	38	39	40
41	42	43	44	45	46	47	48	49	50
51	52	53	54	55	56	57	58	59	60
61	62	63	64	65	66	67	68	69	70
71	72	73	74	75	76	77	78	79	80
81	82	83	84	85	86	87	88	89	90
91	92	93	94	95	96	97	98	99	100

© Macmillan/McGraw-Hill

6A

PATTERNS 1 PREREQUISITE SKILLS

The skills listed in this chart are those identified as major prerequisite skills for students' success in Patterns. Each skill is covered by one or more assessment items from page 6A as shown in the middle column. The right column provides the page numbers for the lessons in this book that reteach Patterns prerequisite skills.

Skill Name	Assessment Items	Lesson Pages
Ordinal Numbers	1–4	T20–T21
Skip Counting by 2s	5	T24–T25

Assessment Goal

This assessment covers skills identified as necessary for success in Patterns.

Getting Started

- Allow students time to look over the assessment. Point out the labels that identify the skills covered.

- Have students find math vocabulary terms used in the assessment. List vocabulary terms on the board as students identify them. If necessary, review the meanings of all essential math vocabulary.

Introducing the Assessment

- Explain to students that these pages will help you know if they are ready to start a new topic in their math textbooks.

- Students who have transferred from another school may not have been introduced to some of these skills. Encourage students to do their best and assure them you will help them learn any needed skills.

Alternative Assessment Strategy

- Oral administration is appropriate for younger students or those whose native language is not English. Read the skills title and directions one section at a time. Check students' understanding by asking them to tell you how they will do the first exercise in the group.

Name _____

Skip Counting by 5s and 10s

Write each missing number.

1. 5, 10, 15, 20, _____, 30, 35, _____

2. 10, 20, _____, 40, 50, _____, 70

3. 25, _____, _____, 40, _____, 50, _____

Counting On

Write the missing number.

4. Start with ____.   I more makes ____.   I more makes ____.

Before, After, Between

Write the number that comes

5. just *after* 9. _____

6. *between* 12 and 14. _____

7. just *before* 20. _____

Name_____

Skip Counting by 5s and 10s

Write each missing number.

1. 5, 10, 15, 20, __25__, 30, 35, __40__

2. 10, 20, __30__, 40, 50, __60__, 70

3. 25, __30__, __35__, 40, __45__, 50, __55__

Counting On

Write the missing number.

4. Start with __3__. I more makes __4__. I more makes __5__.

Before, After, Between

Write the number that comes

5. just *after* 9. __10__

6. *between* 12 and 14. __13__

7. just *before* 20. __19__

7A

Assessment Goal
This assessment covers skills identified as necessary for success in Patterns.

Getting Started
- Allow students time to look over the assessment. Point out the labels that identify the skills covered.
- Have students find math vocabulary terms used in the assessment. List vocabulary terms on the board as students identify them. If necessary, review the meanings of all essential math vocabulary.

Introducing the Assessment
- Explain to students that these pages will help you know if they are ready to start a new topic in their math textbooks.
- Students who have transferred from another school may not have been introduced to some of these skills. Encourage students to do their best and assure them you will help them learn any needed skills.

Alternative Assessment Strategy
- Oral administration is appropriate for younger students or those whose native language is not English. Read the skills title and directions one section at a time. Check students' understanding by asking them to tell you how they will do the first exercise in the group.

PATTERNS 2 PREREQUISITE SKILLS

The skills listed in this chart are those identified as major prerequisite skills for students' success in Patterns. Each skill is covered by one or more assessment items from page 7A as shown in the middle column. The right column provides the page numbers for the lessons in this book that reteach Patterns prerequisite skills.

Skill Name	Assessment Items	Lesson Pages
Skip Counting by 5s and 10s	1-3	T24-T25, T28
Counting On	4	T26-T27
Before, After, Between	5-7	T26-T27

Round to the Nearest Ten

Use the number line.
Round each number to the nearest ten.

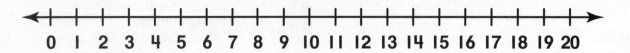

0 1 2 3 4 5 6 7 8 9 10 11 12 13 14 15 16 17 18 19 20

1. 18 _____   **2.** 13 _____

3. 12 _____   **4.** 18 _____

5. 15 _____   **6.** 11 _____

Round to the Nearest Hundred

Use the number line. Round each number
to the nearest hundred.

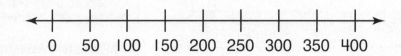

0 50 100 150 200 250 300 350 400

7. 302 _____   **8.** 79 _____

9. 185 _____   **10.** 375 _____

Number Patterns

Find the missing numbers in each counting pattern.

11. 4, 14, _____, 34, 44, _____

Name_____

Round to the Nearest Ten

Use the number line.
Round each number to the nearest ten.

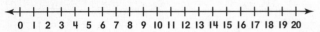

1. 18 __20__   2. 13 __10__

3. 12 __10__   4. 18 __20__

5. 15 __20__   6. 11 __10__

Round to the Nearest Hundred

Use the number line. Round each number
to the nearest hundred.

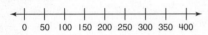

7. 302 __300__   8. 79 __100__

9. 185 __200__   10. 375 __400__

Number Patterns

Find the missing numbers in each counting pattern.

11. 4, 14, __24__, 34, 44, __54__

© Macmillan/McGraw-Hill

8A

Assessment Goal

This assessment covers skills
identified as necessary for success
in Patterns.

Getting Started

- Allow students time to look over
  the assessment. Point out the
  labels that identify the skills
  covered.

- Have students find math vocabulary terms used in the assessment. List vocabulary terms on
  the board as students identify
  them. If necessary, review the
  meanings of all essential math
  vocabulary.

Introducing the Assessment

- Explain to students that these
  pages will help you know if they
  are ready to start a new topic in
  their math textbooks.

- Students who have transferred
  from another school may not
  have been introduced to some
  of these skills. Encourage
  students to do their best and
  assure them you will help them
  learn any needed skills.

Alternative Assessment Strategy

- Oral administration is appropriate for younger students or
  those whose native language is
  not English. Read the skills title
  and directions one section at a
  time. Check students'
  understanding by asking them
  to tell you how they will do the
  first exercise in the group.

PATTERNS 3 PREREQUISITE SKILLS

The skills listed in this chart are those identified as major prerequisite
skills for students' success in Patterns. Each skill is covered by one or
more assessment items from page 8A as shown in the middle column.
The right column provides the page numbers for the lessons in this
book that reteach Patterns prerequisite skills.

Skill Name	Assessment Items	Lesson Pages
Round to the Nearest Ten	1-6	T29-T31
Round to the Nearest Hundred	7-10	T32-T33
Number Patterns	11	T34-T37

Add and Subtract One

Add or subtract.

1. $8 + 1 =$ _____

2. $8 - 1 =$ _____

3. $\begin{array}{r} 4 \\ -\ 1 \\ \hline \end{array}$

4. $\begin{array}{r} 4 \\ +\ 1 \\ \hline \end{array}$

5. $\begin{array}{r} 6 \\ +\ 1 \\ \hline \end{array}$

6. $\begin{array}{r} 6 \\ -\ 1 \\ \hline \end{array}$

7. $6 - 1 =$ _____

8. $6 + 1 =$ _____

Addition Facts to 8

Add.

9. $2 + 5 =$ _____

10. $\begin{array}{r} 4 \\ +\ 4 \\ \hline \end{array}$

Add and Subtract One

Add or subtract.

1. $8 + 1 = \underline{\ \ 9\ \ }$ 2. $8 - 1 = \underline{\ \ 7\ \ }$

3. $\begin{array}{r} 4 \\ -1 \\ \hline 3 \end{array}$ 4. $\begin{array}{r} 4 \\ +1 \\ \hline 5 \end{array}$ 5. $\begin{array}{r} 6 \\ +1 \\ \hline 7 \end{array}$ 6. $\begin{array}{r} 6 \\ -1 \\ \hline 5 \end{array}$

7. $6 - 1 = \underline{\ \ 5\ \ }$ 8. $6 + 1 = \underline{\ \ 7\ \ }$

Addition Facts to 8

Add.

9. $2 + 5 = \underline{\ \ 7\ \ }$ 10. $\begin{array}{r} 4 \\ +4 \\ \hline 8 \end{array}$

9A

OPERATIONS 1 PREREQUISITE SKILLS

The skills listed in this chart are those identified as major prerequisite skills for students' success in Operations. Each skill is covered by one or more assessment items from page 9A as shown in the middle column. The right column provides the page numbers for the lessons in this book that reteach Operations prerequisite skills.

Skill Name	Assessment Items	Lesson Pages
Add and Subtract One	1-8	T38-T39
Addition Facts to 8	9-10	T38-T39, T42-T43

Assessment Goal

This assessment covers skills identified as necessary for success in Operations.

Getting Started

- Allow students time to look over the assessment. Point out the labels that identify the skills covered.

- Have students find math vocabulary terms used in the assessment. List vocabulary terms on the board as students identify them. If necessary, review the meanings of all essential math vocabulary.

Introducing the Assessment

- Explain to students that these pages will help you know if they are ready to start a new topic in their math textbooks.

- Students who have transferred from another school may not have been introduced to some of these skills. Encourage students to do their best and assure them you will help them learn any needed skills.

Alternative Assessment Strategy

- Oral administration is appropriate for younger students or those whose native language is not English. Read the skills title and directions one section at a time. Check students' understanding by asking them to tell you how they will do the first exercise in the group.

Addition Facts to 8

Add.

1. $4 + 3 =$ _____

2. $\begin{array}{r} 4 \\ + 3 \\ \hline \end{array}$

3. $5 + 2 =$ _____

4. $\begin{array}{r} 5 \\ + 2 \\ \hline \end{array}$

5. $2 + 3 =$ _____

6. $\begin{array}{r} 2 \\ + 3 \\ \hline \end{array}$

Subtraction Facts to 8

Subtract.

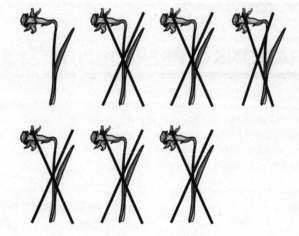

7. $8 - 1 =$ _____

8. $\begin{array}{r} 7 \\ - 6 \\ \hline \end{array}$

Name _____

Addition Facts to 8

Add.

1. $4 + 3 =$ __7__

2.
$$\begin{array}{r} 4 \\ + 3 \\ \hline 7 \end{array}$$

3. $5 + 2 =$ __7__

4.
$$\begin{array}{r} 5 \\ + 2 \\ \hline 7 \end{array}$$

5. $2 + 3 =$ __5__

6.
$$\begin{array}{r} 2 \\ + 3 \\ \hline 5 \end{array}$$

Subtraction Facts to 8

Subtract.

7. $8 - 1 =$ __7__

8.
$$\begin{array}{r} 7 \\ - 6 \\ \hline 1 \end{array}$$

© Macmillan/McGraw-Hill

10A

OPERATIONS 2 PREREQUISITE SKILLS

The skills listed in this chart are those identified as major prerequisite skills for students' success in Operations. Each skill is covered by one or more assessment items from page 10A as shown in the middle column. The right column provides the page numbers for the lessons in this book that reteach Operations prerequisite skills.

Skill Name	Assessment Items	Lesson Pages
Addition Facts to 8	1-6	T40-T43
Subtraction Facts to 8	7-8	T42-T43, T50-T53

Assessment Goal

This assessment covers skills identified as necessary for success in Operations.

Getting Started

- Allow students time to look over the assessment. Point out the labels that identify the skills covered.

- Have students find math vocabulary terms used in the assessment. List vocabulary terms on the board as students identify them. If necessary, review the meanings of all essential math vocabulary.

Introducing the Assessment

- Explain to students that these pages will help you know if they are ready to start a new topic in their math textbooks.

- Students who have transferred from another school may not have been introduced to some of these skills. Encourage students to do their best and assure them you will help them learn any needed skills.

Alternative Assessment Strategy

- Oral administration is appropriate for younger students or those whose native language is not English. Read the skills title and directions one section at a time. Check students' understanding by asking them to tell you how they will do the first exercise in the group.

Addition and Subtraction Facts to 12

Add or subtract.

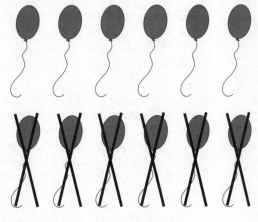

1. $12 - 6 =$ _____

2. $\begin{array}{r} 6 \\ + 6 \\ \hline \end{array}$

Add or Subtract

Write + or −. Then add or subtract.

3.

How many more starfish than clams?

3 ◯ 2 = ____

4.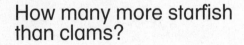

How many in all?

4 ◯ 2 = ____

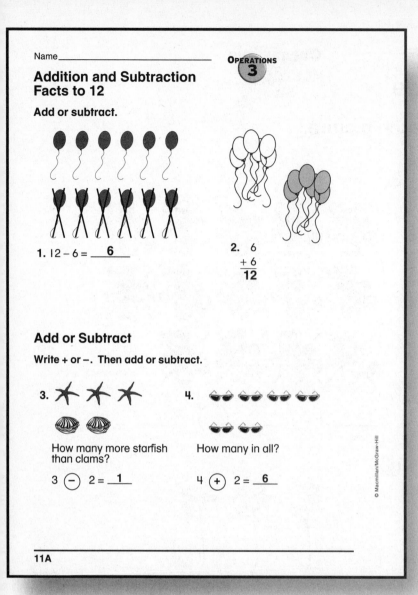

Name_____

Addition and Subtraction Facts to 12

Add or subtract.

1. 12 − 6 = __6__

2. 6
  + 6
  ──
   12

Add or Subtract

Write + or −. Then add or subtract.

3. How many more starfish than clams?

3 ⊖ 2 = __1__

4. How many in all?

4 ⊕ 2 = __6__

© Macmillan/McGraw-Hill

11A

OPERATIONS 3 PREREQUISITE SKILLS

The skills listed in this chart are those identified as major prerequisite skills for students' success in Operations. Each skill is covered by one or more assessment items from page 11A as shown in the middle column. The right column provides the page numbers for the lessons in this book that reteach Operations prerequisite skills.

Skill Name	Assessment Items	Lesson Pages
Addition and Subtraction Facts to 12	1-2	T44-T45
Add or Subtract	3-4	T44-T45, T50-T53

Assessment Goal

This assessment covers skills identified as necessary for success in Operations.

Getting Started

- Allow students time to look over the assessment. Point out the labels that identify the skills covered.

- Have students find math vocabulary terms used in the assessment. List vocabulary terms on the board as students identify them. If necessary, review the meanings of all essential math vocabulary.

Introducing the Assessment

- Explain to students that these pages will help you know if they are ready to start a new topic in their math textbooks.

- Students who have transferred from another school may not have been introduced to some of these skills. Encourage students to do their best and assure them you will help them learn any needed skills.

Alternative Assessment Strategy

- Oral administration is appropriate for younger students or those whose native language is not English. Read the skills title and directions one section at a time. Check students' understanding by asking them to tell you how they will do the first exercise in the group.

Write a Number Sentence

Write a number sentence for each picture.

1.

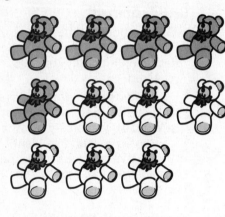

_____ + _____ = _____

2.

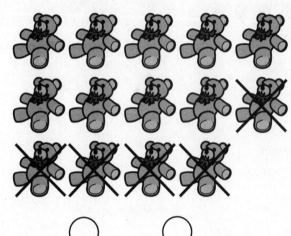

_____ ◯ _____ ◯ _____

3.

_____ + _____ = _____

4.

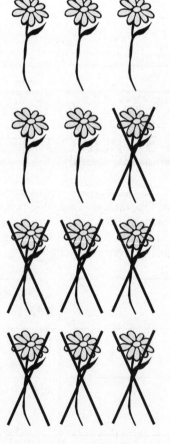

_____ ◯ _____ ◯ _____

Name _____

Write a Number Sentence

Write a number sentence for each picture.

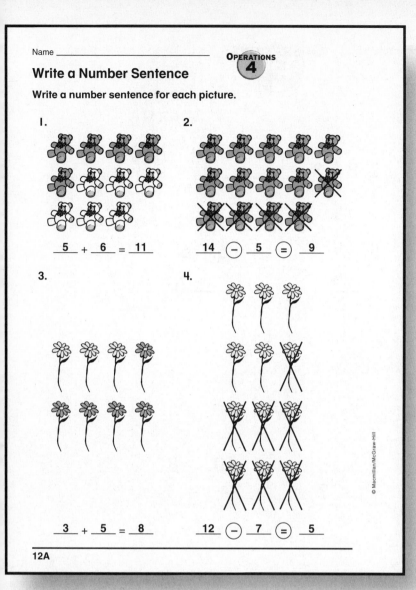

1.

$\underline{5}$ + $\underline{6}$ = $\underline{11}$

2.

$\underline{14}$ (−) $\underline{5}$ (=) $\underline{9}$

3.

$\underline{3}$ + $\underline{5}$ = $\underline{8}$

4.

$\underline{12}$ (−) $\underline{7}$ (=) $\underline{5}$

© Macmillan/McGraw-Hill

12A

OPERATIONS 4 PREREQUISITE SKILLS

The skills listed in this chart are those identified as major prerequisite skills for students' success in Operations. Each skill is covered by one or more assessment items from page 12A as shown in the middle column. The right column provides the page numbers for the lessons in this book that reteach Operations prerequisite skills.

Skill Name	Assessment Items	Lesson Pages
Write a Number Sentence	1-4	T46-T49

Assessment Goal

This assessment covers skills identified as necessary for success in Operations.

Getting Started

- Allow students time to look over the assessment. Point out the labels that identify the skills covered.

- Have students find math vocabulary terms used in the assessment. List vocabulary terms on the board as students identify them. If necessary, review the meanings of all essential math vocabulary.

Introducing the Assessment

- Explain to students that these pages will help you know if they are ready to start a new topic in their math textbooks.

- Students who have transferred from another school may not have been introduced to some of these skills. Encourage students to do their best and assure them you will help them learn any needed skills.

Alternative Assessment Strategy

- Oral administration is appropriate for younger students or those whose native language is not English. Read the skills title and directions one section at a time. Check students' understanding by asking them to tell you how they will do the first exercise in the group.

Addition Facts to 12

Add.

1. $7 + 2 =$ _____

2. $8 + 3 =$ _____

3. $\begin{array}{r} 6 \\ + 5 \\ \hline \end{array}$

4. $\begin{array}{r} 2 \\ + 9 \\ \hline \end{array}$

5. $\begin{array}{r} 4 \\ + 5 \\ \hline \end{array}$

6. $\begin{array}{r} 6 \\ + 4 \\ \hline \end{array}$

Addition Facts to 20

Add.

7. $\begin{array}{r} 9 \\ + 7 \\ \hline \end{array}$

8. $\begin{array}{r} 8 \\ + 9 \\ \hline \end{array}$

9. $\begin{array}{r} 5 \\ + 8 \\ \hline \end{array}$

10. $\begin{array}{r} 8 \\ + 3 \\ \hline \end{array}$

11. $\begin{array}{r} 8 \\ + 7 \\ \hline \end{array}$

12. $\begin{array}{r} 9 \\ + 5 \\ \hline \end{array}$

13. $\begin{array}{r} 7 \\ + 4 \\ \hline \end{array}$

14. $\begin{array}{r} 9 \\ + 9 \\ \hline \end{array}$

Subtraction Facts to 20

Subtract.

15. $\begin{array}{r} 13 \\ - 5 \\ \hline \end{array}$

16. $\begin{array}{r} 15 \\ - 7 \\ \hline \end{array}$

17. $\begin{array}{r} 7 \\ - 3 \\ \hline \end{array}$

18. $\begin{array}{r} 15 \\ - 9 \\ \hline \end{array}$

Addition Facts to 12

Add.

1. $7 + 2 =$ __9__   2. $8 + 3 =$ __11__

3. 6   4. 2   5. 4   6. 6
   $+5$ $+9$ $+5$ $+4$
   ——   ——   ——   ——
   11   11   9   10

Addition Facts to 20

Add.

7. 9   8. 8   9. 5   10. 8
   $+7$ $+9$ $+8$ $+3$
   ——   ——   ——   ——
   16   17   13   11

11. 8   12. 9   13. 7   14. 9
    $+7$ $+5$ $+4$ $+9$
    ——   ——   ——   ——
    15   14   11   18

Subtraction Facts to 20

Subtract.

15. 13   16. 15   17. 7   18. 15
    -5 -7 -3 -9
    ——   ——   ——   ——
     8   8   4   6

© Macmillan/McGraw-Hill

13A

OPERATIONS 5 PREREQUISITE SKILLS

The skills listed in this chart are those identified as major prerequisite skills for students' success in Operations. Each skill is covered by one or more assessment items from page 13A as shown in the middle column. The right column provides the page numbers for the lessons in this book that reteach Operations prerequisite skills.

Skill Name	Assessment Items	Lesson Pages
Addition Facts to 12	1-6	T44-T45
Addition Facts to 20	7-14	T56-T57
Subtraction Facts to 20	15-18	T60-T61

OPERATIONS 5 ASSESSMENT

Assessment Goal

This assessment covers skills identified as necessary for success in Operations.

Getting Started

- Allow students time to look over the assessment. Point out the labels that identify the skills covered.

- Have students find math vocabulary terms used in the assessment. List vocabulary terms on the board as students identify them. If necessary, review the meanings of all essential math vocabulary.

Introducing the Assessment

- Explain to students that these pages will help you know if they are ready to start a new topic in their math textbooks.

- Students who have transferred from another school may not have been introduced to some of these skills. Encourage students to do their best and assure them you will help them learn any needed skills.

Alternative Assessment Strategy

- Oral administration is appropriate for younger students or those whose native language is not English. Read the skills title and directions one section at a time. Check students' understanding by asking them to tell you how they will do the first exercise in the group.

Fact Families

Complete each fact family.

1. $9 + 3 =$ _____

$3 + 9 =$ _____

$12 - 9 =$ _____

$12 - 3 =$ _____

2. $5 + 6 =$ _____

$6 + 5 =$ _____

$11 - 6 =$ _____

$11 - 5 =$ _____

3. $1 + 7 =$ _____

$7 + 1 =$ _____

$8 - 1 =$ _____

$8 - 7 =$ _____

4. $7 + 8 =$ _____

$8 + 7 =$ _____

$15 - 7 =$ _____

$15 - 8 =$ _____

Adding Three or More Numbers

Add.

5. $5 + 1 + 3 + 2 =$ _____

6. $4 + 3 + 2 + 1 =$ _____

7. $7 + 1 + 3 =$ _____

8. $2 + 3 + 4 + 6 =$ _____

Fact Families

Complete each fact family.

1. $9 + 3 = \underline{12}$

    $3 + 9 = \underline{12}$

    $12 - 9 = \underline{3}$

    $12 - 3 = \underline{9}$

2. $5 + 6 = \underline{11}$

    $6 + 5 = \underline{11}$

    $11 - 6 = \underline{5}$

    $11 - 5 = \underline{6}$

3. $1 + 7 = \underline{8}$

    $7 + 1 = \underline{8}$

    $8 - 1 = \underline{7}$

    $8 - 7 = \underline{1}$

4. $7 + 8 = \underline{15}$

    $8 + 7 = \underline{15}$

    $15 - 7 = \underline{8}$

    $15 - 8 = \underline{7}$

Adding Three or More Numbers

Add.

5. $5 + 1 + 3 + 2 = \underline{11}$

6. $4 + 3 + 2 + 1 = \underline{10}$

7. $7 + 1 + 3 = \underline{11}$

8. $2 + 3 + 4 + 6 = \underline{15}$

© Macmillan/McGraw-Hill

14A

OPERATIONS 6 PREREQUISITE SKILLS

The skills listed in this chart are those identified as major prerequisite skills for students' success in Operations. Each skill is covered by one or more assessment items from page 14A as shown in the middle column. The right column provides the page numbers for the lessons in this book that reteach the Operations prerequisite skills.

Skill Name	Assessment Items	Lesson Pages
Fact Families	1-4	T58-T59 T62-T63
Adding Three or More Numbers	5-8	T64-T65

OPERATIONS 6 ASSESSMENT

Assessment Goal

This assessment covers skills identified as necessary for success in Operations.

Getting Started

- Allow students time to look over the assessment. Point out the labels that identify the skills covered.
- Have students find math vocabulary terms used in the assessment. List vocabulary terms on the board as students identify them. If necessary, review the meanings of all essential math vocabulary.

Introducing the Assessment

- Explain to students that these pages will help you know if they are ready to start a new topic in their math textbooks.
- Students who have transferred from another school may not have been introduced to some of these skills. Encourage students to do their best and assure them you will help them learn any needed skills.

Alternative Assessment Strategy

- Oral administration is appropriate for younger students or those whose native language is not English. Read the skills title and directions one section at a time. Check students' understanding by asking them to tell you how they will do the first exercise in the group.

Add Tens

Add.

1. 40
   + 10

2. 20
   + 70

3. 50
   + 30

4. 30 + 40 = _____

5. 60 + 20 = _____

Addition Facts to 20

Add.

6.   8
   + 9

7.   3
   + 7

8.   6
   + 5

9. 15 + 4 = _____

10. 10 + 10 = _____

Add Two-Digit Numbers

Add.

11. 28
   + 34

12. 32
   + 29

13. 61
   + 15

14. 48
   + 12

15. 17
   + 24

16. 34
   + 44

17. 59
   + 28

18. 61
   + 12

Name _____

Add Tens

Add.

1.	40 + 10 **50**	2.	20 + 70 **90**	3.	50 + 30 **80**

4. 30 + 40 = __70__   5. 60 + 20 = __80__

Addition Facts to 20

Add.

6.	8 + 9 **17**	7.	3 + 7 **10**	8.	6 + 5 **11**

9. 15 + 4 = __19__   10. 10 + 10 = __20__

Add Two-Digit Numbers

Add.

11.	28 + 34 **62**	12.	32 + 29 **61**	13.	61 + 15 **76**	14.	48 + 12 **60**

15.	17 + 24 **41**	16.	34 + 44 **78**	17.	59 + 28 **87**	18.	61 + 12 **73**

© Macmillan/McGraw-Hill

15A

OPERATIONS 7 PREREQUISITE SKILLS

The skills listed in this chart are those identified as major prerequisite skills for students' success in Operations. Each skill is covered by one or more assessment items from page 15A as shown in the middle column. The right column provides the page numbers for the lessons in this book that reteach Operations prerequisite skills.

Skill Name	Assessment Items	Lesson Pages
Add Tens	1-5	T54
Addition Facts to 20	6-10	T56-T57
Add Two-Digit Numbers	11-18	T66-T67

OPERATIONS 7 ASSESSMENT

Assessment Goal

This assessment covers skills identified as necessary for success in Operations.

Getting Started

- Allow students time to look over the assessment. Point out the labels that identify the skills covered.
- Have students find math vocabulary terms used in the assessment. List vocabulary terms on the board as students identify them. If necessary, review the meanings of all essential math vocabulary.

Introducing the Assessment

- Explain to students that these pages will help you know if they are ready to start a new topic in their math textbooks.
- Students who have transferred from another school may not have been introduced to some of these skills. Encourage students to do their best and assure them you will help them learn any needed skills.

Alternative Assessment Strategy

- Oral administration is appropriate for younger students or those whose native language is not English. Read the skills title and directions one section at a time. Check students' understanding by asking them to tell you how they will do the first exercise in the group.

Subtract Tens

Subtract.

1. 40
   − 10

2. 80
   − 70

3. 60
   − 30

Subtraction Facts to 20

Subtract.

4. 13
   − 7

5. 16
   − 8

6. 19
   − 2

Subtract Two-Digit Numbers

Subtract.

7. 48
   − 23

8. 62
   − 59

9. 31
   − 18

10. 66
   − 23

11. 47
   − 28

12. 62
   − 17

13. 59
   − 37

14. 36
   − 16

15. 73
   − 45

16. 30
   − 8

17. 21
   − 15

18. 55
   − 39

Name _____

Subtract Tens

Subtract.

1. $\begin{array}{r} 40 \\ -10 \\ \hline \mathbf{30} \end{array}$
2. $\begin{array}{r} 80 \\ -70 \\ \hline \mathbf{10} \end{array}$
3. $\begin{array}{r} 60 \\ -30 \\ \hline \mathbf{30} \end{array}$

Subtraction Facts to 20

Subtract.

4. $\begin{array}{r} 13 \\ -7 \\ \hline \mathbf{6} \end{array}$
5. $\begin{array}{r} 16 \\ -8 \\ \hline \mathbf{8} \end{array}$
6. $\begin{array}{r} 19 \\ -2 \\ \hline \mathbf{17} \end{array}$

Subtract Two-Digit Numbers

Subtract.

7. $\begin{array}{r} 48 \\ -23 \\ \hline \mathbf{25} \end{array}$
8. $\begin{array}{r} 62 \\ -59 \\ \hline \mathbf{3} \end{array}$
9. $\begin{array}{r} 31 \\ -18 \\ \hline \mathbf{13} \end{array}$

10. $\begin{array}{r} 66 \\ -23 \\ \hline \mathbf{43} \end{array}$
11. $\begin{array}{r} 47 \\ -28 \\ \hline \mathbf{19} \end{array}$
12. $\begin{array}{r} 62 \\ -17 \\ \hline \mathbf{45} \end{array}$

13. $\begin{array}{r} 59 \\ -37 \\ \hline \mathbf{22} \end{array}$
14. $\begin{array}{r} 36 \\ -16 \\ \hline \mathbf{20} \end{array}$
15. $\begin{array}{r} 73 \\ -45 \\ \hline \mathbf{28} \end{array}$

16. $\begin{array}{r} 30 \\ -8 \\ \hline \mathbf{22} \end{array}$
17. $\begin{array}{r} 21 \\ -15 \\ \hline \mathbf{6} \end{array}$
18. $\begin{array}{r} 55 \\ -39 \\ \hline \mathbf{16} \end{array}$

© Macmillan/McGraw-Hill

16A

Assessment Goal

This assessment covers skills identified as necessary for success in Operations.

Getting Started

- Allow students time to look over the assessment. Point out the labels that identify the skills covered.

- Have students find math vocabulary terms used in the assessment. List vocabulary terms on the board as students identify them. If necessary, review the meanings of all essential math vocabulary.

Introducing the Assessment

- Explain to students that these pages will help you know if they are ready to start a new topic in their math textbooks.

- Students who have transferred from another school may not have been introduced to some of these skills. Encourage students to do their best and assure them you will help them learn any needed skills.

Alternative Assessment Strategy

- Oral administration is appropriate for younger students or those whose native language is not English. Read the skills title and directions one section at a time. Check students' understanding by asking them to tell you how they will do the first exercise in the group.

OPERATIONS 8 PREREQUISITE SKILLS

The skills listed in this chart are those identified as major prerequisite skills for students' success in Operations. Each skill is covered by one or more assessment items from page 16A as shown in the middle column. The right column provides the page numbers for the lessons in this book that reteach Operations prerequisite skills.

Skill Name	Assessment Items	Lesson Pages
Subtract Tens	1-3	T55
Subtraction Facts to 20	4-6	T60-T61
Subtract Two-Digit Numbers	7-18	T68-T71

Tens and Ones

Write each number.

1.

_____

2.

_____

3.

_____

4.

_____

Circle ten. Write each number.

5.

_____

6.

_____

7.

_____

8.

_____

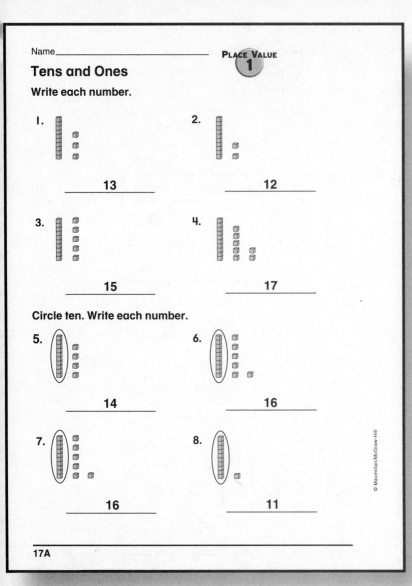

Name_____

Tens and Ones

PLACE VALUE
1

Write each number.

1.   13

2.   12

3.   15

4.   17

Circle ten. Write each number.

5.   14

6.   16

7.   16

8.   11

© Macmillan/McGraw-Hill

17A

PLACE VALUE 1 PREREQUISITE SKILLS

The skills listed in this chart are those identified as major prerequisite skills for students' success in Place Value. Each skill is covered by one or more assessment items from page 17A as shown in the middle column. The right column provides the page numbers for the lessons in this book that reteach Place Value prerequisite skills.

Skill Name	Assessment Items	Lesson Pages
Tens and Ones	1-8	T72-T74

PLACE VALUE 1 ASSESSMENT

Assessment Goal

This assessment covers skills identified as necessary for success in Place Value.

Getting Started

- Allow students time to look over the assessment. Point out the labels that identify the skills covered.
- Have students find math vocabulary terms used in the assessment. List vocabulary terms on the board as students identify them. If necessary, review the meanings of all essential math vocabulary.

Introducing the Assessment

- Explain to students that these pages will help you know if they are ready to start a new topic in their math textbooks.
- Students who have transferred from another school may not have been introduced to some of these skills. Encourage students to do their best and assure them you will help them learn any needed skills.

Alternative Assessment Strategy

- Oral administration is appropriate for younger students or those whose native language is not English. Read the skills title and directions one section at a time. Check students' understanding by asking them to tell you how they will do the first exercise in the group.

Name_____

Place-Value Chart

Write each number.

1.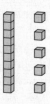

tens	ones
1	2

_____

2.

tens	ones
1	8

_____

3.

tens	ones
1	5

_____

4.

tens	ones
1	4

_____

5.

tens	ones
1	3

_____

6.

tens	ones
1	7

_____

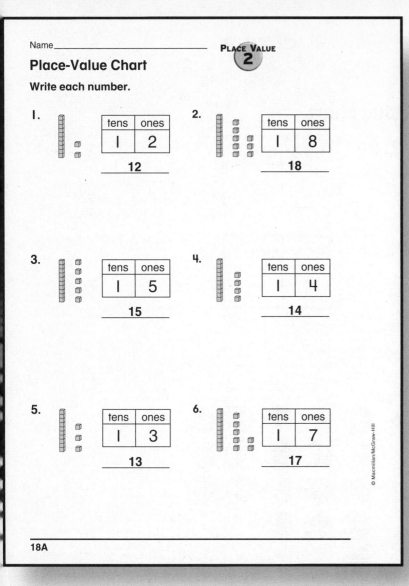

Name_____

Place-Value Chart

Write each number.

1. | tens | ones |
   |------|------|
   | 1 | 2 |

   12

2. | tens | ones |
   |------|------|
   | 1 | 8 |

   18

3. | tens | ones |
   |------|------|
   | 1 | 5 |

   15

4. | tens | ones |
   |------|------|
   | 1 | 4 |

   14

5. | tens | ones |
   |------|------|
   | 1 | 3 |

   13

6. | tens | ones |
   |------|------|
   | 1 | 7 |

   17

© Macmillan/McGraw-Hill

18A

PLACE VALUE 2 PREREQUISITE SKILLS

The skills listed in this chart are those identified as major prerequisite skills for students' success in Place Value. Each skill is covered by one or more assessment items from page 18A as shown in the middle column. The right column provides the page numbers for the lessons in this book that reteach Place Value prerequisite skills.

Skill Name	Assessment Items	Lesson Pages
Place-Value Chart	1-6	T76-T77

Assessment Goal

This assessment covers skills identified as necessary for success in Place Value.

Getting Started

- Allow students time to look over the assessment. Point out the labels that identify the skills covered.
- Have students find math vocabulary terms used in the assessment. List vocabulary terms on the board as students identify them. If necessary, review the meanings of all essential math vocabulary.

Introducing the Assessment

- Explain to students that these pages will help you know if they are ready to start a new chapter in their math textbooks.
- Students who have transferred from another school may not have been introduced to some of these skills. Encourage students to do their best and assure them you will help them learn any needed skills.

Alternative Assessment Strategy

- Oral administration is appropriate for younger students or those whose native language is not English. Read the skills title and directions one section at a time. Check students' understanding by asking them to tell you how they will do the first exercise in the group.

Place Value

Write each number in a place-value chart.

1. 64

tens	ones

2. 29

tens	ones

3. 38

tens	ones

4. 56

tens	ones

Regrouping Ones

Write each number two ways.

5.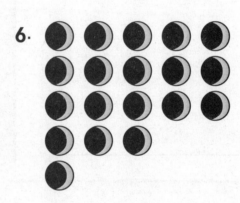

_____ ones

_____ tens _____ ones

6.

_____ ones

_____ tens _____ ones

7.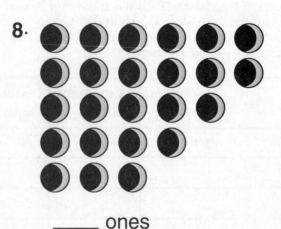

_____ ones

_____ tens _____ ones

8.

_____ ones

_____ tens _____ ones

Name_____

Place Value

Write each number in a place-value chart.

1. 64

tens	ones
6	4

2. 29

tens	ones
2	9

3. 38

tens	ones
3	8

4. 56

tens	ones
5	6

Regrouping Ones

Write each number two ways.

5.

__23__ ones

__2__ tens __3__ ones

6.

__19__ ones

__1__ tens __9__ ones

7.

__20__ ones

__2__ tens __0__ ones

8.

__25__ ones

__2__ tens __5__ ones

© Macmillan/McGraw-Hill

19A

PLACE VALUE 3 PREREQUISITE SKILLS

The skills listed in this chart are those identified as major prerequisite skills for students' success in Place Value. Each skill is covered by one or more assessment items from page 19A as shown in the middle column. The right column provides the page numbers for the lessons in this book that reteach Place Value prerequisite skills.

Skill Name	Assessment Items	Lesson Pages
Place Value	1-4	T78-T81
Regrouping Ones	5-8	T82-T83

Assessment Goal

This assessment covers skills identified as necessary for success in Place Value.

Getting Started

- Allow students time to look over the assessment. Point out the labels that identify the skills covered.
- Have students find math vocabulary terms used in the assessment. List vocabulary terms on the board as students identify them. If necessary, review the meanings of all essential math vocabulary.

Introducing the Assessment

- Explain to students that these pages will help you know if they are ready to start a new topic in their math textbooks.
- Students who have transferred from another school may not have been introduced to some of these skills. Encourage students to do their best and assure them you will help them learn any needed skills.

Alternative Assessment Strategy

- Oral administration is appropriate for younger students or those whose native language is not English. Read the skills title and directions one section at a time. Check students' understanding by asking them to tell you how they will do the first exercise in the group.

Name _____

Place Value

Write each number in a place-value chart.

1. 46

tens	ones

2. 98

tens	ones

3. 17

tens	ones

4. 66

tens	ones

Regrouping Tens and Ones

Write each number two ways.

5.

_____ tens _____ ones

_____ ones

6.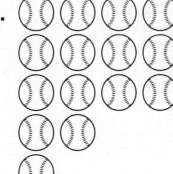

_____ tens _____ ones

_____ ones

7.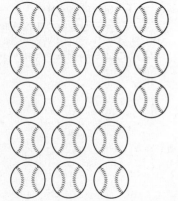

_____ tens _____ ones

_____ ones

8.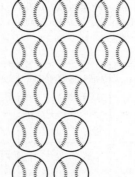

_____ tens _____ ones

_____ ones

Name _____

Place Value
Write each number in a place-value chart.

1. 46

tens	ones
4	6

2. 98

tens	ones
9	8

3. 17

tens	ones
1	7

4. 66

tens	ones
6	6

Regrouping Tens and Ones
Write each number two ways.

5.

__2__ tens __2__ ones

__22__ ones

6.

__1__ tens __5__ ones

__15__ ones

7.

__1__ tens __8__ ones

__18__ ones

8.

__1__ tens __2__ ones

__12__ ones

© Macmillan/McGraw-Hill

20A

PLACE VALUE 4 PREREQUISITE SKILLS

The skills listed in this chart are those identified as major prerequisite skills for students' success in Place Value. Each skill is covered by one or more assessment items from page 20A as shown in the middle column. The right column provides the page numbers for the lessons in this book that reteach Place Value prerequisite skills.

Skill Name	Assessment Items	Lesson Pages
Place Value	1-4	T78-T81
Regrouping Tens and Ones	5-8	T82-T85

PLACE VALUE 4 ASSESSMENT

Assessment Goal
This assessment covers skills identified as necessary for success in Place Value.

Getting Started
- Allow students time to look over the assessment. Point out the labels that identify the skills covered.
- Have students find math vocabulary terms used in the assessment. List vocabulary terms on the board as students identify them. If necessary, review the meanings of all essential math vocabulary.

Introducing the Assessment
- Explain to students that these pages will help you know if they are ready to start a new topic in their math textbooks.
- Students who have transferred from another school may not have been introduced to some of these skills. Encourage students to do their best and assure them you will help them learn any needed skills.

Alternative Assessment Strategy
- Oral administration is appropriate for younger students or those whose native language is not English. Read the skills title and directions one section at a time. Check students' understanding by asking them to tell you how they will do the first exercise in the group.

Numbers to 100

Write how many.

1.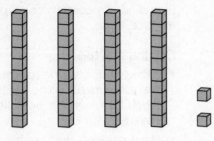

_____

2.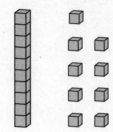

_____

3.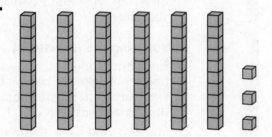

_____

4.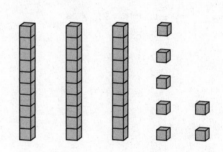

_____

Tens and Ones

Write the number.

5.

tens	ones
7	4

_____

6.

tens	ones
2	9

_____

7.

tens	ones
5	1

_____

8.

tens	ones
3	6

_____

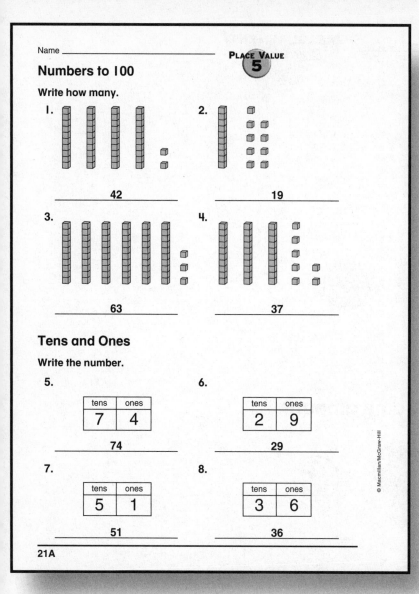

Name _____

Place Value 5

Numbers to 100

Write how many.

1. _____ 42 _____

2. _____ 19 _____

3. _____ 63 _____

4. _____ 37 _____

Tens and Ones

Write the number.

5.

tens	ones
7	4

74

6.

tens	ones
2	9

29

7.

tens	ones
5	1

51

8.

tens	ones
3	6

36

© Macmillan/McGraw-Hill

21A

Assessment Goal

This assessment covers skills identified as necessary for success in Place Value.

Getting Started

- Allow students time to look over the assessment. Point out the labels that identify the skills covered.

- Have students find math vocabulary terms used in the assessment. List vocabulary terms on the board as students identify them. If necessary, review the meanings of all essential math vocabulary.

Introducing the Assessment

- Explain to students that these pages will help you know if they are ready to start a new topic in their math textbooks.

- Students who have transferred from another school may not have been introduced to some of these skills. Encourage students to do their best and assure them you will help them learn any needed skills.

Alternative Assessment Strategy

- Oral administration is appropriate for younger students or those whose native language is not English. Read the skills title and directions one section at a time. Check students' understanding by asking them to tell you how they will do the first exercise in the group.

PLACE VALUE 5 PREREQUISITE SKILLS

The skills listed in this chart are those identified as major prerequisite skills for students' success in Place Value. Each skill is covered by one or more assessment items from page 21A as shown in the middle column. The right column provides the page numbers for the lessons in this book that reteach Place Value prerequisite skills.

Skill Name	Assessment Items	Lesson Pages
Numbers to 100	1-4	T86-T87
Tens and Ones	5-8	T76-T81

Name_____

Identifying Coins

Circle the correct coin.

1. 10¢

2. 25¢

Equal Amounts

Circle the two that show the same amount.

3.

4.

Writing Money Two Ways

Circle the two that show the same amount.

5. 20¢ $0.02 $0.20

6. $0.45 $4.50 45¢

7. $5.00 50¢ $0.50

8. 18¢ $1.80 $0.18

Name_____

Identifying Coins

Circle the correct coin.

1. 10¢

2. 25¢

Equal Amounts

Circle the two that show the same amount.

3.

4.

Writing Money Two Ways

Circle the two that show the same amount.

5. (20¢) $0.02 ($0.20)

6. ($0.45) $4.50 (45¢)

7. $5.00 (50¢) ($0.50)

8. (18¢) $1.80 ($0.18)

22A

MEASUREMENT AND GEOMETRY 1 PREREQUISITE SKILLS

The skills listed in this chart are those identified as major prerequisite skills for students' success in Measurement and Geometry. Each skill is covered by one or more assessment items from page 22A as shown in the middle column. The right column provides the page numbers for the lessons in this book that reteach Measurement and Geometry prerequisite skills.

Skill Name	Assessment Items	Lesson Pages
Identifying Coins	1-2	T88-T89
Equal Amounts	3-4	T90-T91
Writing Money Two Ways	5-8	T88-T89

MEASUREMENT AND GEOMETRY 1 ASSESSMENT

Assessment Goal

This assessment covers skills identified as necessary for success in Measurement and Geometry.

Getting Started

- Allow students time to look over the assessment. Point out the labels that identify the skills covered.

- Have students find math vocabulary terms used in the assessment. List vocabulary terms on the board as students identify them. If necessary, review the meanings of all essential math vocabulary.

Introducing the Assessment

- Explain to students that these pages will help you know if they are ready to start a new topics in their math textbooks.

- Students who have transferred from another school may not have been introduced to some of these skills. Encourage students to do their best and assure them you will help them learn any needed skills.

Alternative Assessment Strategy

- Oral administration is appropriate for younger students or those whose native language is not English. Read the skills title and directions one section at a time. Check students' understanding by asking them to tell you how they will do the first exercise in the group.

Time to the Hour

Write the time.

1.

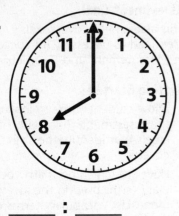

____ : ____

2.

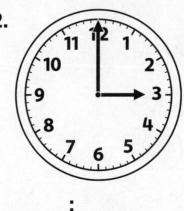

____ : ____

Time to the Half Hour

Write the time.

3.

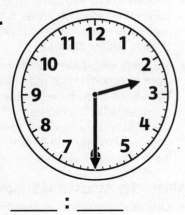

____ : ____

4.

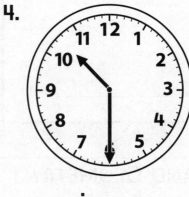

____ : ____

Time to 5 Minutes

Write the time.

5.

____ : ____

6.

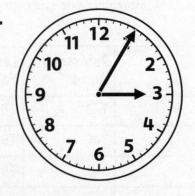

____ : ____

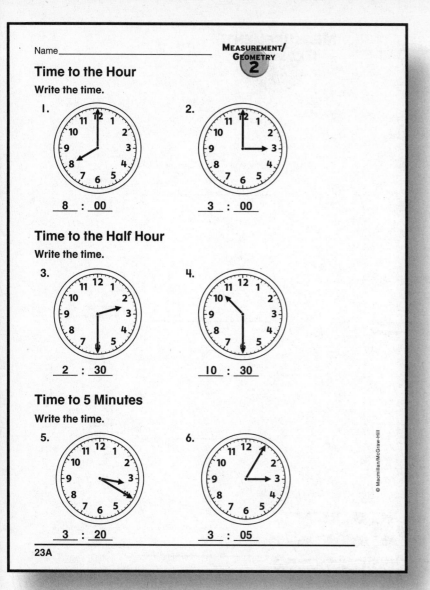

Name_____

Time to the Hour

Write the time.

1.

__8__ : __00__

2.

__3__ : __00__

Time to the Half Hour

Write the time.

3.

__2__ : __30__

4.

__10__ : __30__

Time to 5 Minutes

Write the time.

5.

__3__ : __20__

6.

__3__ : __05__

© Macmillan/McGraw-Hill

23A

MEASUREMENT AND GEOMETRY 2 PREREQUISITE SKILLS

The skills listed in this chart are those identified as major prerequisite skills for students' success in Measurement and Geometry. Each skill is covered by one or more assessment items from page 23A as shown in the middle column. The right column provides the page numbers for the lessons in this book that reteach Measurement and Geometry prerequisite skills.

Skill Name	Assessment Items	Lesson Pages
Time to the Hour	1-2	T92-T93
Time to the Half Hour	3-4	T92-T93
Time to 5 Minutes	5-6	T94

MEASUREMENT AND GEOMETRY 2 ASSESSMENT

Assessment Goal

This assessment covers skills identified as necessary for success in Measurement and Geometry.

Getting Started

- Allow students time to look over the assessment. Point out the labels that identify the skills covered.

- Have students find math vocabulary terms used in the assessment. List vocabulary terms on the board as students identify them. If necessary, review the meanings of all essential math vocabulary.

Introducing the Assessment

- Explain to students that these pages will help you know if they are ready to start a new topic in their math textbooks.

- Students who have transferred from another school may not have been introduced to some of these skills. Encourage students to do their best and assure them you will help them learn any needed skills.

Alternative Assessment Strategy

- Oral administration is appropriate for younger students or those whose native language is not English. Read the skills title and directions one section at a time. Check students' understanding by asking them to tell you how they will do the first exercise in the group.

Explore Length

How long is each one?

1.

_____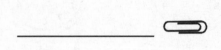

2.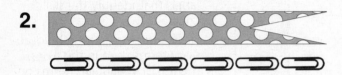

_____

3.

_____

4.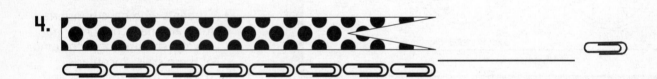

_____

5.

_____

6.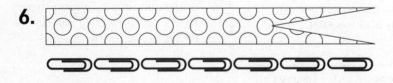

_____

7.

_____

Name_____

Explore Length

How long is each one?

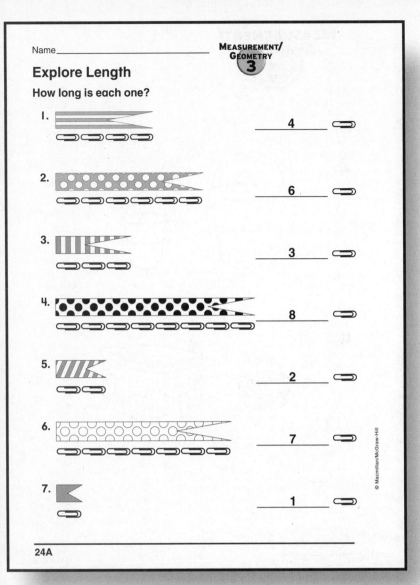

1. _____ 4 ⊂⊃

2. _____ 6 ⊂⊃

3. _____ 3 ⊂⊃

4. _____ 8 ⊂⊃

5. _____ 2 ⊂⊃

6. _____ 7 ⊂⊃

7. _____ 1 ⊂⊃

© Macmillan/McGraw-Hill

24A

MEASUREMENT AND GEOMETRY 3
PREREQUISITE SKILLS

The skills listed in this chart are those identified as major prerequisite skills for students' success in Measurement and Geometry. Each skill is covered by one or more assessment items from page 24A as shown in the middle column. The right column provides the page numbers for the lessons in this book that reteach Measurement and Geometry prerequisite skills.

Skill Name	Assessment Items	Lesson Pages
Explore Length	1-7	T96-T97

MEASUREMENT AND GEOMETRY 3 ASSESSMENT

Assessment Goal

This assessment covers skills identified as necessary for success in Measurement and Geometry.

Getting Started

- Allow students time to look over the assessment. Point out the labels that identify the skills covered.

- Have students find math vocabulary terms used in the assessment. List vocabulary terms on the board as students identify them. If necessary, review the meanings of all essential math vocabulary.

Introducing the Assessment

- Explain to students that these pages will help you know if they are ready to start a new topic in their math textbooks.

- Students who have transferred from another school may not have been introduced to some of these skills. Encourage students to do their best and assure them you will help them learn any needed skills.

Alternative Assessment Strategy

- Oral administration is appropriate for younger students or those whose native language is not English. Read the skills title and directions one section at a time. Check students' understanding by asking them to tell you how they will do the first exercise in the group.

Explore Capacity

Circle the one that holds more.

1.

2.

3.

4.

Explore Weight

Circle the one that is heavier.

5.

6.

7.

8.

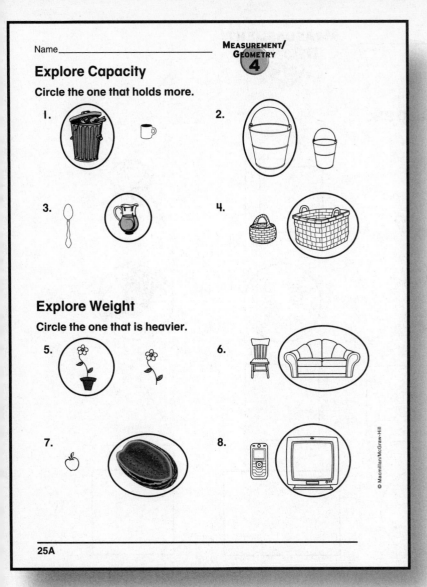

Name_____

Explore Capacity

Circle the one that holds more.

1.

2.

3.

4.

Explore Weight

Circle the one that is heavier.

5.

6.

7.

8.

© Macmillan/McGraw-Hill

25A

MEASUREMENT AND GEOMETRY 4
PREREQUISITE SKILLS

The skills listed in this chart are those identified as major prerequisite skills for students' success in Measurement and Geometry. Each skill is covered by one or more assessment items from page 25A as shown in the middle column. The right column provides the page numbers for the lessons in this book that reteach Measurement and Geometry prerequisite skills.

Skill Name	Assessment Items	Lesson Pages
Explore Capacity	1-4	T98-T99
Explore Weight	5-8	T100-T101

MEASUREMENT AND GEOMETRY 4 ASSESSMENT

Assessment Goal

This assessment covers skills identified as necessary for success in Measurement and Geometry.

Getting Started

- Allow students time to look over the assessment. Point out the labels that identify the skills covered.

- Have students find math vocabulary terms used in the assessment. List vocabulary terms on the board as students identify them. If necessary, review the meanings of all essential math vocabulary.

Introducing the Assessment

- Explain to students that these pages will help you know if they are ready to start a new topic in their math textbooks.

- Students who have transferred from another school may not have been introduced to some of these skills. Encourage students to do their best and assure them you will help them learn any needed skills.

Alternative Assessment Strategy

- Oral administration is appropriate for younger students or those whose native language is not English. Read the skills title and directions one section at a time. Check students' understanding by asking them to tell you how they will do the first exercise in the group.

Same Shape

Circle the same shape or shapes.

1.

2.

3.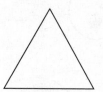

4.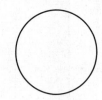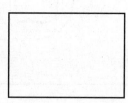

Sides and Corners

Write the number of sides. Write the number of corners.

5.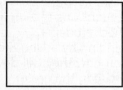

_____ sides

_____ corners

6.

_____ sides

_____ corners

MEASUREMENT/ GEOMETRY 5

Same Shape

Circle the same shape or shapes.

1.

2.

3.

4.

© Macmillan/McGraw-Hill

Sides and Corners

Write the number of sides. Write the number of corners.

5.

___4___ sides

___4___ corners

6.

___3___ sides

___3___ corners

MEASUREMENT AND GEOMETRY 5 PREREQUISITE SKILLS

The skills listed in this chart are those identified as major prerequisite skills for students' success in the Measurement and Geometry. Each skill is covered by one or more assessment items from page 26A as shown in the middle column. The right column provides the page numbers for the lessons in this book that reteach Measurement and Geometry prerequisite skills.

Skill Name	Assessment Items	Lesson Pages
Same Shape	1-4	T102-T105
Sides and Corners	5-6	T106-T107

MEASUREMENT AND GEOMETRY 5 ASSESSMENT

Assessment Goal

This assessment covers skills identified as necessary for success in Measurement and Geometry.

Getting Started

- Allow students time to look over the assessment. Point out the labels that identify the skills covered.

- Have students find math vocabulary terms used in the assessment. List vocabulary terms on the board as students identify them. If necessary, review the meanings of all essential math vocabulary.

Introducing the Assessment

- Explain to students that these pages will help you know if they are ready to start a new topic in their math textbooks.

- Students who have transferred from another school may not have been introduced to some of these skills. Encourage students to do their best and assure them you will help them learn any needed skills.

Alternative Assessment Strategy

- Oral administration is appropriate for younger students or those whose native language is not English. Read the skills title and directions one section at a time. Check students' understanding by asking them to tell you how they will do the first exercise in the group.

Same Size and Shape

Circle the same size and shape.

1.

2.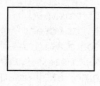

3.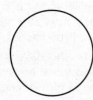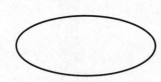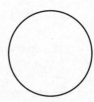

Equal Parts

Circle the shape that shows equal parts.

4.

5.

Name _____

Same Size and Shape

Circle the same size and shape.

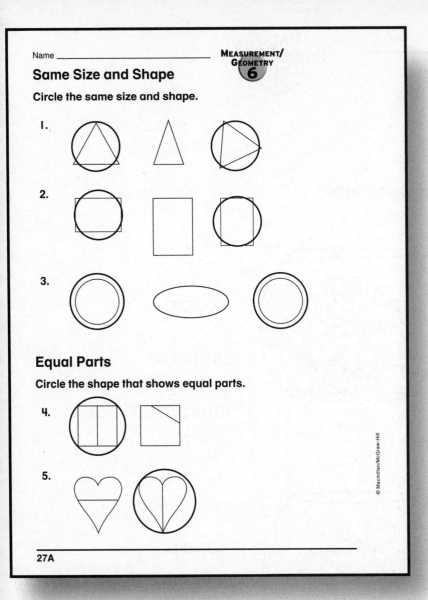

1.

2.

3.

Equal Parts

Circle the shape that shows equal parts.

4.

5.

© Macmillan/McGraw-Hill

27A

Assessment Goal

This assessment covers skills identified as necessary for success in Measurement and Geometry.

Getting Started

- Allow students time to look over the assessment. Point out the labels that identify the skills covered.

- Have students find math vocabulary terms used in the assessment. List vocabulary terms on the board as students identify them. If necessary, review the meanings of all essential math vocabulary.

Introducing the Assessment

- Explain to students that these pages will help you know if they are ready to start a new topic in their math textbooks.

- Students who have transferred from another school may not have been introduced to some of these skills. Encourage students to do their best and assure them you will help them learn any needed skills.

Alternative Assessment Strategy

- Oral administration is appropriate for younger students or those whose native language is not English. Read the skills title and directions one section at a time. Check students' understanding by asking them to tell you how they will do the first exercise in the group.

MEASUREMENT AND GEOMETRY 6 PREREQUISITE SKILLS

The skills listed in this chart are those identified as major prerequisite skills for students' success in Measurement and Geometry. Each skill is covered by one or more assessment items from page 27A as shown in the middle column. The right column provides the page numbers for the lessons in this book that reteach Measurement and Geometry prerequisite skills.

Skill Name	Assessment Items	Lesson Pages
Same Size and Shape	1-3	T108-T109
Equal Parts	4-5	T110-T111

Name_____

Certain, Probable, Impossible

Will it happen?
Circle certain, probable, or impossible.

1. You pick a .

certain

probable

impossible

2. You pick a .

certain

probable

impossible

3. You pick a .

certain

probable

impossible

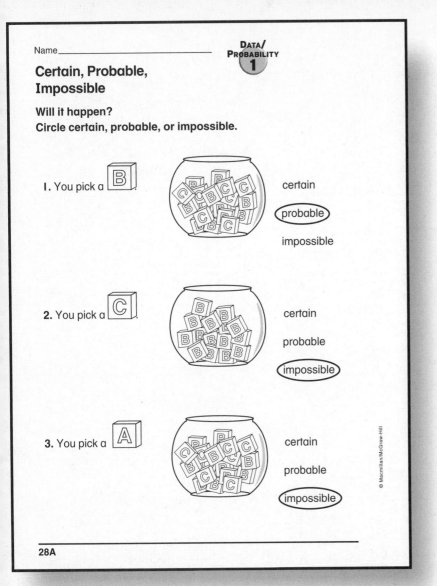

Name_____

Certain, Probable, Impossible

Will it happen?
Circle certain, probable, or impossible.

1. You pick a B.

    certain

    (probable)

    impossible

2. You pick a C.

    certain

    probable

    (impossible)

3. You pick a A.

    certain

    probable

    (impossible)

© Macmillan/McGraw-Hill

28A

DATA AND PROBABILITY 1
PREREQUISITE SKILLS

The skills listed in this chart are those identified as major prerequisite skills for students' success in Data and Probability. Each skill is covered by one or more assessment items from page 28A as shown in the middle column. The right column provides the page numbers for the lessons in this book that reteach Data and Probability prerequisite skills.

Skill Name	Assessment Items	Lesson Pages
Certain, Probable, Impossible	1-3	T112-T113

DATA AND PROBABILITY 1 ASSESSMENT

Assessment Goal
This assessment covers skills identified as necessary for success in Data and Probability.

Getting Started
- Allow students time to look over the assessment. Point out the labels that identify the skills covered.
- Have students find math vocabulary terms used in the assessment. List vocabulary terms on the board as students identify them. If necessary, review the meanings of all essential math vocabulary.

Introducing the Assessment
- Explain to students that these pages will help you know if they are ready to start a new topic in their math textbooks.
- Students who have transferred from another school may not have been introduced to some of these skills. Encourage students to do their best and assure them you will help them learn any needed skills.

Alternative Assessment Strategy
- Oral administration is appropriate for younger students or those whose native language is not English. Read the skills title and directions one section at a time. Check students' understanding by asking them to tell you how they will do the first exercise in the group.

Skill Builder
Lessons and Activities

Activity 1 Lesson Goal

- Compare more than two groups.

What the Student Needs to Know

- Recognize the meaning of *most* and *fewest*.
- Match one-to-one.

Getting Started

Display three circles, four triangles, and five squares. Ask:

- *Which group has more, the circles or the triangles?* (triangles)
- *Which group has more, the triangles or the squares?* (squares)
- *Which group has the most?* (squares)

What Can I Do?

Read the question and the response. Then read and discuss the examples.

- Explain that the words *more* and *fewer* are used to compare two groups. When you compare three groups or more, you use the words *most* and *fewest*.
- Ask students to tell why the words *most* and *fewest* are used in the example. (Three groups of objects are being compared.)

Try It

Point out to students that the question asks them to find the group with the fewest items.

Power Practice

- Suggest to students that they should write down the number of objects in each group.
- Have students complete the practice items. Then review each answer.

Name_____

Most and Fewest

Learn

What Can I Do?
I want to know which group has the fewest.

Count and compare numbers.

Count the □s, △s, and ○s.

| 1 | 2 | 3 | 4 | 5 | 6 | 7 | 8 |

△ ② ③ △ ⑤ ⑥

① ② ③ ④ ⑤ ⑥ ⑦

Write the numbers in order from the **least** to the **greatest.** 6 7 8

The group of □ has the **most.**

The group of △ has the **fewest.**

Try It • Count and compare numbers.

1. △ ② ③ △
   □ ② □
   ① ② ○ ○ ○ ○

2. △ △ △ △ △ △ △
   □ □ □ □ □ □ □ □
   ○ ○ ○ ○ ○ ○ ○ ○ ○

The group of △ has fewest.　　The group of □ has fewest.

Power Practice • Circle the group that has the <u>fewest</u>.

3.

4.

2

© Macmillan/McGraw-Hill

WHAT IF THE STUDENT CAN'T

Recognize the Meaning of *Most* and *Fewest*

Ask students the following questions that involve the concepts *most* or *fewest*. Have students find the solution to each.

- Give the student red, blue, and yellow counters. Ask: *Which group has the most counters? Which group has the fewest counters?*
- Give the student groups of play pennies, nickels, and dimes. Ask: *Which group has the most coins? Which group has the fewest coins?*

Match One-to-One

- Distribute attribute blocks in three shapes. Have the student use one-to-one matchup to determine which group has the most shapes and which group has the fewest.

Complete the Power Practice

- If the student has not used one-to-one matching, ask the student to draw circles containing one item from each of the three groups. Remind the student that the group with no items left over has the fewest.
- Have students count the items in each group aloud before identifying the group with the fewest.

Name_____

Identify Reasonable Estimates

Learn

Use number sense.

Do you think there are fewer than 50 fish?

Do you think there are more than 10 fish?

What Can I Do?
I want to estimate how many.

It looks like there are more than 10 but fewer than 50. A good estimate is 20 or 30 fish.

Group tens to estimate.

You can estimate how many by grouping tens. There are nearly 3 tens, or 30 fish.

Try It • Circle the best estimate.

1. 2 (20) 200

Power Practice • Circle the best estimate.

2. 10 (30) 100

3. (10) 30 50

© Macmillan/McGraw-Hill

3

WHAT IF THE STUDENT CAN'T

Recognize the Meaning of *Greater* and *Less*

Use classroom items and people to ask questions involving greater or less.

- *Are there a greater number of boys or girls in our class?*
- *Is the number of doors in our room greater or less than the number of windows?*
- *Is the number of desks in our classroom greater or less than the number of books in our library?*

Count Ten Items

- Have students locate and count out ten items from inside their desks or cubbies.

Complete the Power Practice

- Discuss each incorrect answer. Have students show each number with hundreds, tens, and ones models. Compare numbers.

Number Sense Skill Builder **T3**

Activity 3 Lesson Goal

- Count on and back on a number line.

What the Student Needs to Know

- Count by 1s.
- Recognize the meanings of *greater* and *less*.

Getting Started

Draw a 0–10 number line on the board. Cover up the number 3. Say:

- *Read the numbers. Which number is missing?* (3)

Repeat, covering a different number.

What Can I Do?

Read the question and the response. Then read and discuss the examples. Ask:

- *When you count on, are the numbers greater or less?* (greater) *In which direction do you move on the number line?* (right)
- *When you count back, are the numbers greater or less?* (less) *In which direction do you move on the number line?* (left)

Try It

- Suggest that students look to the left and right of the number that is missing. To find the number, they could count on from the number to the left or count back from the number to the right.
- Have students check their work by counting from 0 to 10.

Power Practice

- Review the columns of the chart before students begin, and make sure they know where to write the numbers that are 1 less and 1 more.
- Have students complete the practice items. Discuss their answers.

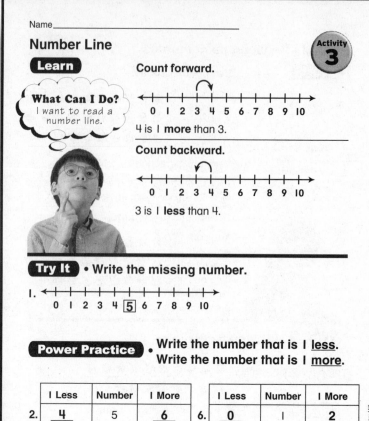

Name _____

Number Line

Activity 3

Learn

What Can I Do? I want to read a number line.

Count forward.

0 1 2 3 4 5 6 7 8 9 10

4 is 1 **more** than 3.

Count backward.

0 1 2 3 4 5 6 7 8 9 10

3 is 1 **less** than 4.

Try It • Write the missing number.

1. 0 1 2 3 4 **5** 6 7 8 9 10

Power Practice • Write the number that is 1 **less**.
• Write the number that is 1 **more**.

	1 Less	Number	1 More			1 Less	Number	1 More
2.	4	5	6	6.		0	1	2
3.	7	8	9	7.		2	3	4
4.	1	2	3	8.		6	7	8
5.	3	4	5	9.		5	6	7

© Macmillan/McGraw-Hill

4

WHAT IF THE STUDENT CAN'T

Count by 1s

- Line up groups of ten students.
- Have students "count off" by 1s.
- Ask students to realign themselves and count off again. Repeat.

Recognize the Meanings of *Greater* and *Less*

- Give the student ten counters and number cards 0–10.
- Have the student pick two cards, model the numbers with counters, and identify which number is greater and which is less.

Complete the Power Practice

- Discuss each incorrect answer. Point out that the numbers in column 1 are supposed to be 1 less, and the numbers in column 3 are supposed to be 1 more. Have the student use a number line to determine the correct answers.
- Have the student read the corrected answers using this wording: "4 is 1 less than 5. 6 is 1 more than 5."

Name_____

Compare Numbers

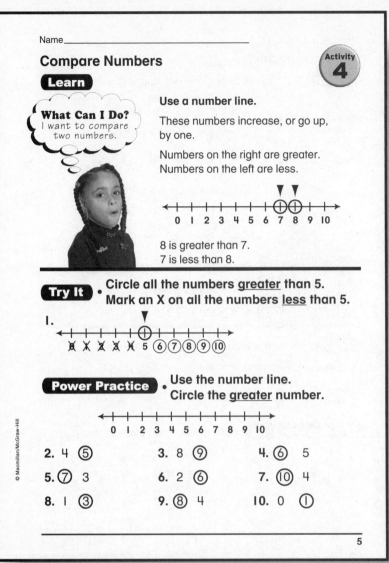

Learn

What Can I Do?
I want to compare two numbers.

Use a number line.

These numbers increase, or go up, by one.

Numbers on the right are greater.
Numbers on the left are less.

0 1 2 3 4 5 6 7 (8)(9) 10

8 is greater than 7.
7 is less than 8.

Try It • Circle all the numbers <u>greater</u> than 5.
• Mark an X on all the numbers <u>less</u> than 5.

1.
X X X X X 5 (6)(7)(8)(9)(10)

Power Practice • Use the number line.
• Circle the <u>greater</u> number.

0 1 2 3 4 5 6 7 8 9 10

2. 4 (5)   3. 8 (9)   4. (6) 5

5. (7) 3   6. 2 (6)   7. (10) 4

8. 1 (3)   9. (8) 4   10. 0 (1)

5

Activity 4

Activity 4 Lesson Goal
• Compare numbers 0–10.

What the Student Needs to Know
• Recognize the meanings of *greater* and *less*.
• Read a number line.

Getting Started
Have students count aloud from 0 to 10. Ask:
• *Which number is the greatest?* (10)

What Can I Do?
Read the question and the response. Then read and discuss the example. Ask:
• *If 8 is to the right of 7, which number is greater?* (8)
• *If 6 is to the left of 7, which number is less?* (6)

Try It
After the directions are read aloud, students may follow these steps:
• Find 5. Look to the right. Those numbers are greater than 5. Circle them.
• Find 5. Look to the left. Those numbers are less than 5. Mark an X on them.

Power Practice
• Have students complete the practice items. Then review each answer, having volunteers use this wording: "5 is greater than 4."

WHAT IF THE STUDENT CAN'T

Recognize the Meanings of *Greater* and *Less*
• Divide a pile of counters unevenly between two students.
• Have the pair guess which one has the greater number and which one has the lesser number.
• Have students count to confirm their guesses. Repeat.

Read a Number Line
• Mark off a 0–10 number line using masking tape on the floor.
• Have students locate the numbers you say aloud by standing on them.

• Have students move left or right to find numbers that are greater or less than the one you assigned them.

Complete the Power Practice
• Discuss each incorrect answer. Have student pairs work together to locate each number on the number line and determine which number comes before (further left) and after (further right). Remind them that numbers on the right are greater.

Activity 5 Lesson Goal

- Compare two groups.

What the Student Needs to Know

- Recognize the meaning of *more* and *fewer*.
- Match one-to-one.
- Count to 12.

Getting Started

Line up four girls and five boys. Ask them to pair off. Then ask:

- *Can all the girls and boys pair off? Who is left over? Are there more girls or more boys?* (more boys)

Repeat using six girls and five boys. Then Ask:

- *How could we use one-to-one matching to see whether there are more boys or girls in our class?* (Line up boys and girls and have them pair off. The group with students left over has more.)

What Can I Do?

Read the question and the response. Then read and discuss the examples. Ask:

- *How can we tell if there are more ants or more spiders?* (Draw a line to match one ant with one spider and see if there are any ants or spiders left over.)

Then Ask:

- *What is another way to compare groups?* (Count how many are in each group. Write a number next to each ladybug and each grasshopper and compare numbers.)

Try It

Have students look back at the ants and spiders above to see how to draw lines to match one-to-one.

Power Practice

- Tell students they may use either strategy to complete Exercises 2–3.
- Have students complete the practice items. Then review each answer.

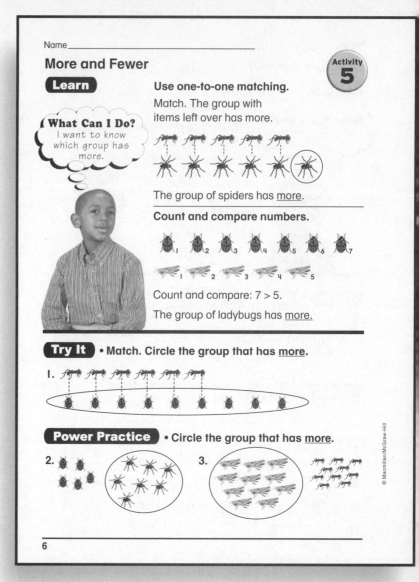

Name_____

More and Fewer

Learn

What Can I Do?
I want to know which group has more.

Use one-to-one matching.
Match. The group with items left over has more.

The group of spiders has <u>more</u>.

Count and compare numbers.

Count and compare: 7 > 5.
The group of ladybugs has <u>more.</u>

Try It • Match. Circle the group that has <u>more</u>.

1.

Power Practice • Circle the group that has <u>more</u>.

2.   3.

6

© Macmillan/McGraw-Hill

WHAT IF THE STUDENT CAN'T

Recognize the Meaning of *More* and *Fewer*

Ask the student the following questions that involve the concepts *more* or *fewer*. Have the student find the solutions.

- *Count the crayons and pencils in your desk. Are there more or fewer crayons than pencils?*
- *Think about the number of school days in a week compared to the number of weekend days. Are there more or fewer school days than weekend days?*

Match One-to-One

- Distribute attribute block squares in two colors. Have the student make pairs to determine which has more.

Count to 12

- Give the student an egg carton and 12 counters. Have the student drop one counter into each compartment of the egg carton, counting as he or she does so.

Complete the Power Practice

- If the student has not used one-to-one matching, ask the student to draw lines to pair up items in the two groups. Remind the student that the group with items left over has more.

Name_____

Greater Than, Less Than

Learn

What Can I Do?
I want to compare two numbers using >, <, or =.

Understand the symbols.

The symbol > means **greater than**.
The open side of the symbol is next to the greater number.

5 > 3 means 5 **is greater than** 3.

The symbol < means **less than**.
The symbol points to the smaller number.

3 < 5 means 3 **is less than** 5.

Use a number line.

Greater numbers are always on the right.
Lesser numbers are always on the left.

0 1 2 ③ 4 ⑤ 6 7 8 9 10

Think: 5 is to the right of 3, so 5 > 3.

Try It • Use the number line. Compare.
Write >, <, or =.

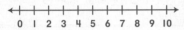
0 1 2 3 4 5 6 7 8 9 10

1. 6 ⓧ 7   2. 3 ⊜ 3   3. 8 ⓧ 10

Power Practice • Compare. Write >, <, or =.

4. 12 ⊜ 10   5. 5 ⊜ 5

6. 6 ⓧ 16   7. 15 ⓧ 16

© Macmillan/McGraw-Hill

7

WHAT IF THE STUDENT CAN'T

Recognize the Meaning of *Great, Greater, More, Most, Fewer, Fewest, Less, and Least*

- On the board, write 8 and 12. Ask: *Which number is greater?* (12) *Which number is less?* (8)
- Then write these sentences on the board:
  __ is less than __.
  __ is greater than __.
  Ask students to complete each sentence using the numbers 8 and 12.
- Do the same for other number pairs from 1–20.

Read a Number Line

On the board, draw a 0–10 number line. Ask the student:

- *Which numbers are less than 6? (0, 1, . . .5)*
- *Which numbers are greater than 3? (4, 5, 6,. . .10)*
- *Which numbers are less than 4? (0, 1, 2, 3)*
- *Which numbers are greater than 7? (8, 9, 10)*

Complete the Power Practice

- Discuss each incorrect answer. Draw a 0–20 number line and have the student use it to compare the numbers.

Activity 6 Lesson Goal
- Compare numbers.

What the Student Needs to Know
- Recognize the meaning of *great, greater, more, most, fewer, fewest, less,* and *least.*
- Read a number line.

Getting Started
Cut out a large tagboard > sign. On the board, write the following number pairs:

- 11   18
- 7   16
- 14   13

Have volunteers come to the board and point to the lesser number in the pair. Then have them point to the greater number in the pair. Help students to say which number is less than the other and which is greater.

What Can I Do?
Read the question and the response. Then read and discuss the examples. Ask:

- *What's an easy way to remember which way to point the "greater than" symbol?* (Always point to the smaller number.)
- *If number A is to the left of number B on a number line, which number is less?* (number A)

Try It
Remind students to first locate the numbers on the number line and then compare.

Power Practice
- Have students complete the practice items. Then review each answer. Discuss the strategies students used to compare the numbers.

Activity 7 Lesson Goal
• Compare numbers to 99.

What the Student Needs to Know
• Recognize the meaning of *greater* and *less*.
• Read a number line.
• Read a place-value chart.

Getting Started
Have students count aloud from 20 to 30. Ask:

• *Which numbers that you said are greater than 25? (26, 27, . . . 30)*

What Can I Do?
Read the question and the response. Then read and discuss the examples. Ask:

• *If 15 is to the right of 13, which number is greater? (15)*

• *If 13 is to the left of 15, which number is less? (13)*

• *How can you use place value to compare the numbers 13 and 15?* (Look at the tens digits. Since they are the same, look at the ones digits. 5 ones is greater than 3 ones, so 15 is greater than 13.)

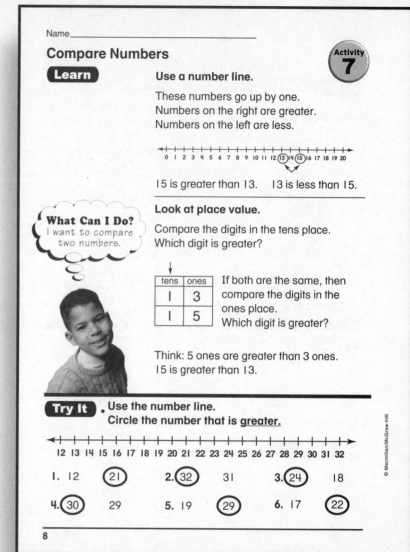

Name_____

Compare Numbers

Learn

Activity 7

Use a number line.

These numbers go up by one.
Numbers on the right are greater.
Numbers on the left are less.

0 1 2 3 4 5 6 7 8 9 10 11 12 (13) 14 (15) 16 17 18 19 20

15 is greater than 13.   13 is less than 15.

What Can I Do?
I want to compare two numbers.

Look at place value.

Compare the digits in the tens place.
Which digit is greater?

tens	ones
1	3
1	5

If both are the same, then compare the digits in the ones place.
Which digit is greater?

Think: 5 ones are greater than 3 ones.
15 is greater than 13.

Try It . Use the number line.
Circle the number that is <u>greater.</u>

12 13 14 15 16 17 18 19 20 21 22 23 24 25 26 27 28 29 30 31 32

1. 12 (21)   2. (32) 31   3. (24) 18

4. (30) 29   5. 19 (29)   6. 17 (22)

8

© Macmillan/McGraw-Hill

WHAT IF THE STUDENT CAN'T

Recognize the Meaning of *Greater* and *Less*
• Give the student a pile of counters. Ask the student to separate the pile into two piles, count the counters, and tell which number is greater and which is less.

Read a Number Line
Draw a 0–10 number line on the board, omitting several numbers. Say:

• *Fill in the missing numbers in order.*
• *Which number is least? (0)*
• *Which numbers is greatest? (10)*
• *Which numbers are less than 4? (0, 1, 2, 3,)*
• *Which numbers are greater than 7? (8, 9, 10)*

Name_____

7. 45 (54)   8. (33) 23

9. 56 (66)   10. 69 (70)

11. (97) 88   12. (17) 16

13. 19 (29)   14. (80) 79

15. (48) 47   16. 47 (57)

17. 73 (83)   18. (82) 28

19. 44 (55)   20. (50) 5

21. 26 (28)   22. (59) 58

23. (63) 36   24. 43 (49)

25. 69 (71)   26. (51) 31

27. 13 (25)   28. 28 (46)

29. 10 (22)   30. 9 (90)

© Macmillan/McGraw-Hill

9

Try It
Remind students to use the number line to determine which number is greater.

Power Practice
- Have students complete the practice items. Then review each answer. Discuss the strategies students used to find the greater number.
- Extend the practice by having students name a number that is greater than either of the numbers shown in each pair. For example, for Exercise 5, 55 is greater than 45 or 54.

WHAT IF THE STUDENT CAN'T

Read a Place-Value Chart
- Write these numbers in a place-value chart: 42, 24, 31, 13, 48, 84. Have the student identify the number of tens and ones in each number and write the two-digit number.

Complete the Power Practice
- Discuss each incorrect answer. Have the student identify the number of tens and ones in each number, compare tens, and then compare ones.

Activity 8 Lesson Goal
• Compare numbers to 99.

What the Student Needs to Know
• Recognize the meaning of *greater* and *less*.
• Read a number line.
• Read a place-value chart.

Getting Started
Have students count aloud from 0 to 20. Ask:

• *Which numbers are greater than 10?* (11, 12, . . . 20)

What Can I Do?
Read the question and the response. Then read and discuss the example. Ask:

• *Which number is to the right of 15?* (16)

• *Which number is greater?* (16)

• *Which number is to the left of 18?* (17)

• *Which number is less?* (17)

• *How can you use place value to compare the numbers 16 and 17?* (Look at the tens digits. Since they are the same, look at the ones digits. 7 ones is greater than 6 ones, so 17 is greater than 16.)

Name_____

Compare Whole Numbers

Learn   Use a number line.

0 1 2 3 4 5 6 7 8 9 10 11 12 13 14 15 16 17 18 19 20

What Can I Do?
I want to compare two numbers.

Each number increases by ones.
The number on the **right** is **greater**. →
← The number on the **left** is **less**.

17 is greater than 16. 16 is less than 17.

Look at place value.

Look at the tens digits. Compare. Which digit is greater?

tens	ones
1	6
1	7

If the tens digits are the same, look at the ones digits. Compare. Which digit is greater?

Think: 7 ones is greater than 6 ones.
17 is greater than 16.

Try It • Use the place-value charts.
Circle the number that is **greater**.

1.

tens	ones
3	5
③	⑨

2.

tens	ones
②	①
1	2

3.

tens	ones
⑧	③
7	3

4.

tens	ones
6	7
⑥	⑧

10

© Macmillan/McGraw-Hill

WHAT IF THE STUDENT CAN'T

Recognize the Meaning of *Greater* and *Less*

• Give a student a pile of counters. Have the student separate the pile into two groups, count each group of counters, and tell which number is greater and which is less.

Read a Number Line
Draw a 0–10 number line on the board. Ask:

• *Which number is the greatest?* (10)

• *Which number is the least?* (0)

• *Which numbers are greater than 5?* (6, 7, 8, 9, 10)

• *Which numbers are less than 5?* (0, 1, 2, 3, 4)

Power Practice • Circle the number that is <u>greater</u>.

5. 68 (86) 6. (24) 23

7. 19 (91) 8. 39 (40)

9. (27) 25 10. (61) 60

11. (13) 11 12. (55) 45

13. (98) 89 14. 67 (77)

15. (56) 50 16. (75) 57

17. 22 (33) 18. (90) 9

19. (86) 68 20. (49) 48

11

© Macmillan/McGraw-Hill

Try It
Remind students to compare tens before comparing ones. If the tens digits differ, they do not need to look at the ones.

Power Practice
• Have students complete the practice items. Then review each answer. Discuss the strategies students used to find the greater number.

WHAT IF THE STUDENT CAN'T

Read a Place-Value Chart
• Write these numbers in a place-value chart: 18, 81, 45, 54, 27, 72. Have the student identify the number of tens and ones in each number and write the two-digit number.

Complete the Power Practice
• Discuss each incorrect answer. Have students identify the number of tens and ones in each number, compare tens, and then compare ones.

Activity 9 Lesson Goal

• Compare numbers to 99.

What the Student Needs to Know

• Identify and use the *greater than* and *less than* signs.
• Read a number line.
• Read a place-value chart.

Getting Started

Cut out a large tagboard > sign. On the board, write number pairs such as the following:

• 25   24
• 36   37
• 92   91

Have volunteers come to the board and arrange the symbol so that it points to the lesser number in the pair. Help students read the resulting inequality aloud; for example, "25 is greater than 24." Remind them to read the inequality from left to right, just as they would read any number sentence.

What Can I Do?

Read the question and the response. Then read and discuss the examples. Ask:

• *Does the greater than and less than symbol point to the greater or lesser number?* (lesser)
• *If number Y is to the right of number X on the number line, which number is less?* (number X)
• *If number A has 3 tens, and number B also has 3 tens, how can you tell which number is greater or less?* (Look at the ones place.)

Name_____

Compare Numbers

Learn

What Can I Do?
I want to compare two numbers.

Use a number line.

These numbers increase or go up by one.

Numbers on the right are greater. →

Numbers on the left are less. ←

```
←+++++++++++⊕+++++++⊕→
  0 1 2 3 4 5 6 7 8 9 10 11 12 13 14 15 16 17 18 19 20
```

19 is greater than 9. So 19 > 9.

9 is less than 19. So 9 < 19.

Look at place value.

Compare the digits in the tens place.
Which digit is greater?

tens	ones
3	5
3	4

If both digits are the same, compare the digits in the ones place. Which digit is greater?

Think: 5 ones is greater than 4 ones. So, 35 is greater than 34.

12

© Macmillan/McGraw-Hill

WHAT IF THE STUDENT CAN'T

Identify and Use the *Greater Than* and *Less Than* Signs

• Use your tagboard greater than sign from Getting Started. Show the student how to flip the sign so that it points either to the left or to the right. Remind the student that the arrow should always point to the lesser number. Have the student write two numbers on the board, use the sign to show the inequality, and read the inequality aloud. Repeat until the student consistently uses the sign correctly.

Read a Number Line

On the board, draw a 0–10 number line. Ask:

• *Which numbers are greater than 6?* (7, 8, 9, 10)
• *Which numbers are less than 6?* (0, 1, 2, . . .5)
• *If a number is to the left of 6, is it greater or less than 6?* (less)
• *If a number is to the right of 6, is it greater or less than 6?* (greater)

Try It • Use the place-value charts.
Circle the number that is *greater*.

1.
tens	ones
2	5
(5	2)

2.
tens	ones
3	1
(3	2)

3.
tens	ones
(7	3)
5	3

4.
tens	ones
8	7
(8	8)

Power Practice • Compare. Write >, <, or =.

5. 38 (<) 83

6. 44 (>) 43

7. 19 (<) 91

8. 89 (<) 90

9. 27 (>) 25

10. 31 (>) 30

11. 11 (=) 11

12. 65 (>) 55

13. 69 (<) 70

14. 97 (=) 97

15. 78 (<) 79

16. 65 (>) 56

17. 53 (>) 33

18. 30 (>) 3

19. 66 (<) 68

20. 100 (>) 10

13

WHAT IF THE STUDENT CAN'T

Read a Place-Value Chart
• Have the student write the numbers in Exercises 5–10 in a place-value chart. Then have the student identify the number of tens and ones in each number and tell which number is greater.

Complete the Power Practice
• Discuss each incorrect answer. If students consistently reverse the symbol, have them read each inequality aloud.
• Students who still have difficulty comparing two-digit numbers should show the numbers using tens and ones models.

Try It
Remind students to look at the tens place first. If those digits are different, they need not look at the ones. If the tens are the same, they must compare the ones.

Power Practice
• Have students complete the practice items. Then review each answer. Discuss the strategies students used to compare the numbers.
• Watch for students who consistently reverse the greater than and "less than" signs. Have these students read their inequalities aloud.

Learn with Partners & Parents
Students can use the ages of members of their households to practice comparing numbers. They should follow these steps:
• List the ages of everyone in your home. If you're not sure, ask.
• Use the ages you found to write as many sentences as possible using the greater than and less than signs. For example, if the ages of people in your home were 8, 10, 38, and 42; you might write:

8 < 10	8 < 38	8 < 42
10 > 8	10 < 38	10 < 42
38 > 8	38 > 10	38 < 42
42 > 8	42 > 10	42 > 38

Activity 10 Lesson Goal

• Order numbers to 99.

What the Student Needs to Know

• Read a hundred chart.
• Count on 1.
• Count back 1.

Getting Started

Give five students number cards 71–75. Have them line up in order in single file and face the class. Ask:

• *Which number comes just after 71?* (72) *Which number comes just before 74?* (73) *Which number comes between 73 and 75?* (74)

Continue with similar questions.

What Can I Do?

Read the question and the response. Then read and discuss the examples. Ask:

• *How could you find the number between two numbers on a hundred chart?* (Point to each of the two numbers and name the number in between.)

• *Would you find the number that comes just after a number by counting on or counting back?* (counting on)

Name_____

Order Numbers

Learn

What Can I Do?
I want to put numbers in order.

Activity **10**

Use a hundred chart.

The numbers are in order from **least** to **greatest**.

1	2	3	4	5	6	7	8	9	10
11	12	13	14	15	16	17	18	19	20
21	22	23	24	25	26	27	28	29	30
31	32	33	34	35	36	37	38	39	40
41	42	43	44	45	46	47	48	49	50
51	52	53	54	55	56	57	58	59	60
61	62	63	64	65	66	67	68	69	70
71	72	73	74	75	76	77	78	79	80
81	82	83	84	85	86	87	88	89	90
91	92	93	94	95	96	97	98	99	100

Think: 36 is just <u>before</u> 37.
38 is just <u>after</u> 37.
37 is <u>between</u> 36 and 38.

Count on or back.

Start with one number, such as 78.
Count on 1. One more is 79.
79 is just <u>after</u> 78.

Start with the same number, 78.
Count back 1. One less is 77.
77 is just <u>before</u> 78.
78 is <u>between</u> 77 and 79.

14

WHAT IF THE STUDENT CAN'T

Read a Hundred Chart

Display a hundred chart. Ask:

• *What is true of all the numbers in column 5 of the hundred chart?* (They all contain 5 ones.)

• *If you move down the column from row to row, how do the numbers change?* (They increase by 10.)

Count On 1

• Place counters in a line. Have the student count them. Then add one counter and have the student count them again. Repeat with other amounts of counters until the student is comfortable counting on without starting from 1.

Try It · Use the hundred chart. Write the number that comes just <u>before</u>, just <u>after</u>, or <u>between</u>.

1. just <u>after</u> 44 __45__

2. <u>between</u> 85 and 87 __86__

3. just <u>before</u> 69 __68__

4. just <u>after</u> 31 __32__

5. <u>between</u> 49 and 51 __50__

6. just <u>before</u> 27 __26__

1	2	3	4	5	6	7	8	9	10
11	12	13	14	15	16	17	18	19	20
21	22	23	24	25	26	27	28	29	30
31	32	33	34	35	36	37	38	39	40
41	42	43	44	45	46	47	48	49	50
51	52	53	54	55	56	57	58	59	60
61	62	63	64	65	66	67	68	69	70
71	72	73	74	75	76	77	78	79	80
81	82	83	84	85	86	87	88	89	90
91	92	93	94	95	96	97	98	99	100

Power Practice · Write the number that comes just <u>before</u>, just <u>after</u>, or <u>between</u>.

7. just after 17 __18__

8. between 55 and 57 __56__

9. just before 96 __95__

10. just after 64 __65__

11. between 76 and 78 __77__

12. just before 21 __20__

13. just after 8 __9__

14. between 93 and 95 __94__

15. just before 2 __1__

16. just after 72 __73__

17. between 81 and 83 __82__

18. just before 100 __99__

19. just after 19 __20__

20. between 19 and 21 __20__

21. just before 40 __39__

22. just after 86 __87__

© Macmillan/McGraw-Hill

15

WHAT IF THE STUDENT CAN'T

Count Back 1

- Have the student count to 10 and then start at 10 and count back 1. Repeat, having the student count to 6, 13, 21, and 34. Then give the student random numbers between 0 and 99 and have him or her count back 1.

Complete the Power Practice

- Discuss each incorrect answer. Have the student use a hundred chart to correct each answer.

Try It

- Students should point to the number or numbers on the hundred chart. Then they can move to the right to find the number after, move to the left to find the number before, or move to the middle to find the number between.

- Discuss what happens in Exercise 5, when the numbers given require moving from one row to the next.

Power Practice

- Have the students complete the practice items. Then review each answer. Discuss the strategies students used to order numbers.

Activity 11 Lesson Goal

• Identify parts of a group.

What the Student Needs to Know

• Recognize *differences*.

• Count parts of a group.

Getting Started

Display 6 attribute blocks—3 large yellow circles and 3 large red circles. Ask:

• *How many circles are there?* (6)

• *How are the circles different?* (They are different colors.)

• *How many different colors do you see?* (2) *So this group of circles has 2 parts—red circles and yellow circles.*

What Can I Do?

Read the question and the response. Then read and discuss the examples. Ask:

• *How can you decide which buttons belong together?* (Look for the buttons with the same size, shape, and color.)

• *Can the parts of a group have different numbers of items?* (yes)

Try It

Have students follow these steps:

• Count how many buttons there are in all.

• Circle the buttons that belong together.

• Count how many buttons are gray.

Power Practice

• Have students complete the practice items. Then review each answer.

Name_____

Parts of a Group

Learn

What Can I Do?
I want to know how many objects are in one part of a group.

Find the parts.

This group has different parts.

2 buttons are large and white.
3 buttons are small and black.
1 button is fancy and gray.

There are 3 different kinds of buttons.
There are 3 parts of the group.

Count, circle, and count.

Count how many in all.
Circle the ones that belong together.
Count the objects in each circle.

Try It • Count, circle, and count. Write how many.

1. How many in all? __8__   2. How many ⚫ ? __2__

Power Practice • Write how many.

Z X W Z Y X Z Z X Z Y Z

3. How many in all? __12__   4. How many Xs? __3__

5. How many Zs? __6__   6. How many Ws? __1__

16

© Macmillan/McGraw-Hill

WHAT IF THE STUDENT CAN'T

Recognize *Differences*

• Give the student the following attribute blocks: 2 red squares, 2 red circles. Have the student identify what is different about the pairs. (shape) Continue with 2 large red squares and 2 small red squares. (size) Continue with 2 large red squares and 2 small red circles. (size and shape)

Count Parts of a Group

• Distribute large attribute blocks that are the same shape but of 3 different colors. Have the student sort the blocks into groups and count the members of each group. Repeat with a different number of blocks.

Complete the Power Practice

• Review any incorrect answers. Have the student use the Count, Circle, Count strategy when necessary.

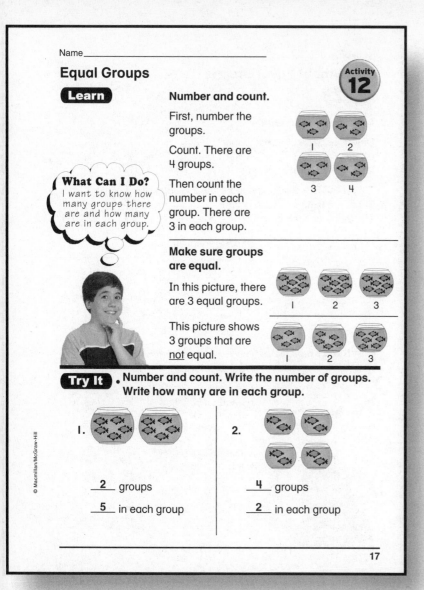

Name_____

Equal Groups

Learn

What Can I Do?
I want to know how many groups there are and how many are in each group.

Number and count.

First, number the groups.

Count. There are 4 groups.

Then count the number in each group. There are 3 in each group.

|1|2|
|3|4|

Make sure groups are equal.

In this picture, there are 3 equal groups.

|1|2|3|

This picture shows 3 groups that are not equal.

|1|2|3|

Try It • Number and count. Write the number of groups. Write how many are in each group.

1. __2__ groups
    __5__ in each group

2. __4__ groups
    __2__ in each group

17

WHAT IF THE STUDENT CAN'T

Count Groups
• Draw 6 circles on the board and draw lines to divide them into three equal groups. Number the groups and have the student count them. Then draw 8 circles and draw lines to divide them into four equal groups. Have the student number and count the groups. Continue with 10 circles divided into five groups.

Recognize the Meaning of *Equal Groups*
• Place four large rubber bands on a desk or table. Give the student 8 counters and ask him or her to make equal groups in each of the circles. Repeat with 12 counters. Then take away one rubber band and have the student work with 6, 9, and 12 counters.

USING THE LESSON

Activity 12 Lesson Goal
• Identify equal groups and the number within each group.

What the Student Needs to Know
• Count groups.
• Recognize the meaning of *equal groups*.

Getting Started
Give each pair of students 12 counters. Say:
• *Make a group of 6. How many are left?* (6) *Do you have equal groups?* (yes) *How many equal groups do you have?* (2)
• *Now make groups of 4. How many equal groups do you have?* (3)
• *Make groups of 3. How many equal groups do you have?* (4)
• *Make 2 groups that are not equal.* (Answers will vary.)

What Can I Do?
Read the question and the response. Then read and discuss the examples. Ask:
• *What is the difference between equal groups and groups that are not equal?* (Equal groups have the same number of items. Groups that are not equal have different numbers of items.)
• Draw 8 circles. Ask a volunteer to draw equal groups of objects in each circle. Discuss different ways of doing this.

Try It
Remind students that they should count and write the number of groups before they count the number in each group.

Activity 13 Lesson Goal

- Divide a group into smaller, equal groups.

What the Student Needs to Know

- Recognize the meaning of *equal groups.*
- Identify *equal groups.*

Getting Started

Give each pair of students 16 counters. Say:

- *Make groups of 8. How many groups do you have?* (2)
- *Now, make groups of 4. How many groups do you have?* (4)
- *Make groups of 2. How many groups do you have?* (8)

What Can I Do?

Read the question and the response. Then read and discuss the examples. Ask:

- *How could you divide the balloons into 4 equal groups?* (4 groups of 4) *8 equal groups?* (8 groups of 2)

Name_____

More About Equal Groups

Learn

Draw lines and count.

Draw lines to show **equal** groups.
Count to check.
Make 2 equal groups of stars.

Think: The line divides the stars into 2 groups.
There are 8 stars in each group.
The 2 groups are equal.

Make 2 equal groups of balloons.

What Can I Do?
I want to divide a group into smaller equal groups.

Use counters.

Count out the same number of counters.

Place the counters in 2 **equal** groups.

© Macmillan/McGraw-Hill

18

WHAT IF THE STUDENT CAN'T

Recognize the Meaning of *Equal Groups*

- Display 12 counters. Separate them into 2 groups of 6 and have the student tell whether the groups are equal. Repeat with 4 groups of 3; 2 groups of 5 and 1 group of 2; 6 groups of 2; 4 groups of 2 and 1 group of 4; and so on.

Identify *Equal Groups*

- Provide the student with 12 counters and an egg carton. Have the student show various ways to make equal groups by placing counters in the cups of the egg carton.

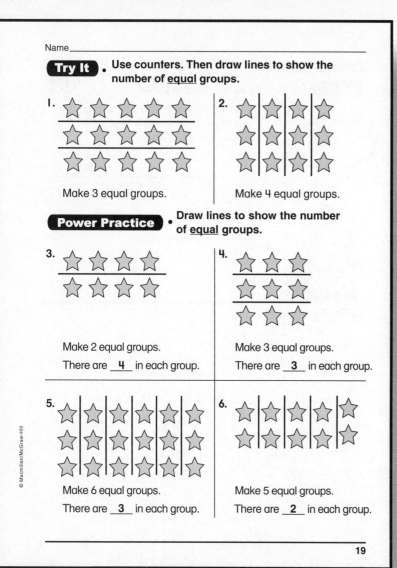

Name_____

Try It . Use counters. Then draw lines to show the number of **equal** groups.

1.
☆ ☆ ☆ ☆ ☆
☆ ☆ ☆ ☆ ☆
☆ ☆ ☆ ☆ ☆

Make 3 equal groups.

2.
☆ ☆ ☆ ☆
☆ ☆ ☆ ☆
☆ ☆ ☆ ☆

Make 4 equal groups.

Power Practice . Draw lines to show the number of **equal** groups.

3.
☆ ☆ ☆ ☆
☆ ☆ ☆ ☆

Make 2 equal groups.
There are __4__ in each group.

4.
☆ ☆ ☆
☆ ☆ ☆
☆ ☆ ☆

Make 3 equal groups.
There are __3__ in each group.

5.
☆ ☆ ☆ ☆ ☆ ☆
☆ ☆ ☆ ☆ ☆ ☆
☆ ☆ ☆ ☆ ☆ ☆

Make 6 equal groups.
There are __3__ in each group.

6.
☆ ☆ ☆ ☆ ☆
☆ ☆ ☆ ☆ ☆

Make 5 equal groups.
There are __2__ in each group.

19

Try It
Remind students that equal groups must have the same number of stars in each.

Power Practice
- Have students complete the practice items. Then review each answer.
- Discuss how students know that the groups they made are equal. (They have the same number of items.)

WHAT IF THE STUDENT CAN'T

Complete the Power Practice
- Discuss each incorrect answer. Have the student model the array pictured with counters. Then give the student a piece of string or yarn to separate the counters into the number of equal groups. Finally, have the student draw the line or lines to show the number of equal groups.

Activity 14 Lesson Goal
- Identify the position of objects using ordinal numbers.

What the Student Needs to Know
- Count to ten.
- Put pictured items in order.

Getting Started
Give each student ten counters. Ask:
- *How many counters do you have? Line them up and count them.* (10)
- *Which counter is first in line? Which is last?*

Name_____

Ordinal Numbers

Learn

Use numbers to order.

What Can I Do?
I want to use numbers to put things in order.

Use the top numbers to count things. Use the bottom numbers to put things in order.

one	two	three	four	five	six	seven	eight	nine	ten
first	second	third	fourth	fifth	sixth	seventh	eighth	ninth	tenth

Count from 1 to 10. Then count the order from first to tenth.

Try It • Draw lines to match.

1. two   fifth
2. five   seventh
3. seven   second
4. one   ninth
5. nine   first
6. four   eighth
7. eight   fourth

20

© Macmillan/McGraw-Hill

WHAT IF THE STUDENT CAN'T

Count to Ten
- Provide the student with a pile of counters. Have the student count off ten.
- Ask the student to write the numbers on a blank 0–10 number line.

Put Pictured Items in Order
- Give the student ten concrete objects to work with, such as pennies, counters, or blocks.
- Have the students put the objects in a line and count them.
- Then have the student start left to right and count the objects by ordinals: first, second, third, and so on.
- Have the student identify selected items, such as the third block, or the tenth block.

Name_____

Power Practice • Follow the directions.

brown blue yellow   red   green   orange

8. Color the **third** duckling yellow.

9. Color the **tenth** duckling orange.

10. Color the **sixth** duckling red.

11. Color the **first** duckling brown.

12. Color the **eighth** duckling green.

13. Color the **second** duckling blue.

Write the word that tells the order.

14. The ___fourth___ fish has stripes.

15. The ___second___ fish has spots.

16. The ___tenth___ fish is the biggest fish of all.

17. The ___fifth___ fish is the smallest fish of all.

18. The ___seventh___ fish is white.

first 1st	second 2nd	third 3rd	fourth 4th	fifth 5th
sixth 6th	seventh 7th	eighth 8th	ninth 9th	tenth 10th

© Macmillan/McGraw-Hill

21

Read the question and the response. Then read and discuss the examples. Ask:

- *How is the word* ten *like* tenth? *How is the word* four *like* fourth? (Both just add -*th* to the counting number to form the ordinal number.)

- Point out other similarities between the counting numbers and the ordinals; for example, *third* begins with the same two letters as *three,* and *fifth* begins with the same two letters as *five.*

Try It

Have students try to complete the matching without looking at the chart.

Power Practice

- Provide crayons. Have students complete the practice items. Then review each answer.

WHAT IF THE STUDENT CAN'T

Complete the Power Practice

Suggest that students follow these steps for Exercises 6–10:

- Find the ordinal number in the direction.

- Match the ordinal number to the counting number. For example, for *third,* think *three.*

- Count from left to right. Color the duckling the correct color.

Suggest that students follow these steps for Exercises 11–14:

- Find the fish named in the direction.

- Count to find the ordinal number.

- Use the list in the box to find the ordinal number to write in the box.

Activity 15 Lesson Goal
- Count to 100.

What the Student Needs to Know
- Count to 10.
- Order numbers.
- Compare numbers.

Getting Started
Have students count aloud from 0 to 10. Ask:
- *Which is greater, 8 or 9?* (9) *Which is less, 5 or 6?* (5)
- *Put these numbers in order: 4, 3, 5.* (3, 4, 5) *Put these numbers in order: 8, 10, 9.* (8, 9, 10)

What Can I Do?
Read the question and the response. Then read and discuss the examples. Ask:
- *What is true of all the numbers in the first column of the hundred chart?* (The ones digit is 1.)
- *What is true of all the numbers in the last column of the hundred chart?* (The ones digit is 0.)
- *If you move your finger down any column, how do the numbers change?* (They increase by 10.)

Name_____

Number Chart

Learn

What Can I Do?
I don't remember how to count by tens.

Find patterns in a hundreds chart.

Here are the first three rows of a hundreds chart.

1	2	3	4	5	6	7	8	9	10
11	12	13	14	15	16	17	18	19	20
21	22	23	24	25	26	27	28	29	30

A hundreds chart shows the order of numbers. It shows number patterns, too.
How can the chart help you count by 10s?
How can it help you count by 5s?
How can you tell which numbers are **greater**?
How can you tell which numbers are **less**?

Try It • Fill in the missing numbers.

1.

1	2	3	4	5	6	7	8	9	10
11	12	13	14	**15**	16	17	18	19	**20**
21	22	23	24	**25**	26	27	28	29	**30**
31	32	33	34	**35**	36	37	38	39	**40**
41	42	43	44	**45**	46	47	48	49	**50**
51	52	53	54	**55**	56	57	58	59	**60**
61	62	63	64	**65**	66	67	68	69	**70**

22

WHAT IF THE STUDENT CAN'T

Count to 10
- Place a number of counters between 1 and 10 on the student's desk. Ask the student to count them.
- Provide opportunities for the students to help distribute classroom materials by counting out items, such as 10 pencils, crayons, scissors, and so on.

Order Numbers
- Distribute number cards 0–10 and have students mix them and line them up in order.

Name_____

2.

1	2	3	4	5	6	7	8	9	10
11	**12**	13	**14**	15	**16**	17	**18**	19	20
21	**22**	23	**24**	25	**26**	27	**28**	29	30
31	**32**	33	**34**	35	**36**	37	**38**	39	40
41	**42**	43	**44**	45	**46**	47	**48**	49	50
51	**52**	53	**54**	55	**56**	57	**58**	59	60

3.

1	2	3	4	**5**	6	7	8	9	**10**
11	12	13	14	**15**	16	17	18	19	**20**
21	**22**	**23**	24	**25**	26	27	28	29	**30**
31	32	33	34	**35**	36	37	**38**	39	**40**
41	42	43	44	**45**	46	47	**48**	49	**50**
51	**52**	53	54	55	56	57	58	59	60
61	**62**	**63**	**64**	65	66	**67**	**68**	**69**	70
71	**72**	**73**	74	**75**	**76**	77	**78**	79	**80**
81	**82**	83	84	85	**86**	**87**	**88**	89	90
91	92	93	**94**	95	96	**97**	98	**99**	100

23

Try It
Remind students that they may use number patterns to determine what numbers are missing. Then they can check their work by counting.

Power Practice
- Have students complete the practice items. Then review each answer.
- *What is the number pattern shown by the missing numbers in Exercise 2?* (The numbers increase by 10.)

WHAT IF THE STUDENT CAN'T

Compare Numbers
- Draw a 0–10 number line on the board. Say one of the numbers and have students name the numbers on the number line that are less than and the numbers on the number line that are greater than that number.

Complete the Power Practice
- Discuss each incorrect answer. Have students count aloud from 1 to 100 to check their responses.

Activity 16 Lesson Goal
- Skip count by 2s

What the Student Needs to Know
- Read a hundred chart.
- Identify the ones digit.

Getting Started
Line up ten students and give them number cards 1–10. Say:
- *Count the people.* (1, 2, 3, 4, 5, 6, 7, 8, 9, 10)

Ask every other student to step forward. Say:
- *Every other person stepped forward. What are their numbers?* (2, 4, 6, 8, 10)

What Can I Do?
Read the question and the response. Then read and discuss the examples. Ask:
- *What is true about all the numbers you count when you count by 2s?* (They all end with the digit 2, 4, 6, 8, or 0.)
- *What number comes after 20 when you count by 2s?* (22)

Try It
Some students may need to count aloud to fill in the missing numbers.

Power Practice
- Tell students to look back at the hundred chart if they have trouble.
- Ask students to check their work by looking at the ones digits in their answers.

Name _____

Skip Counting by 2s

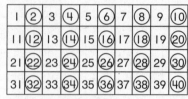

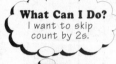

What Can I Do?
I want to skip count by 2s.

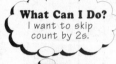

Activity 16

Learn

Use a hundred chart.

Here are the first 4 rows of a hundreds chart. Start with 2 and count every other number.

1	②	3	④	5	⑥	7	⑧	9	⑩
11	⑫	13	⑭	15	⑯	17	⑱	19	⑳
21	㉒	23	㉔	25	㉖	27	㉘	29	㉚
31	㉜	33	㉞	35	㊱	37	㊳	39	㊵

Use number patterns.

Look at the ones digits.

2 4 6 8 10 1<u>2</u> 1<u>4</u> 1<u>6</u> 1<u>8</u> 2<u>0</u>

Use the pattern "2, 4, 6, 8, 0" to decide what comes next.

Try It • Fill in the missing numbers.

1.

1	2	3	4	5	6	7	8	9	10
11	12	13	14	15	16	17	18	19	**20**
21	**22**	23	**24**	25	**26**	27	**28**	29	**30**
31	**32**	33	**34**	35	**36**	37	**38**	39	**40**
41	**42**	43	**44**	45	**46**	47	**48**	49	**50**

Power Practice • Write each missing number.

2. 2, 4, __6__, 8, 10, __12__

3. 32, __34__, 36, 38, 40, __42__

4. 80, 82, __84__, __86__, 88, 90

5. 66, 68, __70__, 72, __74__, 76

24

© Macmillan/McGraw-Hill

WHAT IF THE STUDENT CAN'T

Read a Hundred Chart
Display a hundred chart. Ask:
- *What is true of all the numbers in column 3 of the hundred chart?* (The digit in the ones place is always 3.)
- *As you move down any column, how do the numbers change?* (They increase by 10.)

Identify the Ones Digit
- Have the student choose ten numbers in the hundred chart and identify the digit in the ones place in each number.

Complete the Power Practice
- Have the student count aloud and fill in each missing number.
- Remind the student that each number he or she writes should have a 2, 4, 6, 8, or 0 in the ones place.

Name_____

Skip Count by 5s and 10s

Learn

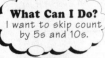

What Can I Do?
I want to skip count by 5s and 10s.

Use number patterns.

Look at the ones digits.

5 10 15 20 25 30

Counting by 5s.

Use the pattern to decide what number comes next.

10 20 30 40 50 60

Counting by 10s.

Try It • Fill in the missing numbers.

1.

1	2	3	4	5	6	7	8	9	10
11	12	13	14	**15**	16	17	18	19	**20**
21	22	23	24	**25**	26	27	28	29	**30**
31	32	33	34	**35**	36	37	38	39	40

Power Practice • Write each missing number.

2. 25, 30, __35__, 40, 45, __50__

3. 40, __50__, 60, 70, 80, __90__

4. 50, 55, __60__, __65__, 70, 75

5. 20, 30, __40__, 50, __60__, 70

© Macmillan/McGraw-Hill

25

WHAT IF THE STUDENT CAN'T

Read a Hundred Chart
- Display a hundred chart. Have students identify the number that is 1 more than 6 (7), 10 more than 6 (16), 1 more than 65 (66), 10 more than 65 (75), 1 more than 29 (30), 10 more than 29 (39), and so on.

Identify the Ones Digit
- Use number cards 1–99. Have the student pick ten cards. Ask him or her to identify the ones digit in each number.

Complete the Power Practice
- Make sure the student can identify whether he or she is counting by 5s or 10s in each case.
- Have the student count aloud and fill in each missing number.

Activity 17 Lesson Goal
- Skip count by 5s and 10s.

What the Student Needs to Know
- Read a hundred chart.
- Identify the ones digit.

Getting Started
Display a hundred chart. Ask:
- *What is true of all the numbers in the last column of the hundred chart?* (The ones digit is 0.)
- *If you move down that column, how do the numbers change?* (They increase by 10.)

What Can I Do?
Read the question and the response. Then read and discuss the examples. Ask:
- *What is true about all the numbers you count when you count by 5s?* (The ones digit is 5 or 0.)
- *What comes after 60 when you count by 10s?* (70) by 5s? (65)

Try It
Counting aloud may help some students to fill in the missing numbers.

Power Practice
- Tell students to refer to the hundred chart only if they have trouble.
- Remind students to check their work by looking at the ones digits in their answers.

Activity 18 Lesson Goal
- Count on by 1s.

What the Student Needs to Know
- Read a number line.
- Count by 1s.
- Draw a given number of objects.

Getting Started
Give students this problem:

- *Jenny is 7. How old will she be on her next birthday? (8) How old will she be on the birthday after that? (9) How old will she be on the birthday after that? (10)*

What Can I Do?
Read the question and the response. Then read and discuss the examples. Ask:

- *Start at 4 on the number line. Go up 1. Then go up 1 more. Where are you? (6)*
- *Start by drawing 4 objects. Draw 1 more. Then draw 1 more. How many objects have you drawn? (6 objects)*

Try It
Students might follow these steps:
- Point to the number on the number line.
- Move to the right to find 1 more.
- Write the number.

Power Practice
- Have students complete the practice items. Then review each answer.

Name_____

Counting On

Learn

What Can I Do?
I want to count on to find how many in all.

Use a number line.
Each number increases or goes up by one. Move to the right to count on one.

0 1 2 3 4 5 6 7 8 9 10

4 and 1 more is 5. 1 more is 6.

Draw a picture.
Draw the number you have.
Draw 1 more. Count. ○○○○○◌ 5
Draw 1 more. Count. ○○○○○○◌ 6

Try It • Use the number line.
Find 1 more.

0 1 2 3 4 5 6 7 8 9 10

1. 3 and 1 more = __4__   2. 6 and 1 more = __7__

3. 9 and 1 more = __10__   4. 8 and 1 more = __9__

Power Practice • Write each missing number.

5. Start with 5. 1 more makes __6__. 1 more makes __7__.

6. Start with 3. 1 more makes __4__. 1 more makes __5__.

7. Start with 7. 1 more makes __8__. 1 more makes __9__.

   1 more makes __10__. 1 more makes __11__.

26

© Macmillan/McGraw-Hill

WHAT IF THE STUDENT CAN'T

Read a Number Line
- Draw a 0–10 number line on the board. Have the student locate and circle: 5, the number that is 1 more than 5 (6); 7, the number that is 1 more than 7 (8).

Count by 1s
- Line up 5 counters. Have the student count them. Add 1 more. Have the student tell how many there are now. If necessary, the student may count the whole group. Repeat with different numbers of counters until the student does not need to return to 1 to count on.

Draw a Given Number of Objects
- Have the student practice by having them draw 3 flowers, 4 flowerpots, 5 trees, 6 rabbits, and so on. Have the student count the number of objects aloud.

Complete the Power Practice
- Have the student count on with counters to model Exercises 5–7.

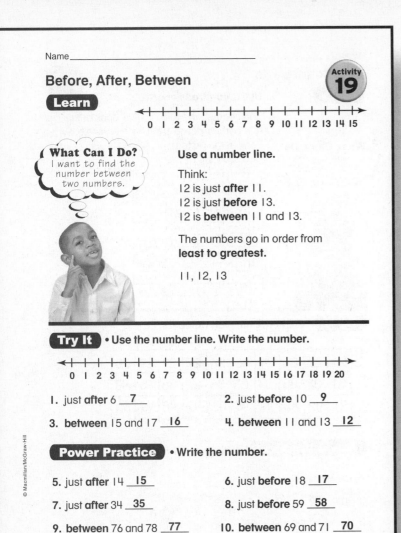

Name _____

Before, After, Between

Learn

Activity **19**

0 1 2 3 4 5 6 7 8 9 10 11 12 13 14 15

What Can I Do?
I want to find the number between two numbers.

Use a number line.

Think:
12 is just **after** 11.
12 is just **before** 13.
12 is **between** 11 and 13.

The numbers go in order from **least to greatest.**

11, 12, 13

Try It • Use the number line. Write the number.

0 1 2 3 4 5 6 7 8 9 10 11 12 13 14 15 16 17 18 19 20

1. just **after** 6 __7__

2. just **before** 10 __9__

3. **between** 15 and 17 __16__

4. **between** 11 and 13 __12__

Power Practice • Write the number.

5. just **after** 14 __15__

6. just **before** 18 __17__

7. just **after** 34 __35__

8. just **before** 59 __58__

9. **between** 76 and 78 __77__

10. **between** 69 and 71 __70__

© Macmillan/McGraw-Hill

27

WHAT IF THE STUDENT CAN'T

Read a Number Line
- Draw a 0–10 number line on the board. Have the student locate and circle: 5, a number less than 5, and a number greater than 5. Then ask the student to do the same for 9.

Count Forward 1
- Place counters in a line. Have the student count them. Then add one counter and have the student count again. Repeat with other numbers of counters.

Count Back 1
- Have the student count to 5 and then start at 5 and count back 1. Repeat, having the student count to 8, 14, 20, and 36, counting back 1 each time.

Complete the Power Practice
- Have the student demonstrate counting on to find the number after and counting back to find the number before.

Activity 19 Lesson Goal
- Identify numbers that come *just before, just after,* and *between* other numbers.

What the Student Needs to Know
- Read a number line.
- Count forward 1.
- Count back 1.

Getting Started
Give five students the number cards 1–5. Have them line up in order in single file. Ask:
- *Which number comes just after 1?* (2) *Which number comes just before 4?* (3) *Which number comes between 3 and 5?* (4)

Continue with similar questions.

What Can I Do?
Read the question and the response. Then read and discuss the examples. Ask:
- *How would you find the number between two numbers on a number line?* (Point to each of the two numbers and name the number that is in between.)
- *Would you find the number that comes just before a number by counting on or counting back?* (counting back)

Try It
Students might follow these steps:
- Point to the number or numbers on the number line.
- Move to the right to find the number just after.
- Move to the left to find the number just before.
- Move to the middle to find the number between.

Power Practice
- Have the students complete the practice items. Then review each answer.

Activity 20 Lesson Goal
• Skip count by 5s.

What the Student Needs to Know
• Read a hundred chart.
• Identify the ones digit.

Getting Started
Show students how to count fives on their fingers. Display the fingers of one hand one at a time and count:

• *1, 2, 3, 4, 5.*

Write 5 on the board. Begin again, counting:

• *6, 7, 8, 9, 10.*

Write 10 on the board. Have students imitate you as you continue to count from 15 through 50.

What Can I Do?
Read the question and the response. Then read and discuss the examples. Ask:

• *What is true about all the numbers you count when you count by 5s?* (The ones digit is 5 or 0.)

• *What comes after 50 when you count by 5s?* (55) *What comes after 85 when you count by 5s?* (90)

Try It
Some students may need to count aloud to fill in the missing numbers.

Power Practice
• Have students complete the practice items. Tell them to look back at the hundred chart if they have trouble.

Name_____

Skip Count by 5s

Learn

Activity
20

What Can I Do?
I want to skip count by 5s.

Use a hundreds chart.

The chart shows the numbers from 1 to 100. Look at the pattern for skip counting by 5s.

Look at the ones digits.

5, 10, 15, 20, 25, 30

1	2	3	4	5	6	7	8	9	10
11	12	13	14	15	16	17	18	19	20
21	22	23	24	25	26	27	28	29	30
31	32	33	34	35	36	37	38	39	40
41	42	43	44	45	46	47	48	49	50
51	52	53	54	55	56	57	58	59	60
61	62	63	64	65	66	67	68	69	70
71	72	73	74	75	76	77	78	79	80
81	82	83	84	85	86	87	88	89	90
91	92	93	94	95	96	97	98	99	100

Try It • Fill in the missing numbers.

1.

21	22	23	24	**25**	26	27	28	29	**30**
31	32	33	34	**35**	36	37	38	39	40
41	42	43	44	**45**	46	47	48	49	**50**

Power Practice • Write each missing number.

2. 15, 20, __25__ , 30, 35, __40__

3. 30, __35__ , 40, 45, 50, __55__

4. 10, 15, __20__ , __25__ , 30, 35

28

WHAT IF THE STUDENT CAN'T

Read a Hundred Chart
• Display a hundred chart. Have the student identify all the numbers that contain 5 ones (5, 15, 25,. . . 95) and all the numbers that contain 0 ones (10, 20, 30,. . .100). Circle all these numbers on the chart and ask the student to count with you by 5s to 100.

Identify the Ones Digit
• Have the student choose ten numbers in the hundred chart and identify the digit in the ones place in each number.

Complete the Power Practice
• Have the student count aloud and fill in each missing number. Watch for students who need to return to 5 each time; they may need additional practice.

• Remind the student that each number he or she writes should have a 5 or 0 in the ones place.

Name_____

Round to the Nearest Ten

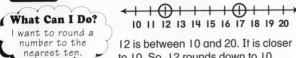

Activity 21

Learn

What Can I Do?

I want to round a number to the nearest ten.

Use a number line.

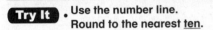

10 11 12 13 14 15 16 17 18 19 20

12 is between 10 and 20. It is closer to 10. So, 12 rounds down to 10.

17 is between 10 and 20. It is closer to 20. So 17 rounds up to 20.

Use the ones digit.

If the ones digit is less than 5, round down. Round 14 down to 10.

If the ones digit is 5 or greater, round up. Round 15 up to 20.

Try It
• Use the number line.
Round to the nearest <u>ten</u>.

1. 31 __30__   30 31 32 33 34 35 36 37 38 39 40

2. 58 __60__   50 51 52 53 54 55 56 57 58 59 60

Power Practice
• Look at the ones digit. Round each number to the nearest <u>ten</u>.

3. 73 __70__   4. 19 __20__   5. 25 __30__

6. 54 __50__   7. 36 __40__   8. 88 __90__

9. 42 __40__   10. 65 __70__   11. 7 __10__

© Macmillan/McGraw-Hill

29

WHAT IF THE STUDENT CAN'T

Count by 10s
• Have the student use tens models to show tens from 10 to 100. Then have the student count the models by tens.

Read a Number Line
• Draw a 70–80 number line on the board. Have students locate a number you say and name the ten to the left (70) and the ten to the right (80).

Identify the Ones Digit
• Students may practice identifying the ones digit by writing the numbers in items 3-11 in place-value charts.

Complete the Power Practice
• Review the rules for rounding: down if the ones digit is 0–4, up if the ones digit is 5–9.

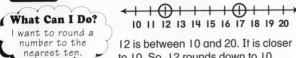

USING THE LESSON

Activity 21 Lesson Goal
• Round numbers to the nearest ten.

What the Student Needs to Know
• Count by 10s.
• Read a number line.
• Identify the ones digit.

Getting Started
Have students count by 10s to 100. Ask:
• *How many tens are in 40?* (4) *How many tens are in 70?* (7)

What Can I Do?
Read the question and the response. Then read and discuss the examples. Ask:
• *What does it mean when you say "17 rounds up to 20"?* (20 is the nearest ten to 17, and it is greater, so you have to round up.)
• *What does it mean when you say "12 rounds down to 10"?* (10 is the nearest ten to 12, and it is less, so you have to round down.)
• *Would you round 35 up or down? Why?* (Up; you round up when the ones digit is 5 or greater.)

Try It
Suggest that students find the number on the number line first and then look at the tens to the left and the right to determine which is closer.

Power Practice
• Have students complete the practice items. Then review each answer.

Activity 22 Lesson Goal

- Round numbers to the nearest ten.

What the Student Needs to Know

- Count by 10s.
- Read a number line.
- Identify the ones digit.

Getting Started

- Have students count by 10s to 100.
- Display a hundred chart and have students locate the 10s. (10, 20, 30, . . . 100)

What Can I Do?

Read the question and the response. Then read and discuss the examples. Ask:

- *What does it mean when you say "18 rounds up to 20"?* (20 is the nearest ten to 18, and it is greater, so you have to round up.)
- *What does it mean when you say "32 rounds down to 30"?* (30 is the nearest ten to 32, and it is less, so you have to round down.)
- *Would you round 55 up or down? Why?* (Up; you round up when the ones digit is 5 or greater.)

Name_____

Round to the Nearest Ten

Learn

What Can I Do?
I want to round a number to the nearest ten.

Activity 22

Use a number line.

The number 18 is between 10 and 20. It is closer to 20. So 18 rounds up to 20.

10 11 12 13 14 15 16 17 18 19 20

The number 32 is between 30 and 40. It is closer to 30. So 32 rounds down to 30.

30 31 32 33 34 35 36 37 38 39 40

Use the ones digit.

If the ones digit is less than 5, round down. If it is 5 or greater, round up.

Round 64 down to 60. Round 65 up to 70.

Try It . Use the number line. Round to the nearest <u>ten</u>.

1. 51 __50__ 50 51 52 53 54 55 56 57 58 59 60

2. 17 __20__ 10 11 12 13 14 15 16 17 18 19 20

3. 34 __30__ 30 31 32 33 34 35 36 37 38 39 40

30

© Macmillan/McGraw-Hill

WHAT IF THE STUDENT CAN'T

Count by 10s

- Give the student 10 play dimes and have the student count by tens to 1 dollar.
- Have the student use tens models to show the tens from 10 to 100. Then have the student count the models by tens.

Read a Number Line

- Draw a 0–10 number line on the board. Have students locate a number you say, the number that is 1 less, and the number that is 1 greater.

Name_____

4. 81 ___80___   5. 24 ___20___   6. 38 ___40___

7. 62 ___60___   8. 33 ___30___   9. 74 ___70___

10. 45 ___50___   11. 13 ___10___   12. 9 ___10___

13. 78 ___80___   14. 65 ___70___   15. 44 ___40___

16. 26 ___30___   17. 77 ___80___   18. 88 ___90___

© Macmillan/McGraw-Hill

31

Suggest that students use these steps:

- Find the number on the number line.
- Find the tens on either side of that number.
- Decide which ten is closer to the number.
- Write that ten.

Power Practice

- If students have trouble, they might draw a number line to help them.
- Have students complete the practice items. Then review each answer.

Learn with Partners & Parents

Have students use the ages of people in their families to practice rounding to the nearest ten.

- Give each student a hundred chart to take home.
- Have students circle numbers on the hundred chart that represent family members' ages.
- Tell students to round each family member's age to the nearest ten and write a sentence for each person; for example, *To the nearest ten, Grandpa Dennis is 70. To the nearest ten, I am 10.*

WHAT IF THE STUDENT CAN'T

Identify the Ones Digit

- Have students practice identifying the ones digit by writing the numbers in Exercises 4-18 in place-value charts.

Complete the Power Practice

- Review the rules for rounding: round down if the ones digit is 0–4; round up if the ones digit is 5–9.
- Have students circle the ones digit before rounding the number.

Activity 23 Lesson Goal
• Round numbers to the nearest hundred.

What the Student Needs to Know
• Read a number line.
• Identify the tens digit.

Getting Started
Have students count by 100s to 1,000. Say:

• *222 is between 200 and 300. Between which two hundreds is 450? 760? 546? 812?* (400 and 500; 700 and 800; 500 and 600; 800 and 900)

What Can I Do?
Read the question and the response. Then read and discuss the examples. Ask:

• *What does it mean when you say "222 rounds down to 200"?* (200 is the nearest hundred to 222, and it is less, so you have to round down.)

• *What does it mean when you say "275 rounds up to 300"?* (300 is the nearest hundred to 275, and it is greater, so you have to round up.)

• *Would you round 450 up or down? Why?* (Up; you round up when the tens digit is 5 or greater.)

Try It
Suggest that students use these steps:

• Find the number on the number line.
• Find the hundreds on either side of that number.
• Decide which hundred is closer to the number.
• Write that hundred.

Name_____

Round to the Nearest Hundred

Learn

Use a number line.

The number 222 is between 200 and 300. It is closer to 200.

So 222 <u>rounds down</u> to 200.

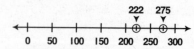

The number 275 is between 200 and 300. It is closer to 300.

So 275 <u>rounds up</u> to 300.

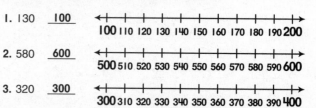

What Can I Do?
I want to round a number to the nearest hundred.

Use the digit in the tens place.

Look at the tens digit.

> If it is less than 5, round down.
> If it is 5 or greater, round up.

Round 149 down to 100.
Round 150 up to 200.

Try It • Use the number line.
Round to the nearest <u>hundred</u>.

1. 130 ___100___
   100 110 120 130 140 150 160 170 180 190 200

2. 580 ___600___
   500 510 520 530 540 550 560 570 580 590 600

3. 320 ___300___
   300 310 320 330 340 350 360 370 380 390 400

32

© Macmillan/McGraw-Hill

WHAT IF THE STUDENT CAN'T

Read a Number Line
• On the board, draw a number line that is marked in 10s from 100 to 200. Cover up or erase some of the numbers and have the student fill them in.

• Use the number line above. Have the student locate (1) two numbers that are greater than 110; (2) two numbers that are less than 150. Continue with other numbers.

Identify the Tens Digit
• Have students use Exercises 1–5 in Try It. Ask them to write the five numbers and underline the tens digits.

Name_____

4. 258 __300__
200 210 220 230 240 250 260 270 280 290 300

5. 441 __400__
400 410 420 430 440 450 460 470 480 490 500

6. 348 __300__
300 310 320 330 340 350 360 370 380 390 400

7. 527 __500__
500 510 520 530 540 550 560 570 580 590 600

Power Practice • Round each number to the nearest <u>hundred</u>.

8. 730 __700__   9. 195 __200__

10. 253 __300__   11. 543 __500__

12. 236 __200__   13. 858 __900__

14. 142 __100__   15. 659 __700__

16. 75 __100__   17. 360 __400__

18. 715 __700__   19. 907 __900__

20. 455 __500__   21. 346 __300__

22. 188 __200__   23. 220 __200__

33

Power Practice

- If students have trouble, they might draw a number line to help them.
- Have students complete the practice items. Then review each answer.

Learn with Partners & Parents

Have students use books in their classroom or at home to practice rounding.

- Choose ten books. Each book should have at least 50 pages. Look at the page number on the last page of each one.
- Round the number of pages to the nearest hundred.
- How many books have page numbers that round to 100? That round to 200 or 300? Write their titles.

WHAT IF THE STUDENT CAN'T

Complete the Power Practice

- Discuss each incorrect answer. Review the rules for rounding: down if the tens digit is 0–4, up if the tens digit is 5–9 to the nearest hundred.
- Have students circle the tens digit before rounding the number.

Activity 24 Lesson Goal
• Skip count by 2s, 3s, 4s, or 5s.

What the Student Needs to Know
• Read a hundred chart.
• Complete a number pattern.

Getting Started
Line up twelve students. Have them count off by 1s. Give each student a number card from 1–12 to hold up. Then ask every other student to step forward. Ask:

• *What numbers do you see? (2, 4, 6, 8, 10, 12) That's the same as counting by 2s.*

Realign the students and ask every third student to step forward. Ask:

• *What numbers do you see now? (3, 6, 9, 12) That's the same as counting by 3s.*

Repeat, asking every fourth student to step forward. (4, 8, 12)

What Can I Do?
Read the question and the response. Then read and discuss the examples. Ask:

• *What is true about all the numbers you count when you count by 5s?* (The ones digit is either 5 or 0.)

• *When you count by 2s and by 4s, the numbers you count have some things in common. What are they?* (They are even numbers; the numbers you count when you count by 4s are also numbers you count when you count by 2s.)

Name_____

Skip Counting

Learn

Use a hundreds chart.

A hundreds chart shows all the numbers from 1 to 100.

1	2	3	4	5	6	7	8	9	10
11	12	13	14	15	16	17	18	19	20
21	22	23	24	25	26	27	28	29	30
31	32	33	34	35	36	37	38	39	40
41	42	43	44	45	46	47	48	49	50
51	52	53	54	55	56	57	58	59	60
61	62	63	64	65	66	67	68	69	70
71	72	73	74	75	76	77	78	79	80
81	82	83	84	85	86	87	88	89	90
91	92	93	94	95	96	97	98	99	100

Start at 2. Stop at every other number.

Start at 3. Stop at every 3rd number.

Start at 4. Stop at every 4th number.

Start at 5. Stop at every 5th number.

What Can I Do?
I want to skip count by 2s, 3s, 4s, or 5s.

Use number patterns.

Look at the ones digits when you count:

by 2s: 2 4 6 8 10 12 14 16 18 20

by 4s: 4 8 12 16 20 24 28 32 36 40

by 5s: 5 10 15 20 25 30 35 40 45 50

by 3s: 3 6 9 12 15 18 21 24 27

© Macmillan/McGraw-Hill

34

WHAT IF THE STUDENT CAN'T

Read a Hundred Chart
• Display a hundred chart. Have the student identify all the numbers that have 5 in the ones place (5, 15, 25,. . . 95) and all the numbers that have 0 in the ones place (10, 20, 30,. . .100). Then have the student point to each number as he or she counts by 2s.

Complete a Number Pattern
Have the student continue each of these patterns by saying the next three numbers:

• 15, 20, 25, 30, ?, ?, ? (35, 40, 45)

• 42, 44, 46, 48, ?, ?, ? (50, 52, 54)

• 63, 66, 69, 72, ?, ?, ? (75, 78, 81)

• 12, 16, 20, 24, ?, ?, ? (28, 32, 36)

Try It • Fill in the missing numbers.

1.

1	2	3	4	5	6	7	8	9	**10**
11	12	13	14	**15**	16	17	18	19	20
21	22	23	24	**25**	26	27	28	29	**30**
31	32	33	34	**35**	36	37	38	39	40

2.

71	72	73	74	75	76	77	78	79	80
81	82	83	**84**	85	86	**87**	88	89	**90**
91	92	**93**	94	95	96	97	98	99	100

Power Practice • Write the missing numbers in each skip counting pattern.

3. 60, __65__, 70, 75, 80, __85__, __90__, __95__

4. 21, 24, __27__, __30__, 33, 36, __39__, __42__

5. 64, 68, __72__, 76, __80__, 84, 88, __92__, __96__

6. 40, 44, __48__, 52, __56__, 60, __64__, __68__, 72, 76

7. 30, 35, __40__, __45__, 50, 55, __60__, __65__, 70

8. 86, 88, __90__, __92__, __94__, 96, 98, __100__

© Macmillan/McGraw-Hill

35

Try It
Some students may need to count aloud to fill in the missing numbers.

Power Practice
• Tell students to figure out the rule before filling in the missing numbers.
• Have students complete the practice items. Tell them to look back at the hundred chart if they have trouble.

Activity 25 Lesson Goal

- Identify and complete a number pattern.

What the Student Needs to Know

- Count by 1s.
- Count by 10s.

Getting Started

Display a hundred chart. Say:

- *Read the first row aloud. Each number in the row is one more than the one before it. 2 is one more than 1. 3 is one more than 2, and so on. So we can say that the pattern for this row is that each number goes up by one.*

- Now *read the last column aloud. What is the pattern?* (Each number goes up by 10.)

What Can I Do?

Read the question and the response. Then read and discuss the examples. Ask:

- *What is true of the ones digits when the pattern is Add One?* (The ones digits go up by 1.)

- *What is true of the ones digits when the pattern is Add Ten?* (The ones digits remain the same.)

Name _____

Number Patterns

Learn

What Can I Do?
I want to figure out a number pattern.

Read the pattern aloud.

Reading aloud helps you "hear" the pattern.
Try reading these numbers aloud.
What number comes next?

44, 45, 46, 47, 48, ___?___

23, 33, 43, 53, 63, ___?___

Find the rule.

Read this pattern:

34, 44, 54, 64, 74, ___?___

Think: 44 is 10 more than 34.
54 is 10 more than 44.
64 is 10 more than 54.
The rule is Add ten.

Read this pattern:

36, 37, 38, 39, 40, ___?___

Think: 37 is 1 more than 36.
38 is 1 more than 37.
39 is 1 more than 38.
The rule is Add one.

© Macmillan/McGraw-Hill

36

WHAT IF THE STUDENT CAN'T

Count by 1s

- Give the student a number to start with; for example, 16. Have the student count by 1s until you say "Stop." Repeat with another starting number until the student seems comfortable counting by 1s from any starting point.

Name_____

1. 11, 21, 31, 41, 51   Add one   (Add ten)

2. 68, 69, 70, 71, 72   (Add one)   Add ten

3. 97, 98, 99, 100, 101   (Add one)   Add ten

4. 46, 56, 66, 76, 86   Add one   (Add ten)

5. 19, 29, 39, 49, 59   Add one   (Add ten)

Power Practice • Write the missing numbers in each counting pattern.

6. 20, 30, __40__, 50, 60, __70__, __80__, 90

7. 43, __44__, 45, 46, 47, __48__, 48, 49, __50__, __51__, 53

8. 15, 25, __35__, __45__, 55, 65, __75__, __85__, 95

9. 26, 27, __28__, 29, __30__, 31, 32, __33__, 34, __35__

10. 33, 43, __53__, 63, 73, __83__, __93__

11. 48, __49__, 50, 51, 52, __53__, 53, __54__, __55__, 56

12. 42, 52, __62__, __72__, 82, 92

13. 17, 27, __37__, __47__, 57, __67__, 77

WHAT IF THE STUDENT CAN'T

Count by 10s
- Provide a hundred chart and have the student read the numbers in the last column. Cover some of the numbers and have the student recite the numbers again. Continue by having the student read the numbers in the other columns.

Complete the Power Practice
- Have the student identify the rule or pattern for each set of numbers.
- Ask the student to count aloud and fill in each missing number.

Try It
Counting aloud may help some students to identify the pattern.

Power Practice
- Post a hundred chart for students to refer to if necessary.
- Remind students to check their work by looking at the ones digits in the number patterns.

USING THE LESSON

Activity 26 Lesson Goal
- Add and subtract one.

What the Student Needs to Know
- Count to ten.
- Read a number line.

Getting Started
Have students count aloud from 0 to 10. Then have them count backward from 10 to 0.

What Can I Do?
Read the question and the response. Then read and discuss the examples. Ask:
- *How could you write "7 and 1 more" as a number sentence?* $(7 + 1 = 8)$
- *How could you write "7 and 1 less" as a number sentence?* $(7 - 1 = 6)$

Try It
Students might follow these steps:
- Find the first number on the number line. Put your finger there.
- To add 1, move your finger to the right one space. To subtract 1, move your finger to the left one space.

Power Practice
- Have students complete the practice items. Then review each answer.

Name_____

Add and Subtract One

Learn

What Can I Do? I want to add and subtract one.

Use a number line.
Count on one to **add** 1.
Count **back** one to subtract 1.

0 1 2 3 4 5 6 ⑦ 8 9 10

$7 + 1 = 8$
$7 - 1 = 6$

Try It • Use the number line. Add or subtract.

0 1 2 3 4 5 6 7 8 9 10

1. $4 + 1 = $ __5__

2. $4 - 1 = $ __3__

3. $5 + 1 = $ __6__

4. $5 - 1 = $ __4__

Power Practice • Add or subtract.

5. $6 + 1 = $ __7__

6. $6 - 1 = $ __5__

7. $9 + 1 = $ __10__

8. $9 - 1 = $ __8__

9. $8 + 1 = $ __9__

10. $8 - 1 = $ __7__

38

© Macmillan/McGraw-Hill

WHAT IF THE STUDENT CAN'T

Count to Ten
- Mix number cards 0–10 and have the student line them up in order.
- Place a number of counters between 1 and 10 on the student's desk. Ask the student to count them.

Read a Number Line
- Draw a 0–10 number line on the board. Omit some of the numbers and have the student write them.

- Draw a 0–10 number line on the board. Say one of the numbers and have the student name the number that comes just before and just after that number.

Complete the Power Practice
- Discuss each incorrect answer. Use counting on and counting back on a number line to help students see their errors: *6 + 1 is the same as 6 and 1 more = 7. 6 – 1 is the same as 6 and 1 less = 5.*

Name_____

Addition Facts to 12

Activity 27

Learn

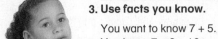

What Can I Do?
I want to know an addition fact. Here are three ways.

1. Draw a picture.

A picture can help you add.

$5 + 6 = ?$
$5 + 6 = 11$

2. Use doubles.

$4 + 4 = 8$ $5 + 5 = 10$ $6 + 6 = 12$

3. Use facts you know.

You want to know $7 + 5$.
You know $7 + 3 = 10$.
Think: 5 is 2 more than 3.
$7 + 5$ must be 2 more than $7 + 3$.
So, $7 + 5 = 12$.

Try It • Add.

1. $9 + 3 = \underline{12}$ 2. $7 + 2 = \underline{9}$ 3. $8 + 4 = \underline{12}$

Power Practice • Add.

4. $8 + 3 = \underline{11}$ 5. $6 + 4 = \underline{10}$ 6. $8 + 1 = \underline{9}$

7. $3 + 9 = \underline{12}$ 8. $5 + 5 = \underline{10}$ 9. $6 + 5 = \underline{11}$

10. $\begin{array}{r} 9 \\ +2 \\ \hline 11 \end{array}$ 11. $\begin{array}{r} 7 \\ +3 \\ \hline 10 \end{array}$ 12. $\begin{array}{r} 6 \\ +6 \\ \hline 12 \end{array}$ 13. $\begin{array}{r} 6 \\ +3 \\ \hline 9 \end{array}$ 14. $\begin{array}{r} 7 \\ +4 \\ \hline 11 \end{array}$

© Macmillan/McGraw-Hill

39

WHAT IF THE STUDENT CAN'T

Count from 0–12

- Provide the student with a 0–12 number line.
- Ask the student to count the numbers on the number line aloud with you as he or she points to each number.
- When the student can count easily on the number line, have the student count objects such as blocks or counters and write each number on a paper.

Complete the Power Practice

- Discuss each incorrect answer. Have the students use counters to model each incorrect answer.

Activity 27 Lesson Goal

- Use addition facts to 12.

What the Student Needs to Know

- Count from 0–12.
- Add using manipulatives.

Getting Started

Give each student 12 counters. Say:

- *Count to find out how many counters you have.* (12) *Separate your counters into two groups. What addition number sentence can you make for these groups?* Record students' number sentences on the board.
- *What other addition number sentences can we make with these counters?*

What Can I Do?

Read the question and the response. Then read and discuss the examples. Ask:

- *When might it be a good idea to draw a picture to solve an addition sentence?* (Possible answer: when the numbers are small enough to picture easily.)
- *What other doubles facts do you know?* (Possible answers: $3 + 3 = 6$, $2 + 2 = 4$, $1 + 1 = 2$, $0 + 0 = 0$)
- *Could you use the doubles fact $5 + 5 = 10$ to help you solve $7 + 5$?* (yes) *How?* (7 is 2 more than 5, so $7 + 5$ is 2 more than $5 + 5$, so $7 + 5 = 12$.)

Try It

Have students complete additions.

Power Practice

Have students complete the practice items. Then review each answer.

Activity 28 Lesson Goal

• Add facts to 8 horizontally or vertically.

What the Student Needs to Know

• Recognize *plus* and *equal* signs.
• Draw a picture to match a number sentence.

Getting Started

On the board, draw a row of 3 Xs next to a row of 4 Xs. Say:

• *How many Xs are in the first group? (3) How many are in the second group? (4) How many Xs are there in all? (7)*

Erase the row of Xs and redraw them as a row of 3 Xs above a row of 4 Xs. Ask:

• *How many Xs are in the first group? (3) How many are in the second group? (4) How many Xs are there in all? (7) Does it matter if the groups are across or down? (no)*

What Can I Do?

Read the question and the response. Then read and discuss the example. Ask:

• *What is the difference between the first 2 + 3 example and the second 2 + 3 example? (One is written across, and the other is written down.)*

• *What is the difference in the answers? (There is no difference; the answers are the same.)*

Have volunteers come to the board and draw their own across and down pictures for the example 2 + 3.

Try It

Read the directions aloud. Make sure students understand that adding across or down yields the same answer.

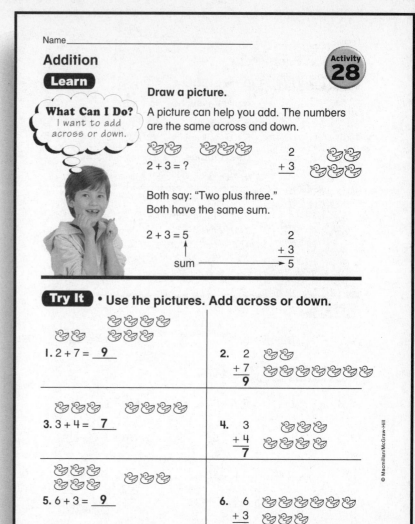

WHAT IF THE STUDENT CAN'T

Recognize *Plus* and *Equal* Signs

• Write a variety of addition number sentences on the board and have the student read them aloud.

• Write number sentences with circles in place of the plus and equal signs. For example:

2 ☐ 4 ☐ 6

• Have the student supply the signs and read the sentences aloud.

Draw a Picture to Match a Number Sentence

• Supply counters and have the student model a given number sentence using counters first. Then have the student draw or trace the counters.

Power Practice • Add. If you need to, draw a picture.

7. $2 + 6 =$ __8__

8.
$$\begin{array}{r} 2 \\ + 6 \\ \hline 8 \end{array}$$

9. $7 + 4 =$ __11__

10.
$$\begin{array}{r} 7 \\ + 4 \\ \hline 11 \end{array}$$

11. $3 + 8 =$ __11__

12.
$$\begin{array}{r} 3 \\ + 8 \\ \hline 11 \end{array}$$

13. $5 + 3 =$ __8__

14.
$$\begin{array}{r} 5 \\ + 3 \\ \hline 8 \end{array}$$

41

Power Practice

- After students have completed the problems, volunteers may share the drawings they used to solve them.

- Ask students to tell whether they find it easier to add across or down. Remind them that the answer is the same either way. If they have trouble adding across, they can always rewrite the number sentence as a vertical exercise.

Learn with Partners & Parents

Students can use plastic spoons and forks to set up horizontal and vertical addition problems. Have them follow these steps.

- Choose two numbers to add, from 0–4.

- Model the numbers with forks and spoons. Place the models across or down.

- Write an addition sentence or a vertical problem to match the fork-and-spoon model. Find the sum.

WHAT IF THE STUDENT CAN'T

Complete the Power Practice

- Have the students identify the exercises that should have the same answers. (5 and 6; 7 and 8; 9 and 10; 11 and 12)

- Discuss each incorrect answer. Have the student use counters to model any fact he or she missed.

Activity 29 Lesson Goal
- Add facts to 8.

What the Student Needs to Know
- Find one more.
- Draw a picture to match a number sentence.

Getting Started
Line up three students on one side of the room and three on the other side. Ask:
- *How many students are in the first group?* (3) *How many students are in the second group?* (3)

Move one student from group 2 to group 1. Say:
- *3 and 1 more is 4.*

Continue moving one student at a time. Then ask:
- *How many students are there in all?* (6) *So 3 + 3 = 6.*

What Can I Do?
Read the question and the response. Then read and discuss the examples. Ask:
- *What are the numbers being added in the first example?* (4 and 2)
- *What are the numbers being added in the second example?* (4 and 2)
- *How can drawing a picture help you add?* (You can count the items in the picture to find the sum.)
- *If you had to solve the number sentence 3 + 4, what would you draw to help you find the sum?* (You would draw a group of 3 items and a group of 4 items.)

Try It
Point out that students may use the pictures to help them add. Alternatively, they may count on to find the sums.

Name_____

Addition Facts to 8

Learn

What Can I Do?
I want to find sums to 8. Here are two ways.

Count on.
Start with the **greater number.**
Count on to find the sum.

4 + 2 = ?

Think: 4 and 1 is 5, and 1 more is 6.

Draw a picture.
Use a picture to help you add.

4 + 2 = ?

Draw 4 circles and 2 more circles.

○○○○ ○○

Count all the circles to find the sum.

Try It • Add.

1. 3 + 4 = __7__

2. 5
   + 3
   ___
   8

3. 4 + 4 = __8__

△△△△ △△△△ △

4. 2
   + 4
   ___
   6

42

© Macmillan/McGraw-Hill

WHAT IF THE STUDENT CAN'T

Find One More
- Supply counters and number cards 0–9. Have the student pick a card, model the number with counters, and then find one more using a counter. Once the student is comfortable modeling one more, have the student try finding one more without the counters.

Draw a Picture to Match a Number Sentence
- Write a variety of addition facts on the board, and have the student tell how many objects he or she would draw. For example, given the number sentence 3 + 2 = ?, the student should respond that he or she would draw a group of 3 items and a group of 2 items.

Power Practice • Add. Count on or draw a picture.

5. $3 + 3 =$ **6**　　　　**6.** $1 + 5 =$ **6**

7. $2 + 3 =$ **5**　　　　**8.** $4 + 3 =$ **7**

9.
$$\begin{array}{r} 5 \\ +\ 2 \\ \hline 7 \end{array}$$

10.
$$\begin{array}{r} 3 \\ +\ 5 \\ \hline 8 \end{array}$$

11.
$$\begin{array}{r} 2 \\ +\ 6 \\ \hline 8 \end{array}$$

12.
$$\begin{array}{r} 6 \\ +\ 1 \\ \hline 7 \end{array}$$

13.
$$\begin{array}{r} 6 \\ +\ 2 \\ \hline 8 \end{array}$$

14.
$$\begin{array}{r} 2 \\ +\ 5 \\ \hline 7 \end{array}$$

43

Power Practice
- Tell students that it is up to them to decide whether it is easier for them to draw a picture or count on to add. If they do not need to use either strategy, they may add on their own.
- Volunteers may share any drawings they used to solve the problems.

WHAT IF THE STUDENT CAN'T

Complete the Power Practice
- Have the student discuss the strategy he or she used to find each sum.
- Discuss each incorrect answer. Have the student model with counters any fact he or she missed.

Activity 30 Lesson Goal
- Add and subtract facts to 12.

What the Student Needs to Know
- Draw a picture to match a number sentence.
- Recognize *plus* and *minus* signs.
- Add doubles.

Getting Started
Choose 10 students to come to the front of the room. Ask:
- *How many ways can you arrange yourselves to make 2 groups?*

Have volunteers count the students to find the number in each group and write the resulting addition sentence.

What Can I Do?
Read the question and the response. Then read and discuss the examples. Ask:
- *When you put two groups together, are you adding or subtracting?* (adding)
- *When you take some items away from a group, are you adding or subtracting?* (subtracting)
- *You want to solve the problem 12 − 5. Why would it help to find the answer to 10 − 5 first?* (If you know the answer to 10 − 5 = 5, then adding 2 to the answer would solve the problem 12 − 5.)

Try It
You may wish to have students circle the signs before they begin their computations.

Power Practice
- Tell students that it is up to them to decide whether it is easier for them to draw a picture or use facts they already know. If they do not need to use either strategy, they may add and subtract on their own.
- Volunteers may share any drawings they used to solve the problems.

Name_____

Addition and Subtraction Facts to 12

Activity 30

Learn

Draw a picture.

A picture can help you add or subtract.

4 + 6 = ?

What Can I Do?
I forgot an addition or subtraction fact!

The **plus sign** means add. 4 + 6 = 10

$$\begin{array}{r} 11 \\ -3 \\ \hline 8 \end{array}$$

The **minus sign** means subtract. 11 − 3 = 8

Use facts you know.

You forgot 12 − 5. You know 10 − 5 = 5.
Think: 12 is 2 more than 10.
12 − 5 must be 2 more than 10 − 5.
So, 12 − 5 = 7.

Try It • Watch the signs. Add or subtract.

1. 2 + 9 = __11__

2. $$\begin{array}{r} 12 \\ -8 \\ \hline 4 \end{array}$$

3. 9 − 7 = __2__

4. $$\begin{array}{r} 3 \\ +7 \\ \hline 10 \end{array}$$

44

© Macmillan/McGraw-Hill

WHAT IF THE STUDENT CAN'T

Draw a Picture to Match a Number Sentence
- Write related addition and subtraction facts on the board and have students first model each one with counters and then draw a picture for each. For example, you might write 5 + 6 = ? and 11 − 6 = ?

Recognize *Plus* and *Minus* Signs
- Write a variety of addition and subtraction number sentences on the chalkboard and have students read them aloud. Then have students add or subtract to solve the problem.
- Write addition and subtraction number sentences on the board. Ask students to circle the sign in each addition sentence. Repeat the activity asking the students to circle the sign in each subtraction sentence. Then have students add or subtract to solve the problem.

Name_____

 Power Practice • Add or subtract. Draw a picture or use facts you know.

5. $2 + 7 = \underline{\ 9\ }$

6.
$$\begin{array}{r} 5 \\ + 6 \\ \hline 11 \end{array}$$

7. $11 - 4 = \underline{\ 7\ }$

8.
$$\begin{array}{r} 8 \\ + 4 \\ \hline 12 \end{array}$$

9. $10 - 9 = \underline{\ 1\ }$

10.
$$\begin{array}{r} 9 \\ - 4 \\ \hline 5 \end{array}$$

11. $5 + 7 = \underline{\ 12\ }$

12.
$$\begin{array}{r} 11 \\ - 6 \\ \hline 5 \end{array}$$

13. $6 + 4 = \underline{\ 10\ }$

14.
$$\begin{array}{r} 12 \\ - 8 \\ \hline 4 \end{array}$$

© Macmillan/McGraw-Hill

45

Learn with Partners & Parents

Play a game of *Concentration* to review and reinforce addition and subtraction facts to 12.

• Write each of these facts on a card: 1 + 2, 3 – 0, 2 + 2, 9 – 5, 0 + 5, 12 – 7, 2 + 4, 11 – 5, 6 + 1, 10 – 3, 3 + 5, 12 – 4, 6 + 3, 11 – 2.

• Players mix the cards and lay them facedown. The first player turns up two cards. If their answers are the same, the player keeps the cards and goes again. If not, the player replaces the cards, and the next player has a turn.

• When all cards have been picked, the player with the most pairs wins.

• Make a new set of cards with different facts and play again.

WHAT IF THE STUDENT CAN'T

Add Doubles

• Make flash cards with doubles from 1 + 1 to 6 + 6. Have students work in pairs to practice adding doubles.

Complete the Power Practice

• Have students discuss the strategy they used to find each sum or difference.

• Discuss each incorrect answer. Have the student model any fact he or she missed using counters.

Activity 31 Lesson Goal

- Write an addition or subtraction number sentence to match a picture.

What the Student Needs to Know

- Recognize *plus* and *minus* signs.
- Count objects in an array.

Getting Started

On the board, draw a group of 3 circles and a group of 5 circles. Ask:

- *Would I add or subtract to find how many in all?* (add)

  Write: $3 + 5 = 8$

  Cross out 3 circles. Ask:

- *Would I add or subtract to find how many are left?* (subtract)

  Write: $8 - 3 = 5$

What Can I Do?

Read the question and the response. Then read and discuss the examples. Ask:

- *What sign do you use to find how many in all?* (plus sign)
- *What sign do you use to find how many are left?* (a minus sign)
- *When you subtract 6 from 10, what number do you write first?* (10) *Why?* (The greater number comes first in a subtraction sentence.)

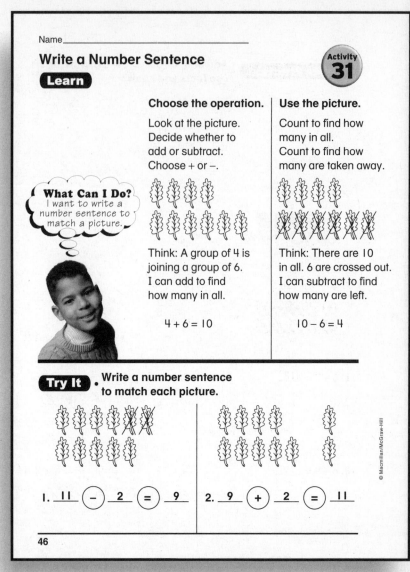

Recognize *Plus* and *Minus* Signs

- Write several addition and subtraction sentences on the board. Ask students to circle the sign in each addition sentence and read the sentence aloud. Repeat the activity, asking students to circle the subtraction signs and read each subtraction sentence. Then have student solve each problem.

Count Objects in an Array

- Place counters in a line. Have the student count them. Mix the counters and place them in an array. Have the student count them again. Repeat with a different number of counters.

Name _____

Power Practice • Write a number sentence to match each picture.

3. 10 (−) 4 (=) 6

_____

4. 6 (+) 6 (=) 12

_____

5. 4 (+) 7 (=) 11

_____

6. 12 (−) 9 (=) 3

© Macmillan/McGraw-Hill

_____

47

Suggest that students keep the following in mind:

• When there are two groups of items, you should add the groups.
When there is one group of items and several items are crossed out, you should subtract the items that are crossed out from the total number of items.

• Count the group or groups. Write the numbers on the lines.

• Write = in the second circle.

• Check your number sentence against the picture. Does it make sense?

Power Practice

• Remind students to choose the operation first and to use numbers that correspond to the items in the pictures.

• Have students share their work by reading their addition and subtraction sentences aloud.

WHAT IF THE STUDENT CAN'T

Complete the Power Practice

• Have the student explain how he or she might decide whether to add or subtract.

• Discuss each incorrect answer. Be sure the student understands that when writing subtraction sentences, he or she should count the total number of items and subtract the crossed-out items from that number. Have the student count the objects in each picture to check his or her work.

Activity 32 Lesson Goal

- Write an addition or subtraction sentence to match a picture.

What the Student Needs to Know

- Recognize *plus* and *minus* signs.
- Count objects in an array.

Getting Started

On the board, draw a group of 4 squares and a group of 7 squares. Ask:

- *Would I add or subtract to find how many in all?* (add)

Write: 4 + 7 = 11

Cross out 4 squares. Ask:

- *Would I add or subtract to find how many are left?* (subtract)

Write: 11 – 4 = 7

What Can I Do?

Read the question and the response. Then read and discuss the examples. Ask:

- *What sign do you use to find how many in all?* (a plus sign)
- *What sign do you use to find how many are left?* (a minus sign)
- *When you subtract 6 from 13, what number do you write first?* (13) *Why?* (The greater number comes first in a subtraction sentence.)

Name_____

Write a Number Sentence

Learn

Choose the operation.

Look at the picture. Decide whether to add or subtract. Choose + or − for your number sentence.

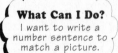

What Can I Do?
I want to write a number sentence to match a picture.

Think: The model planes are all the same. I can **add** to find how many in all. 7 + 6 = 13

Think: There are 13 planes in all. 6 are crossed out. I can **subtract** to find out how many are left. 13 − 6 = 7

Use numbers from the picture.

Think: I can count to find how many in all. One group has 6. One group has 7.
6 + 7 = 13

Think: I can count how many in all. I can count the number being subtracted. There are 13 in all. Seven are being subtracted. 13 − 7 = 6

48

© Macmillan/McGraw-Hill

WHAT IF THE STUDENT CAN'T

Recognize *Plus* and *Minus* Signs

- Write number sentences with circles in place of the plus and minus signs. For example:

  8 ◯ 6 = 14; 14 ◯ 6 = 8

- Have students supply the signs and read the number sentences aloud.

Count Objects in an Array

- Place two groups of counters on a desk or table. Have the student count the number in each group. Rearrange the counters in an array and have the student count again.

Name _____

Try It • Write a number sentence for each picture.

1.

$$16 \;(-)\; 8 \;(=)\; 8$$

2.

$$9 \;(+)\; 5 \;(=)\; 14$$

Power Practice • Write a number sentence for each picture.

3.

$$18 \;(-)\; 9 \;(=)\; 9$$

4.

$$6 \;(+)\; 8 \;(=)\; 14$$

5.

$$5 \;(+)\; 7 \;(=)\; 12$$

6.

$$15 \;(-)\; 9 \;(=)\; 6$$

7.

$$15 \;(-)\; 7 \;(=)\; 8$$

8.

$$7 \;(+)\; 9 \;(=)\; 16$$

49

Try It

Suggest that students use these steps:

- Choose the operation. Write + or – in the first circle.
- Count the group or groups. Write the numbers on the lines.
- Write = in the second circle.
- Add or subtract and write the answer.
- Check your number sentence against the picture. Does it make sense?

Power Practice

- Remind students to choose the operation first and to use numbers that correspond to the items in the pictures.
- Have students share their work by reading their number sentences aloud.

WHAT IF THE STUDENT CAN'T

Complete the Power Practice

- Have the student explain how he or she would decide whether to add or subtract.
- Discuss each incorrect answer. Have the student count the objects in each picture to check his or her work.

Operations Skill Builder **T49**

Activity 33 Lesson Goal

- Subtract facts to 8.

What the Student Needs to Know

- Find one less.
- Draw a picture to match a subtraction sentence.

Getting Started

Line up five students in the front of the classroom. Ask:

- *How many students are in the group?* (5)

Have one student sit down. Say:

- *5 and 1 less is 4.*

Have another student sit down. Then ask:

- *How many students sat down?* (2) *How many students are left?* (3) So 5 – 2 = 3.

What Can I Do?

Read the question and the response. Then read and discuss the examples. Ask:

- *Why do you start subtracting with the greater number?* (You can't subtract a greater number from a lesser number; you are subtracting a lesser number from a greater number.)

- *Why is 7 – 1 – 1 the same as 7 – 2?* (Subtracting 2 is the same as subtracting 1 twice.)

- *If you had to solve the number sentence 4 – 3, what would you draw? What would you cross out?* (You would draw a group of 4 items and cross out 3 of them.)

Name_____

Subtraction Facts to 8

Learn

Count back.
Start with the **greater number.**
Count back to find the difference.

$7 - 2 = ?$

Think: 7 and 1 less is 6, and 1 less is 5.

Draw a picture.
Use a picture to help you subtract.

$7 - 2 = ?$

Draw 4 circles. Cross out 1 circle.

Count the circles that are left to find the difference.

Try It • Subtract.

1. $2 - 1 = \underline{1}$

2. $\begin{array}{r} 6 \\ -3 \\ \hline 3 \end{array}$

3. $7 - 3 = \underline{4}$

4. $\begin{array}{r} 8 \\ -6 \\ \hline 2 \end{array}$

50

© Macmillan/McGraw-Hill

WHAT IF THE STUDENT CAN'T

Find One Less

- On the board, draw a 0–10 number line. Supply number cards 1–10. Have students pick a number, point to the number on the number line, and move their fingers back one to find one less. Once students are competent at this skill, have them use the number cards without the number line.

Draw a Picture to Match a Subtraction Sentence

- Give students several subtraction sentences, such as the following:

  $7 - 5 = 2$
  $6 - 2 = 4$
  $8 - 3 = 5$

- Have the student use connecting cubes or counters to model each sentence. Then ask him or her to draw a picture to represent each sentence. You may want students to work in pairs, taking turns modeling with counters and drawing pictures.

• Subtract. Count back or use a picture.

5. $8 - 2 =$ **6**

6. $5 - 3 =$ **2**

△△◿◿◿

7. $8 - 6 =$ **2**

⌀⌀◯◯
◯◯◯◯

8. $7 - 4 =$ **3**

✦✦✦✦✦
✦✦

9.
   6
 -2
 ──
   4
△△△
△◿◿

10.
   3
 -2
 ──
   1
▢◿▢

11.
   8
 -5
 ──
   3
✦✦✦✦
✦✦✦✦

12.
   4
 -3
 ──
   1
◯⌀◯⌀

WHAT IF THE STUDENT CAN'T

Complete the Power Practice

- Have the student discuss the strategy he or she used to find each answer.
- Discuss each incorrect answer. Have the student use counters to model any fact he or she missed.

Try It

Explain that the pictures show the subtraction problems. The number of things in all is the number of things shown in the picture. The number of things subtracted is the number of things crossed out in the pictures. Students may use the picture or the count back strategy to find each answer.

Power Practice

- Tell students that if they do not need to use either strategy, they may subtract on their own.
- Suggest that students check their work by adding. Give them this example: $8 - 2 = 6$; $6 + 2 = 8$.

Activity 34 Lesson Goal
- Choose the operation to solve a problem.

What the Student Needs to Know
- Recognize *plus* and *minus* signs.
- Use counters to model a problem.

Getting Started
Line up three girls and two boys. Ask:

- *How many students are there in all? How did you find out?* (5; put groups together; added)

- *How many more girls are there than boys? How did you find out?* (1 more; compared groups; subtracted)

What Can I Do?
Read the question and the response. Then read and discuss the examples. Ask:

- *What sign do you use in a number sentence to show how many in all?* (plus sign) *to show how many more?* (minus sign)

- *When you join two groups, do you add or subtract?* (add) *When you compare two groups, do you add or subtract?* (subtract)

Name_____

Add or Subtract

Learn

Use word clues.
How many in all? means **add**.
How many more? means **subtract**.

How many balls in all? $4 + 2 = 6$

How many more soccerballs than baseballs? $4 - 2 = 2$

What Can I Do?
How do I know whether to add or subtract?

Act it out.
Use counters. Act out the problem.

How many in all?   How many more?

Think: I can put the groups together and count.

Think: I can see which group has more and count to find how many more.

Try It . Look for clue words. Write + or –. Then add or subtract.

1.

How many more baseballs than soccerballs?

$5 \ominus 3 = \underline{2}$

2.

How many in all?

$6 \oplus 4 = \underline{10}$

52

© Macmillan/McGraw-Hill

WHAT IF THE STUDENT CAN'T

Recognize *Plus* and *Minus* Signs
- Write number addition and subtraction sentences on the board. Ask students to circle the sign in each addition sentence. Repeat the activity, asking the student to circle the sign in each subtraction sentence. Then have the student solve the problem.

Use Counters to Model a Problem
- Give the student 20 counters. Ask the student to model number sentences like these:
  $2 + 3 = 5$, $16 - 9 = 7$,
  $4 + 8 = 12$, $9 - 5 = 4$,
  $6 + 8 = 14$, $11 - 2 = 9$.

- Ask the student to use counters to model Problems 3–10.

Name _____

Power Practice • Write + or −.
Then add or subtract.

3.

How many in all?

7 (+) 2 = __9__

4.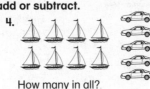

How many in all?

8 (+) 5 = __13__

5.

How many more planes than boats?

6 (−) 4 = __2__

6.

How many in all?

5 (+) 5 = __10__

7.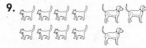

How many more cars than planes?

9 (−) 4 = __5__

8.

How many more cats than dogs?

11 (−) 6 = __5__

9.

How many in all?

8 (+) 3 = __11__

10.

How many more planes than cars?

8 (−) 7 = __1__

© Macmillan/McGraw-Hill

53

Try It
Remind students that each item requires two steps: (1) choosing a plus or minus sign and (2) solving the number sentence.

Power Practice
- You may want to suggest that students go through the exercises first, looking for clue words and writing the plus or minus signs. When they have completed that task, they may go back and add or subtract to solve the number sentences.
- Have students complete the practice items. Then review each answer.

Learn with Partners & Parents
Students can practice choosing the operation by using spoons and forks.
- Display several spoons and forks. Ask:
- *How many spoons and forks are there in all? Do you add or subtract to find out?* (add)
- *Are there more spoons or more forks? How many more? Do you add or subtract to find out?* (subtract)

WHAT IF THE STUDENT CAN'T

Complete the Power Practice
- Have the student read aloud any problems they answered incorrectly and repeat the clue words. Then have the student solve the problem again.
- Watch for students who choose the operation correctly but need additional help with addition and subtraction facts.

USING THE LESSON

Activity 35 Lesson Goal
- Add multiples of ten.

What the Student Needs to Know
- Add facts to 10.
- Use tens models.

Getting Started
- Have students count by 10s to 100.
- Display a hundred chart and have students locate the 10s. (10, 20, 30, . . . 100)

What Can I Do?
Read the question and the response. Then read and discuss the examples. Ask:
- If 2 + 3 = 5, what is 20 + 30? (50) *Why?* (2 ones plus 3 ones equals 5 ones, so 2 tens plus 3 tens equals 5 tens.)

Try It
Have students complete the addition sentences in this section. Ask students to read the addition sentences and their answers aloud.

Power Practice
- Have students complete the practice items. Then review each answer.
- Watch for students who leave out the zero in their answers.

Name_____

Add Tens

Learn

What Can I Do?
I want to add tens.

Use addition facts.

Think: 3 + 4 = 7,   5 + 1 = 6,
so 30 + 40 = 70.   so 50 + 10 = 60.

Draw a picture.

Picture tens blocks.
Add them.

Think: 4 + 2 = 6,
so 4 tens + 2 tens = 6 tens
6 tens = 60

4 tens + 2 tens

Try It • Add.

1. 3 + 5 = __8__,   so   30 + 50 = __80__.

2. 8 + 1 = __9__,   so   80 + 10 = __90__.

3. 2 + 7 = __9__,   so   20 + 70 = __90__.

4. 3 + 2 = __5__,   so   30 + 20 = __50__.

Power Practice • Add.

5.	6.	7.	8.	9.	10.
20	30	10	50	60	40
+ 40	+ 10	+ 70	+ 40	+ 20	+ 40
60	40	80	90	80	80

54

WHAT IF THE STUDENT CAN'T

Add Facts to 10
- Write addition facts on flash cards and have students work in pairs to quiz each other.
- Review facts to 10. Have students write the facts that still cause them difficulty, take them home, and practice them with a parent or sibling.

Use Tens Models
- Give the student a handful of tens models and have him or her count by tens to find the total. Take some models away and have the student find the total again. Add some models and repeat.

Complete the Power Practice
- Give the student tens models and have him or her model any incorrect items.
- Remind students to add the ones before adding the tens, just as they would for any two-digit number. This will prevent their forgetting the placeholder zero.

Name_____

Subtract Tens

Learn

What Can I Do?
I want to subtract tens.

Use subtraction facts.

Think: 9 − 4 = 5, so
90 − 40 = 50

6 − 3 = 3, so
60 − 30 = 30

Draw a picture.

Picture tens blocks.
Subtract them.

Think: 5 − 2 = 3, so
5 tens − 2 tens = 3 tens
3 tens = 30

Activity 36

Try It • Subtract.

1. 6 − 5 = __1__, so 60 − 50 = __10__

2. 7 − 2 = __5__, so 70 − 20 = __50__

3. 4 − 1 = __3__, so 40 − 10 = __30__

4. 8 − 4 = __4__, so 80 − 40 = __40__

Power Practice • Subtract.

5.	6.	7.	8.	9.	10.
40	30	60	50	70	90
− 30	− 10	− 40	− 30	− 40	− 50
10	20	20	20	30	40

© Macmillan/McGraw-Hill

55

Activity 37 Lesson Goal
- Add facts to 20.

What the Student Needs to Know
- Add doubles.
- Add or subtract one.

Getting Started
Give each pair of students 10 counters. Ask:

- *How many ways can you arrange the counters in 2 groups?*

Have volunteers write the resulting groups as number sentences.

(1 + 9 = 10, 2 + 8 = 10, 3 + 7 = 10, . . . 9 + 1 = 10)

What Can I Do?
Read the question and the response. Then read and discuss the examples. Ask:

- *How does knowing that 6 + 6 = 12 help you know the answer to 6 + 7?* (Because 7 is 1 more than 6, the answer will be 1 more than 12, or 13.)

- *How does knowing that 8 + 8 = 16 help you know the answer to 8 + 7?* (Because 7 is 1 less than 8, the answer will be 1 less than 16, or 15.)

Try It
You may wish to have students describe the relationship between the sentences in each pair before finding the sums.

Power Practice
- Ask students to recall addition facts they learned earlier in the year.
- Have students complete the practice items. Then review each answer.

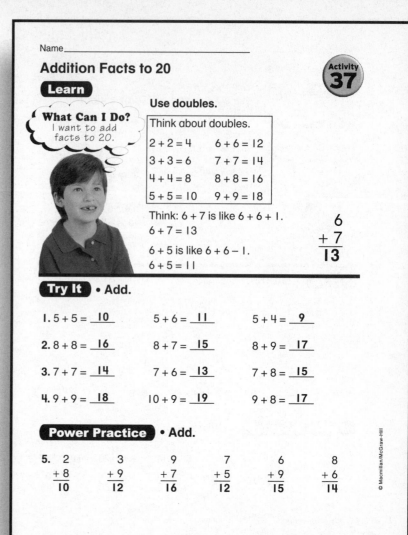

Name_____

Addition Facts to 20

Activity **37**

Learn

What Can I Do? I want to add facts to 20.

Use doubles.

Think about doubles.

2 + 2 = 4	6 + 6 = 12
3 + 3 = 6	7 + 7 = 14
4 + 4 = 8	8 + 8 = 16
5 + 5 = 10	9 + 9 = 18

Think: 6 + 7 is like 6 + 6 + 1.
6 + 7 = 13

6 + 5 is like 6 + 6 − 1.
6 + 5 = 11

$$\begin{array}{r} 6 \\ + 7 \\ \hline 13 \end{array}$$

Try It • Add.

1. 5 + 5 = __10__   5 + 6 = __11__   5 + 4 = __9__

2. 8 + 8 = __16__   8 + 7 = __15__   8 + 9 = __17__

3. 7 + 7 = __14__   7 + 6 = __13__   7 + 8 = __15__

4. 9 + 9 = __18__   10 + 9 = __19__   9 + 8 = __17__

Power Practice • Add.

5.
$$\begin{array}{r} 2 \\ +8 \\ \hline 10 \end{array} \quad \begin{array}{r} 3 \\ +9 \\ \hline 12 \end{array} \quad \begin{array}{r} 9 \\ +7 \\ \hline 16 \end{array} \quad \begin{array}{r} 7 \\ +5 \\ \hline 12 \end{array} \quad \begin{array}{r} 6 \\ +9 \\ \hline 15 \end{array} \quad \begin{array}{r} 8 \\ +6 \\ \hline 14 \end{array}$$

56

© Macmillan/McGraw-Hill

WHAT IF THE STUDENT CAN'T

Add Doubles
- Make flash cards with doubles from 1 + 1 to 6 + 6. Have students work in pairs to practice adding doubles.

Add or Subtract One
- Line up 9 counters. Have the student count them. Add 1 more. Have the student state the result as a number sentence ("9 plus 1 equals 10.") Take away 1 counter and have the student state the result. ("10 minus 1 equals 9.") Repeat with other numbers of counters.

Complete the Power Practice
- Discuss each incorrect answer. Have the student model any fact he or she missed using counters.

Name_____

Addition Facts to 20

Activity
38

Learn

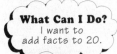

What Can I Do?
I want to add facts to 20.

Use doubles.

Think about doubles.

2 + 2 = 4	6 + 6 = 12
3 + 3 = 6	7 + 7 = 14
4 + 4 = 8	8 + 8 = 16
5 + 5 = 10	9 + 9 = 18

Think: 5 + 6 is like ⌊5 + 5⌋ + 1
$$5 + 6 = 11 \qquad 10 + 1$$

5 + 5 is like ⌊5 + 5⌋ − 1
$$5 + 4 = 9 \qquad 10 - 1$$

Use turnaround facts.

If you know one fact, then you really know two facts.

Think: 4 + 5 = 9, so 5 + 4 = 9
8 + 6 = 14, so 6 + 8 = 14

Try It • Add.

1. 5 + 5 = __10__   5 + 4 = __9__   5 + 6 = __11__

2. 7 + 7 = __14__   7 + 6 = __13__   7 + 8 = __15__

3. 9 + 9 = __18__   9 + 10 = __19__   9 + 8 = __17__

4. 8 + 8 = __16__   8 + 7 = __15__   8 + 9 = __17__

Power Practice • Add.

5. 7	6. 5	7. 3	8. 5	9. 4	10. 2
+6	+6	+4	+4	+3	+3
13	11	7	9	7	5

57

WHAT IF THE STUDENT CAN'T

Add Doubles
- Make flash cards with doubles from 1 + 1 to 6 + 6. Have students work in pairs to practice adding doubles.

Add or Subtract One
- Mix number cards 1–9 and place them face down. Have the student turn up a card, add 1, and give the sum. Repeat until all cards have been turned up. Then mix the cards and repeat the game, having the student subtract 1 this time.

Use the Commutative Property of Addition
- On index cards, write numbers from fact families such as 3, 4, 7; 2, 8, 10; 7, 6, 13; 4, 8, 12; and so on. Have the student pick a card and write the two addition sentences that can be made with those numbers. Repeat with other cards.

Complete the Power Practice
- Discuss each incorrect answer. Have the student model any fact he or she missed using counters.

Activity 38 Lesson Goal
- Add facts to 20.

What the Student Needs to Know
- Add doubles.
- Add or subtract one.
- Use the Commutative Property of Addition.

Getting Started
- Hold up flash cards with facts to 20 and have students take turns giving the sums. Ask students to write any facts that still cause them trouble. They should practice these facts at home.

What Can I Do?
Read the question and the response. Then read and discuss the examples. Ask:
- *How does knowing 5 + 5 help you know 5 + 6?* (Because 6 is 1 more than 5, the answer will be 1 more than 10, or 11.)
- *How does knowing 8 + 8 help you know 8 + 7?* (Because 7 is 1 less than 8, the answer will be 1 less than 16, or 15.)

Try It
You may wish to have students describe the relationship between the sentences in each pair before finding the sums.

Power Practice
- Ask students to skim the items and answer the ones that are easiest for them first before going back to the others.
- Have students complete the practice items. Then review each answer.

Activity 39 Lesson Goal

- Use the Commutative Property of Addition.

What the Student Needs to Know

- Draw a picture to match a number sentence.
- Recall addition facts to 20.

Getting Started

Display a group of 7 shapes and a group of 6 shapes. Ask:

- *Would I add or subtract to find how many in all?* (add)

Write: 7 + 6 = 13

Flip the displays so that the group of 6 shapes is on the left. Ask:

- *Would I add or subtract to find how many in all?* (add)

Write: 6 + 7 = ? Ask:

- *What is the sum? How do you know?* (13; it will be the same as 7 + 6.)

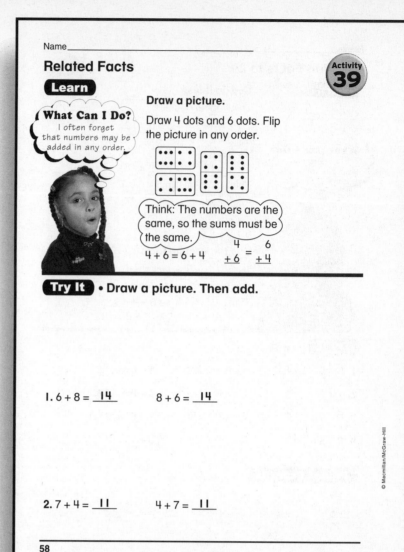

Name_____

Related Facts

Learn

What Can I Do?
I often forget that numbers may be added in any order.

Draw a picture.

Draw 4 dots and 6 dots. Flip the picture in any order.

Think: The numbers are the same, so the sums must be the same.

$4 + 6 = 6 + 4$

$\begin{array}{r} 4 \\ +6 \\ \hline \end{array} = \begin{array}{r} 6 \\ +4 \\ \hline \end{array}$

Try It • Draw a picture. Then add.

1. $6 + 8 =$ __14__ $8 + 6 =$ __14__

2. $7 + 4 =$ __11__ $4 + 7 =$ __11__

58

© Macmillan/McGraw-Hill

WHAT IF THE STUDENT CAN'T

Draw a Picture to Match a Number Sentence

- Supply counters and ask students to model a given addition fact to 20. Then have them draw or trace the counters, flip the picture, and give both number sentences; for example, 4 + 6 = 10 and 6 + 4 = 10.
- Ask students to work with a partner or in small groups to draw pictures to illustrate some of the addition facts to 20.

Recall Addition Facts to 20

- Make up flash cards with addition facts to 20 and have pairs of students quiz each other.
- Have students work in teams in an "Addition Facts Bee." Line up two teams and give the first player in Team 1 a fact to solve. If he or she solves it correctly, that team goes again. If not, the fact goes to Team 2. Continue until everyone has had two chances to find a sum.

Name_____

Power Practice • Add.

3. 5 + 8 = _13_

8 + 5 = _13_

4. 7 + 6 = _13_

6 + 7 = _13_

5. 9 + 7 = _16_

7 + 9 = _16_

6. 4 + 9 = _13_

9 + 4 = _13_

7. 3 + 6 = _9_

6 + 3 = _9_

8. 8 + 4 = _12_

4 + 8 = _12_

9. 3 + 9 = _12_

9 + 3 = _12_

10. 7 + 8 = _15_

8 + 7 = _15_

11. 6 + 8 = _14_

8 + 6 = _14_

12. 5 + 7 = _12_

7 + 5 = _12_

59

What Can I Do?

Read the question and the response. Then read and discuss the examples. Ask:

- *What can dominoes teach you about addition facts?* (They can show you that the sum is the same no matter how you order the addends.)

- *If you know that 4 + 6 = 10, what other addition fact do you know?* (6 + 4 = 10)

- *If you know that 7 + 5 = 12, what other addition fact do you know?* (5 + 7 = 12)

Try It

Tell students that they may choose any object to draw for their addition pictures. Discuss their answers.

Power Practice

- Suggest that students complete the facts they know first, and use those facts to find the sums they don't immediately know.

- Have students complete the practice items. Then review their answers.

WHAT IF THE STUDENT CAN'T

Complete the Power Practice

- Provide paper and pencil and have students draw pictures for the facts they missed.

- If students found two different sums for the facts in a pair, provide counters and have them model the facts.

Operations Skill Builder **T59**

Activity 40 Lesson Goal

• Subtract facts to 20.

What the Student Needs to Know

• Add doubles.

• Recognize the inverse relation-ship between addition and subtraction.

• Read a place-value chart.

Getting Started

Give each pair of students 10 counters. Say:

• *How many different ways can you take away counters from 10?*

Have volunteers write the resulting groups as number sentences.

(10 – 1 = 9, 10 – 2 = 8, 10 – 3 = 7, . . .10 – 9 = 1)

What Can I Do?

Read the question and the response. Then read and discuss the examples. Ask:

• *How does knowing 5 + 5 = 10 help you know 10 – 5 = 5?* (Because subtracting 5 from 10 is the opposite of adding 5 + 5.)

• *Why is it important to line up the digits when you subtract?* (So that tens and ones are clearly shown and understood.)

Try It

You may wish to have students describe the relationship between the sentences in each pair before finding the differences.

Power Practice

• Ask students to recall subtraction facts they learned earlier in the year.

• Have students complete the practice items. Then review each answer.

Name _____

Subtraction Facts to 20

Activity 40

Learn

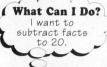
What Can I Do?
I want to subtract facts to 20.

Use doubles.

Think about doubles:
5 + 5 = 10 and 10 – 5 = 5.

You can use doubles to find 11 – 6.

Think: 11 is 1 more than 10.
11 – 5 is 1 more than 10 – 5.
So, 11 – 5 = 6.

Try It • Subtract.

1. 16 – 8 = __8__

17 – 8 = __9__

2. 14 – 7 = __7__

15 – 7 = __8__

3. 8 – 4 = __4__

9 – 4 = __5__

4. 12 – 6 = __6__

13 – 6 = __7__

Power Practice • Subtract.

5. 12	6. 13	7. 16	8. 13	9. 14	10. 17
−8	−9	−7	−5	−8	−9
4	4	9	8	6	8

60

© Macmillan/McGraw-Hill

WHAT IF THE STUDENT CAN'T

Add Doubles

• Have the student use doubles flash cards to practice doubles addition from 1 + 1 to 9 + 9. Ask the student to model each double addition with connecting cubes.

Recognize the Inverse Relationship Between Addition and Subtraction

• Give the student a variety of subtraction doubles facts and have them check their answers using addition.

Complete the Power Practice

• Discuss each incorrect answer. Have the student model any fact he or she missed using counters.

Name_____

Subtraction Facts to 20

Activity
41

Learn　Use doubles.

Think about doubles.

2 + 2 = 4	4 − 2 = 2
3 + 3 = 6	6 − 3 = 3
4 + 4 = 8	8 − 4 = 4
5 + 5 = 10	10 − 5 = 5
6 + 6 = 12	12 − 6 = 6
7 + 7 = 14	14 − 7 = 7
8 + 8 = 16	16 − 8 = 8
9 + 9 = 18	18 − 9 = 9

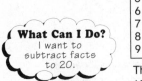

What Can I Do?
I want to subtract facts to 20.

Think: 13 − 6 is one more than 12 − 6.
13 − 6 = 7

Use fact families.

If you know one fact, then
you may know other facts.

Think: 15 − 8 = 7, so 15 − 7 = 8
9 − 3 = 6, so 9 − 6 = 3

Try It　• Subtract.

1. 14 − 7 = __7__,　so　15 − 7 = __8__

2. 10 − 5 = __5__,　so　11 − 5 = __6__

3. 6 − 3 = __3__,　so　7 − 3 = __4__

Power Practice　• Subtract.

4. 11 − 8 = __3__　　5. 14 − 9 = __5__　　6. 17 − 8 = __9__

61

© Macmillan/McGraw-Hill

WHAT IF THE STUDENT CAN'T

Read a Place-Value Chart
- Give the student tens and ones models and have them show these numbers: 15, 28, 34. Then have them use their models to write the numbers in a place-value chart.

Complete the Power Practice
- Discuss each incorrect answer. Have students show each number with tens and ones models.

USING THE LESSON

Activity 41 Lesson Goal
- Subtract facts to 20.

What the Student Needs to Know
- Add doubles.
- Recognize the inverse relationship between addition and subtraction.
- Read a place-value chart.

Getting Started
Give each pair of students 12 counters. Say: *Subtract 6. Write the number sentence for this action.* 12 − 6 = 6. Now put the counters back into a pile and give each pair of students one more counter. Without actually moving counters, ask students to subtract 6. *What is the number sentence you just demonstrated?* 13 − 6 = 7. Subtract 6 counters to check your answer. Ask: *How did knowing the double 12 − 6 help you find 13 − 6?*

What Can I Do?
Read the question and the response. Then read and discuss the examples. Ask:
- *How does knowing 9 + 9 = 18 help you know 18 − 9 = 9?* (Because subtracting 9 from 18 is the opposite of adding 9 + 9.)

Try It
You may wish to have students describe the relationship between the sentences in each pair before finding the differences.

Power Practice
- Ask students to recall subtraction facts they learned earlier in the year.
- Have students complete the practice items. Then review each answer.

Operations Skill Builder **T61**

Activity 42 Lesson Goal

- Complete a family of addition and subtraction facts.

What the Student Needs to Know

- Write a number sentence.
- Use the Commutative Property of Addition.
- Recall addition and subtraction facts to 20.

Getting Started

Display a group of 5 shapes and a group of 8 shapes. Ask:

- *If I asked how many shapes there are in all, what number sentence would you write?* (5 + 8 = 13)

Flip the felt board. Ask:

- *What number sentence describes this picture now?* (8 + 5 = 13)

Take away 5 shapes. Ask:

- *What number sentence would describe what I just did?* (13 − 5 = 8)

Replace the 5 shapes. Take away 8 shapes. Ask:

- *What number sentence would describe what I just did?* (13 − 8 = 5)

What Can I Do?

Read the question and the response. Then read and discuss the examples. Ask:

- *When you add two numbers, which is the greatest number in an addition sentence?* (the last number; the sum)
- *When you subtract one number from another, which is the greatest number in a subtraction sentence?* (the first number)

Name_____

Fact Families

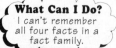 **Learn**   Write number sentences.

Begin with an addition fact. Then put the same numbers together in different addition and subtraction sentences.

What Can I Do? I can't remember all four facts in a fact family.

$$7 + 8 = 15 \qquad 8 + 7 = 15$$

$$15 - 8 = 7 \qquad 15 - 7 = 8$$

Addition sentences and subtraction sentences that use the same numbers are called a **fact family**.

Try It • Complete each fact family.

1. 6 + 8 = __14__

   8 + 6 = __14__

   14 − 8 = __6__

   14 − 6 = __8__

2. 7 + 3 = __10__

   3 + 7 = __10__

   10 − 7 = __3__

   10 − 3 = __7__

3. 8 + 5 = __13__

   __5__ + __8__ = __13__

   13 − 8 = __5__

   __13__ − __5__ = __8__

62

WHAT IF THE STUDENT CAN'T

Write a Number Sentence

- Display two groups of counters and have the student write the two related addition sentences. Take away one group and have the student write the related subtraction sentence. Then take away the other group and have the student write the other related subtraction sentence.

Use the Commutative Property of Addition

- Give the student dominoes and have the student say and write the two addition sentences represented by each one.

Name_____

Power Practice • Complete each fact family.

4. 7 + 6 = _13_

  _6_ + _7_ = _13_

  13 − 7 = _6_

  _13_ − _6_ = _7_

5. 8 + 9 = _17_

  _9_ + _8_ = _17_

  17 − 8 = _9_

  _17_ − _9_ = _8_

6. 6 + 4 = _10_

  _4_ + _6_ = _10_

  _10_ − _6_ = _4_

  _10_ − _4_ = _6_

7. 5 + 9 = _14_

  _9_ + _5_ = _14_

  _14_ − _5_ = _9_

  _14_ − _9_ = _5_

8. 5 + 5 = _10_

  _10_ − _5_ = _5_

9. 9 + 9 = _18_

  _18_ − _9_ = _9_

Use the numbers. Write the fact family.

10. 5, 6, 11

  5 + 6 = 11

  6 + 5 = 11

  11 − 5 = 6

  11 − 6 = 5

11. 7, 9, 16

  7 + 9 = 16

  9 + 7 = 16

  16 − 7 = 9

  16 − 9 = 7

63

CHALLENGE

Try It

Remind students that a fact family contains only three numbers, and the numbers are the same from fact to fact. Discuss their answers.

Power Practice

- Have students complete the practice items. Then review their answers.

WHAT IF THE STUDENT CAN'T

Recall Addition and Subtraction Facts to 20

- Make up flash cards with addition and subtraction facts to 20 and have pairs of students quiz each other and model each fact with counters.

Complete the Power Practice

- Provide paper and pencil and have students draw pictures for the facts they missed.
- Remind students that all four facts in a family contain the same three numbers.

Operations Skill Builder **T63**

Activity 43 Lesson Goal
- Add three or more numbers.

What the Student Needs to Know
- Make a 10.
- Use the Commutative Property of Addition.

Getting Started
On the board, draw the following:

O O

O O O

O O O O

O O O O O

Ask:

- *How could you add all four groups of circles?* (Add the first two groups; then add the third group to that sum; then add the fourth group to that sum.)

  Have the students find the sum. (14)

What Can I Do?
Read the question and the response. Then read and discuss the examples. Ask:

- *Why does it help to find 10?* (It's easy to add 10 to other numbers.)

- *Why can you check addition by adding the numbers in a different direction?* (Changing the order of addends does not change the sum.)

Name_____

Adding Three or More Numbers

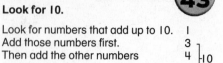

Learn

What Can I Do?
I want to add 3 or more numbers.

Look for 10.

Look for numbers that add up to 10.   1
Add those numbers first.   3
Then add the other numbers   4 }10
                                                        +7

Think: $3 + 7 = 10$. Add $1 + 4 = 5$. Then add $10 + 5 = 15$.

Add in stages.

Add the first two numbers.   4 }6
Then add the third number.   2
Then add the fourth number.   1
Check by adding the numbers   +6
in a different direction.

Think: $4 + 2 = 6$. Add $6 + 1 = 7$, then $7 + 6 = 13$.
$6 + 1 + 2 + 4 = 13$

Try It • Look for 10. Add.

1.   5
     4]
     6]
   + 2

    17

2.   5
     2]
     1]
   + 8

    16

3. $1 + 9 + 7 =$ __17__

4. $5 + 4 + 5 + 4 =$ __18__

64

© Macmillan/McGraw-Hill

WHAT IF THE STUDENT CAN'T

Make a 10
- Give the student ten counters. Have him or her group the counters in as many ways as possible to make two groups that add up to 10.
  $(1 + 9, 2 + 8, \ldots 9 + 1)$

Use the Commutative Property of Addition
Ask the student questions like these:

- *If $3 + 4 = 7$, what is $4 + 3$?* (7)
- *If $9 + 2 = 11$, what is $2 + 9$?* (11)

Have the student model similar addition pairs using counters.

Power Practice • Add.

5.	6	6.	2	7.	5
	4		2		7
	3		9		+5
	+7		+8		17
	20		21		

8.	4	9.	3	10.	4
	5		7		4
	1		+7		4
	+6		17		+8
	16				20

11. $3 + 6 + 1 =$ __10__   12. $4 + 7 + 3 =$ __14__

13. $9 + 1 + 4 + 3 =$ __17__   14. $5 + 5 + 6 + 2 =$ __18__

15. $2 + 3 + 4 + 5 + 6 + 7 =$ __27__   16. $8 + 2 + 7 + 3 =$ __20__

17. $1 + 5 + 3 + 7 + 5 =$ __21__   18. $6 + 2 + 8 + 4 =$ __20__

19. $1 + 3 + 3 + 4 + 6 =$ __17__   20. $4 + 5 + 1 + 6 =$ __16__

Try It

- Remind students that they will not always be able to find 10 in an addition problem. Exercises 1–4, however, all include 10.
- Suggest that students check their answers by adding in the other direction.

Power Practice

- Remind students to check their addition by adding in the other direction.
- Have students complete the practice items. Then discuss their answers.

WHAT IF THE STUDENT CAN'T

Complete the Power Practice

- Have students work out incorrect problems as you observe. Watch for students who add only three out of four addends or who cannot hold a sum in their heads long enough to add it to the next number.
- Provide counters for students to use to model any incorrect problems.

Activity 44 Lesson Goal

• Add two-digit numbers, with and without regrouping.

What the Student Needs to Know

• Regroup ones as tens and ones.
• Check addition.

Getting Started

Use tens and ones models to show the numbers 13 and 18. Ask:

• *How many tens are in each number? How many ones are in each number?* (1 ten, 3 ones; 1 ten, 8 ones)

Put the models together. Say:

• *I'm adding 13 and 18. Now how many tens do I have? How many ones do I have?* (2 tens, 11 ones)

• *What can I do with 11 ones?* (Regroup as 1 ten and 1 one.)

• *Now how many tens do I have? How many ones do I have?* (3 tens, 1 one)

What Can I Do?

Read the question and the response. Then read and discuss the examples. Ask:

• *Why can you add 6 ones and 3 ones without regrouping?* (They add up to 9 ones, which is less than the 10 ones needed for regrouping.)

• *Why do you need to regroup when you add 6 ones and 7 ones?* (They add up to 13 ones, which is more than 10 ones or 1 ten.)

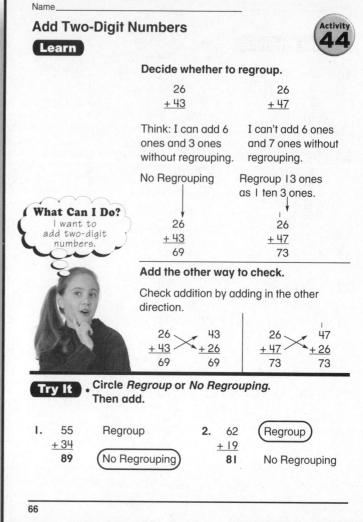

WHAT IF THE STUDENT CAN'T

Regroup Ones as Tens and Ones

• Give the student 18 ones models and 5 tens models. Have the student show addends like these: 32 + 18; 17 + 25; 29 + 17. After showing the addends, have the student put the models together and regroup any groups of 10 ones for 1 ten before finding the sum. Encourage the student to talk about each step of the process.

Check Addition

• Display addition fact cards to 18 and have the student use counters to model the facts.

• Then ask the student to check the addition by adding the numbers in a different direction and using counters to model the new fact.

Name _____

3. 28   (Regroup)   **4.** 31   Regroup
       + 17   + 27
        45   No Regrouping   58   (No Regrouping)

5. 24   (Regroup)   **6.** 16   (Regroup)
       + 48   + 27
        72   No Regrouping   43   No Regrouping

Power Practice • **Add. Check by adding in the other direction.**

7.   32   **8.**   40   **9.**   57
        + 8   + 22   + 27
         40   62   84

10. 33   **11.** 64   **12.** 65
        + 29   + 31   + 6
         62   95   71

13. 42   **14.** 35   **15.** 86
        + 52   + 45   + 12
         94   80   98

16. 14   **17.** 21   **18.** 47
        + 68   + 67   + 39
         82   88   86

19. 13   **20.** 53   **21.** 46
        + 18   + 8   + 19
         31   61   65

© Macmillan/McGraw-Hill

67

- Remind students that they need only look at the ones digits to know whether or not to regroup. If the ones add up to less than 10, no regrouping is needed. If they add up to 10 or more, you must regroup.
- Make sure students realize that they are to add as well as to circle the correct choice.

Power Practice

- If necessary, provide additional paper for students to check their answers.
- Have students complete the practice items. Then review each answer.

WHAT IF THE STUDENT CAN'T

Complete the Power Practice

- Discuss each incorrect answer. Have the student tell which addition problems require regrouping and which do not.
- Watch for students who consistently fail to add the regrouped ten. Remind them to write the 1 above the tens after they add the ones.

Activity 45 Lesson Goal

- Subtract two-digit numbers, with and without regrouping.

What the Student Needs to Know

- Regroup tens and ones as ones.
- Check subtraction.

Getting Started

Use tens and ones models to show the number 43. Ask:

- *How many tens are there? How many ones are there?* (4 tens, 3 ones)

Say:

- *I want to subtract 15. How many tens and ones is that?* (1 ten, 5 ones)

- *How can I subtract 5 ones when I only have 3 ones?* (Regroup 1 ten as 10 ones, add it to the 3 ones to make 13 ones.)

- *Now how many tens do I have? How many ones do I have?* (3 tens, 13 ones) *So if I subtract 5 ones, I have 8 ones left. If I subtract 1 ten, I have 2 tens left. My answer is 2 tens, 8 ones, or 28.*

Name_____

Subtract Two-Digit Numbers

Learn

Decide whether to regroup.

$$\begin{array}{r} 55 \\ -33 \\ \hline \end{array} \qquad \begin{array}{r} 55 \\ -38 \\ \hline \end{array}$$

Think: I can subtract 3 ones from 5 ones without regrouping. | I can't subtract 8 ones from 5 ones without regrouping.

No Regrouping | Regroup 1 ten 5 ones as 15 ones.

$$\begin{array}{r} 55 \\ -33 \\ \hline 22 \end{array} \qquad \begin{array}{r} {}^{4\ 15} \\ \cancel{55} \\ -38 \\ \hline 17 \end{array}$$

What Can I Do?
I want to subtract two-digit numbers.

Add to check.

Check your subtraction by adding.

$$\begin{array}{r} 55 \\ -33 \\ \hline 22 \end{array} \diagup \begin{array}{r} 22 \\ +33 \\ \hline 55 \end{array} \qquad \begin{array}{r} 55 \\ -38 \\ \hline 17 \end{array} \diagup \begin{array}{r} {}^{1} \\ 17 \\ +38 \\ \hline 55 \end{array}$$

Try It · Circle *Regroup* or *No Regrouping*. Then subtract.

1.
$$\begin{array}{r} 64 \\ -14 \\ \hline 50 \end{array}$$
Regroup

(No Regrouping)

2.
$$\begin{array}{r} 47 \\ -19 \\ \hline 28 \end{array}$$
(Regroup)

No Regrouping

© Macmillan/McGraw-Hill

68

WHAT IF THE STUDENT CAN'T

Regroup Tens and Ones as Ones

- Give the student 5 tens models and 15 ones models. Have the student show numbers like these: 43, 25, 32. After modeling the numbers, have the student demonstrate how to subtract 15 from each number, regrouping 1 ten as 10 ones where needed. Encourage the student to talk about each step in the process.

Check Addition

- Display subtraction fact cards to 18 and have the student tell the difference and explain how he or she might add to check.

- Ask the student to write the addition fact for each subtraction fact.

Name_____

3. 50 (Regroup) **4.** 42 Regroup
  − 25   − 31
  25 No Regrouping 11 (No Regrouping)

5. 83 (Regroup) **6.** 37 (Regroup)
  − 14   − 29
  69 No Regrouping 8 No Regrouping

Power Practice • Subtract. Check by adding.

7. 92   **8.** 45   **9.** 56
  − 6   − 32   − 17
  86   13   39

10. 82   **11.** 56   **12.** 98
  − 48   − 21   − 57
  34   35   41

13. 72   **14.** 85   **15.** 36
  − 58   − 29   − 18
  14   56   18

16. 66   **17.** 74   **18.** 48
  − 65   − 26   − 29
  1   48   19

19. 63   **20.** 47   **21.** 59
  − 35   − 28   − 21
  28   19   38

© Macmillan/McGraw-Hill

69

WHAT IF THE STUDENT CAN'T

Complete the Power Practice

- Discuss each incorrect answer. Have the student tell which subtraction problems require regrouping and which do not.

- Watch for students who consistently have answers that are too great by ten. Remind them to cross out the tens and write 1 less ten whenever regrouping occurs.

What Can I Do?

Read the question and the response. Then read and discuss the examples. Ask:

- *Why can you subtract 3 ones from 5 ones without regrouping?* (3 is less than 5.)

- *Why do you need to regroup when you subtract 8 ones from 5 ones?* (8 is greater than 5, and you can't subtract a greater number from a lesser number.)

Try It

- Remind students that they need only look at the ones digits to know whether or not to regroup. If there are more ones in the number being subtracted, you must regroup.

- Make sure students complete each subtraction, as well as circling the correct choice.

Power Practice

- Provide additional paper, if necessary, so that students can check their answers.

- Have students complete the practice items. Then review each answer.

Activity 46 Lesson Goal

- Subtract two-digit numbers, with and without regrouping.

What the Student Needs to Know

- Recognize when regrouping is necessary.
- Add two-digit numbers, with and without regrouping.
- Rename tens and ones as ones.

Getting Started

Give each group of students 5 tens models and 15 ones models. Ask them to show these number sentences:

- 55 – 25 = ? (30)
- 55 – 26 = ? (29)

Discuss the regrouping students had to do to complete the second example: regrouping 1 ten and 5 ones as 15 ones and then subtracting 6 ones from 15 ones.

What Can I Do?

Read the question and the response. Then read and discuss the examples. Ask:

- *How can you tell by looking at two numbers whether you'll have to regroup?* (If the number of ones in the lesser number is greater than the number of ones in the greater number, you will have to regroup.)
- *Why does it work to check subtraction by adding?* (In subtraction, you take a lesser number away from a greater number. In addition, you add the two lesser numbers to form the greater number.)

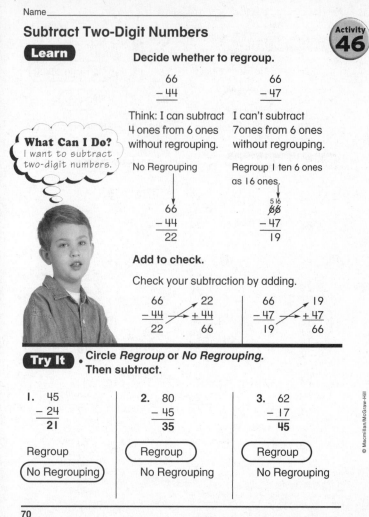

WHAT IF THE STUDENT CAN'T

Recognize When Regrouping Is Necessary

- Review Exercises 4–24 and have the student tell by looking at the ones digits which items require regrouping.

Add Two-Digit Numbers, With and Without Regrouping

- Provide the student with number cards 0–99. Have the student draw two cards, write the numbers, and add them. Repeat several times.

Rename Tens and Ones as Ones

Distribute tens and ones models. Have the student show these regroupings:

- *Regroup 1 ten 6 ones.* (16 ones)
- *Regroup 4 tens 5 ones.* (3 tens 15 ones)
- *Regroup 3 tens 2 ones.* (2 tens 12 ones)
- *Regroup 2 tens 4 ones.* (1 ten 14 ones)

Name_____

Power Practice • Subtract.
Check by adding.

4. 22
   − 8
    14

5. 83
   − 12
    71

6. 76
   − 27
    49

7. 43
   − 25
    18

8. 94
   − 33
    61

9. 67
   − 7
    60

10. 32
    − 18
     14

11. 65
    − 25
     40

12. 46
    − 17
     29

13. 94
    − 65
     29

14. 54
    − 20
     34

15. 58
    − 39
     19

16. 23
    − 15
     8

17. 67
    − 28
     39

18. 55
    − 51
     4

19. 86
    − 44
     42

20. 57
    − 29
     28

21. 34
    − 14
     20

22. 62
    − 19
     43

23. 74
    − 37
     37

24. 49
    − 23
     26

71

© Macmillan/McGraw-Hill

Try It
• Remind students to look at the ones digit of each number to decide whether to regroup or not.
• Make sure that students complete step (1) Circle "Regroup" or "No Regrouping" and step (2) Complete the subtraction.

Power Practice
• Remind students to check their subtraction by adding.
• Have students complete the practice items. Then discuss their answers.

WHAT IF THE STUDENT CAN'T

Complete the Power Practice
• Review with the student any exercises that were done incorrectly one-on-one. Have the student explain how he or she knew whether or not to regroup. Then watch as the student completes the subtraction again. Look for problems that involve regrouping, alignment of digits, or adding instead of subtracting.

Activity 47 Lesson Goal

- Write whole numbers for hundreds, tens, and ones.

What the Student Needs to Know

- Skip count by 10s and 100s.
- Use a place value chart to understand place value.

Getting Started

Find out what students know about hundreds, tens, and ones. Say:

- *Let's count to twenty. I'll start: 1, 2, 3, ... Now you continue counting to 20.*
- *Now let's count to 100 by tens. I'll start: 10, 20, 30... . Now you continue to count to 100.*
- *Let's count to 900 by hundreds. I'll start: 100, 200, 300... . Now you continue to 900.*

What Can I Do?

Read the question and the response. Draw a place-value chart on the board. Ask:

- *I want to write 6 in my place value chart. Where do I write the 6?* (in the ones column)
- *I want to write 40 in my place value chart. How many tens are in 40?* (4) *Where should I write the 4 in my chart?* (in the tens column) *How many ones are in 40?* (0) *What do I write in the ones place in my chart?* (0)
- *I want to write 200 in my place value chart. How many hundreds are in 200?* (2) *Where do I write the 2 in my place-value chart?* (in the hundreds place) *How many tens are in 200?* (0) *What do I write in the tens place in my chart?* (0) *What do I write in the ones place in my chart?* (0)

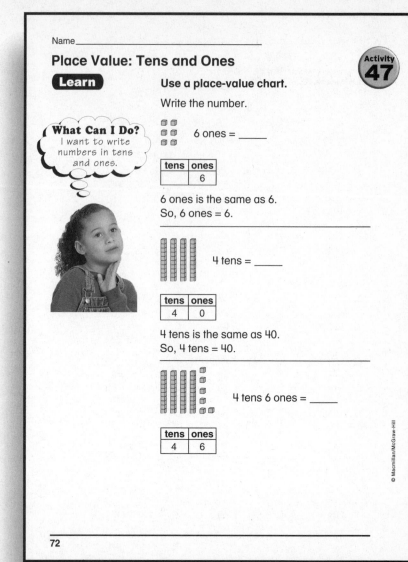

WHAT IF THE STUDENT CAN'T

Skip Count by 10s and 100s

- Provide more practice skip counting by tens by using base ten blocks. The student can use tens blocks, setting down one tens block at a time as he or she says, "10, 20, 30, ..."
- When the student can skip count by tens with ease, have him or her use hundreds blocks and set one down each time as he or she says, "100, 200, 300, ..."

Use a Place-Value Chart to Understand Place Value

- Have the student use connecting cubes and a place value mat to model numbers such as 2, 5, 12, 15, 22, and 25.
- For numbers greater than or equal to 10, the student can connect cubes to make 10-cube trains and place the leftover cubes in the ones column.
- Then the student can write each number in a place-value chart as follows.

tens	ones
2	5

Name_____

Try It • Fill in each place-value chart.

Write the number.

1.
tens	ones
5	0

5 tens = __50__

2.
tens	ones
3	4

3 tens 4 ones = __34__

Write each number.

3. 3 tens = __30__

4. 7 ones = __7__

5. 7 tens 8 ones = __78__

6. 4 tens I one = __41__

Power Practice • Write each number.

7. 2 tens = __20__

8. I ten 9 ones = __19__

9. 8 tens = __80__

10. 4 ones = __4__

11. I ten I one = __II__

12. 6 tens 5 ones = __65__

13. 7 tens = __70__

14. 2 tens 3 ones = __23__

15. 5 ones = __5__

16. 9 tens = __90__

17. 8 tens 7 ones = __87__

18. 4 tens 4 ones = __44__

73

WHAT IF THE STUDENT CAN'T

Complete the Power Practice

- Discuss each incorrect answer. Have the student use base ten models and a place-value mat to model any exercise he or she missed. Then have the student write the number in a place-value chart.

- Have the student point to the hundreds, tens, and ones place in each number and explain what the number in each place means.

Try It

Have students write the numbers in the place-value charts. Ask:

- *How many tens are in the first model?* (5) *Look at the place-value chart. Where do we write this 5?* (in the tens place) *How many ones are there?* (0) *What do we write in the ones place?* (0) *What number does 5 tens equal?* (50) *Let's check. Skip count by tens to count the models.* (10, 20, 30, 40, 50)

- *Does the number 400 have 4 tens or 4 hundreds?* (4 hundreds)

Power Practice

- Have students complete the practice items. Then review each answer.

Activity 48 Lesson Goal
- Write two-digit numbers.

What the Student Needs to Know
- Count ten items.
- Identify tens and ones.

Getting Started
Display a tens model and a ones model. Ask:

- *Which model stands for 1 one? Which model stands for 1 ten? What number do the models stand for when I put them together? (11)*

What Can I Do?
Read the question and the response. Then read and discuss the examples. Ask:

- *What number has 1 ten and 2 ones? (12) 1 ten and 3 ones? (13) 1 ten and 4 ones? (14)*

- *What is the least number you can make that has a tens digit and a ones digit? (10)*

Try It
Students who are having trouble might try counting on from 10 before they write the number.

Power Practice
- Point out that students may circle any 10 ones to make 1 ten.

- Have students complete the practice items and share their answers.

WHAT IF THE STUDENT CAN'T

Count Ten Items
- Place ten counters in a line. Have the student count them. Mix the counters and place them out in random order. Have the student count them again.

- Find opportunities to have the student count a variety of classroom objects to 10. For example, you may ask the student to count pencils, crayons, books, sheets of paper, and so on.

Identify Tens and Ones
- Write these numbers in a place-value chart: 12, 15, 18. Have the student identify the number of tens and ones in each number.

- Play Place-Value Bingo with students. Instead of calling out a number such as "12," call out "1 ten, 2 ones" and have students mark the appropriate number. Be sure the numbers on the prepared Bingo cards fall within the range of 0–19. Continue with calls such as "2 ones," "1 ten," "6 ones," and so on.

Complete the Power Practice
- Discuss each incorrect answer. Look for common errors such as reversed place value or incorrect counting.

- Have students show each number with tens and ones models.

Name_____

Greater Than, Less Than

Learn

Use a number line.

Numbers on the **right** are greater. →
← Numbers on the **left** are less.

What Can I Do?
I want to find the greater number.

0 1 2 3 4 5 6 7 8 9 10 11 12 13 14 15 16 17 18 19 20

Think: 14 is to the left of 16.
So, 14 is less than 16.

Compare place values.

Look at the tens place. Which digit is greater?
If both are the same look at the ones place.
Which digit is greater?
6 is greater than 4.
So, 16 is greater than 14.

tens	ones
1	4
1	6

Try It • Use the number line.
Circle the *greater* number.

0 1 2 3 4 5 6 7 8 9 10 11 12 13 14 15 16 17 18 19 20

1. (12)　2

2. 15　(17)

Power Practice • Circle the number that is *greater*.

3. (71)　17

4. 12　(21)

5. (33)　22

Circle the number that is *less*.

6. 68　(67)

7. (50)　51

8. (39)　40

© Macmillan/McGraw-Hill

75

WHAT IF THE STUDENT CAN'T

Recognize the Meaning of *Greater* and *Less*

Ask the student questions involving greater or less.

- Is the number of pets at your house greater or less than the number of people?
- Is the number of adults at your house greater or less than the number of children?

Read a Number Line

- Draw a 0–10 number line on the board. Have the student locate and circle: 3, a number less than 3, and a number greater than 3. Then have the student do the same for the number 7.

Read a Place-Value Chart

- Write these numbers in a place-value chart: 14, 41, 29, 92, 58, 85. Have the student identify the number of tens and ones in each number and write the two-digit number.

Complete the Power Practice

- Discuss each incorrect answer. Have the student show each number with tens and ones models and compare the numbers.

Activity 49 Lesson Goal

- Compare numbers to 99.

What the Student Needs to Know

- Recognize the meaning of *greater* and *less*.
- Read a number line.
- Read a place-value chart.

Getting Started

On the board, draw a 0–10 number line. Ask:

- *Which number comes just after 8?* (9) *Which is greater, 8 or 9?* (9)
- *Which number comes just before 8?* (7) *Which is greater, 7 or 8?* (8)

What Can I Do?

Read the question and the response. Then read and discuss the examples. Ask:

- *If the number line continued to the right, what would the next number be?* (15) *Would it be greater or less than 14?* (greater)
- *The numbers 14 and 16 have the same digit in the tens place. Where do you look to figure out which number is greater?* (the ones place)

Try It

Suggest that students follow these steps:

- Find each number on the number line. Mark it.
- See which number is on the right. That number is greater.

Power Practice

- Have students complete the exercises. Discuss their answers.
- Ask: *Which strategy did you use? Was the strategy you used for Exercise 5 the same one you used for Exercise 6?* (Answers will vary.)

Place Value Skill Builder **T75**

Activity 50 Lesson Goal

- Identify place value in a two-digit number.

What the Student Needs to Know

- Count ten items.
- Identify place value.
- Read a place-value chart.

Getting Started

Display 2 tens models and 3 ones models. Ask:

- *What number do these make when I put them together?* (23)
- *How many tens are in 23?* (2) *How many ones are in 23?* (3)

Repeat, using 3 tens blocks and 2 ones blocks.

What Can I Do?

Read the question and the response. Then read and discuss the examples. Ask:

- *Why do you think tens are on the left and ones on the right in a place-value chart?* (That's the way they are arranged in a two-digit number.)
- *How would the place-value chart change to show the number 43?* (The 4 would be in the tens place, and the 3 would be in the ones place.)
- *What number is 4 tens with 3 left over?* (43)

Name_____

Place-Value Chart

Learn

Use a place-value chart.

This place-value chart shows tens and ones. Tens are on the left. Ones are on the right.

tens	ones
1	9

What Can I Do? I want to write a number as tens and ones.

There is 1 ten and 9 ones in 19.

This shows 1 ten with 9 ones.

tens	ones
1	9

Try It • Write each number in a place-value chart.

1. 15

tens	ones
1	5

2. 17

tens	ones
1	7

3. 20

tens	ones
2	0

4. 12

tens	ones
1	2

76

WHAT IF THE STUDENT CAN'T

Count Ten Items

- Have the student draw a picture of 10 objects. Ask the student to count the objects aloud.

Identify Place Value

- Write a two-digit number on each of 20 cards. Have one student in a pair hold up a card and the other student say the number of tens and ones in the number. Then have students reverse roles.

Power Practice • Write each number.

5. __6__ | tens | ones |
          | | 6 |

6. __13__ | tens | ones |
          | 1 | 3 |

7. __11__ | tens | ones |
          | 1 | 1 |

8. __2__ | tens | ones |
          | | 2 |

9. __18__ | tens | ones |
          | 1 | 8 |

10. __16__ | tens | ones |
           | 1 | 6 |

11. __10__ | tens | ones |
           | 1 | 0 |

12. __14__ | tens | ones |
           | 1 | 4 |

13. __20__ | tens | ones |
           | 2 | 0 |

14. __12__ | tens | ones |
           | 1 | 2 |

15. __9__ | tens | ones |
           | | 9 |

16. __5__ | tens | ones |
           | | 5 |

© Macmillan/McGraw-Hill

77

WHAT IF THE STUDENT CAN'T

Read a Place-Value Chart
- Write these numbers in a place-value chart: 28, 82, 19, 91, 46, 64. Have the student identify the number of tens and ones in each number and write the two-digit number.

Complete the Power Practice
- Discuss each incorrect answer. Have students read the number of tens and ones aloud and then say the two-digit number.
- Have students show each number with tens and ones models.

Try It
Have students say the number aloud and then state the number of tens and ones: "Fifty-nine. Five tens, nine ones."

Power Practice
- Have students write the number for each place-value chart. Discuss their answers.
- *How would item 5 change if the 2 were in the tens place and the 5 were in the ones place?* (The number would be 25.)
- *How would item 14 change if the 2 were in the tens place and the 8 were in the ones place?* (The number would be 28.)

Learn with Partners & Parents
Use a large collection of pennies (99 or fewer) to study place value.
- Dump the pennies and have children stack tens until they have made as many piles of tens as they can.
- Have children count the piles and the leftover pennies and write the two-digit number represented by the tens and ones.
- Repeat with a different number of pennies.

USING THE LESSON

Activity 51 Lesson Goal
- Identify place value in two-digit numbers.

What the Student Needs to Know
- Read a place-value chart.
- Distinguish *left* from *right*.
- Identify two-digit numbers.

Getting Started
Draw a place-value chart on the board. Ask:
- *Which column shows the tens?* (the left column) *Which column shows the ones?* (the right column)
- *How would you write the number 56 in the chart?* (5 on the left, 6 on the right)

Name_____

Place Value

Activity **51**

What Can I Do?
I want to know the number of tens and ones in a number.

Use a place-value chart.

Write the number 34 in a place-value chart.

tens	ones
3	4

34 has 3 tens and 4 ones.

Understanding place value.

The ones digit is on the right. The tens digit is to the left of the ones digit.

The 4 tells how many **ones** are in 34.
The 3 tells how many **tens** are in 34.

Try It • Write each number in a place-value chart.

1. 78

tens	ones
7	8

2. 39

tens	ones
3	9

3. 14

tens	ones
1	4

4. 60

tens	ones
6	0

• Draw lines to match.

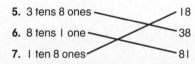

5. 3 tens 8 ones ———— 18
6. 8 tens 1 one ———— 38
7. 1 ten 8 ones ———— 81

78

© Macmillan/McGraw-Hill

WHAT IF THE STUDENT CAN'T

Read a Place-Value Chart
- Play *Place-Value Bingo* with students. Instead of calling out a number, such as "38," call out "3 tens, 8 ones," and have students mark the appropriate number. Continue to play the game in this manner until someone has "Bingo."

Distinguish *Left* from *Right*
- Write the digits 0–9 on large cards. Mix them and have the student pick two cards to make a two-digit number. Have the student place his or her hands on the cards and tell which digit is on the left (the tens digit) and which digit is on the right (the ones digit). Then have the student say the number. Continue with other numbers.

Power Practice • Write each number in a place-value chart.

8. 15

tens	ones
1	5

9. 63

tens	ones
6	3

10. 75

tens	ones
7	5

11. 96

tens	ones
9	6

12. 53

tens	ones
5	3

13. 87

tens	ones
8	7

Power Practice • Write the number ot tens and ones.

14. 82 __8__ tens __2__ ones   15. 47 __4__ tens __7__ ones

16. 24 __2__ tens __4__ ones   17. 90 __9__ tens __0__ ones

18. 55 __5__ tens __5__ ones   19. 78 __7__ tens __8__ ones

20. 29 __2__ tens __9__ ones   21. 44 __4__ tens __4__ ones

22. 11 __1__ tens __1__ ones   23. 57 __5__ tens __7__ ones

24. 72 __7__ tens __2__ ones   25. 40 __4__ tens __0__ ones

26. 93 __9__ tens __3__ ones   27. 68 __6__ tens __8__ ones

© Macmillan/McGraw-Hill

79

What Can I Do?

Read the question and the response. Then read and discuss the examples. Ask:

- *In the number 34, what does the 4 stand for?* (4 ones) *What does the 3 stand for?* (3 tens)

- *How do you know that 34 is the same as 30 + 4?* (34 is 3 tens, or 30, plus 4 ones)

Try It

To prepare students for the addition of two-digit numbers, suggest that they write the ones first and the tens next.

Power Practice

- Have students complete the practice items. Discuss their answers.

- Point out that 8 tens 2 ones is the same as 80 + 2; 4 tens 7 ones is the same as 40 + 7, and so on.

WHAT IF THE STUDENT CAN'T

Identify Two-Digit Numbers

- Give the student base ten blocks for tens and ones and a place-value mat. Have the student take several tens blocks and skip count to find how many there are.

- Then have the student put those blocks in the tens place on the place-value mat and record the number in a place-value chart.

- Have the student repeat for other groups of tens.

- Show the student how to count on by ones from the tens. Have the student model numbers such as 42, 35, 67, 92, and 48 on the place-value mat.

Complete the Power Practice

- Discuss each incorrect answer. Have students show each number with tens and ones models.

Activity 52 Lesson Goal

• Write two-digit numbers.

What the Student Needs to Know

• Identify place value.

• Count ten items.

Getting Started

Display 3 tens models and 3 ones models. Ask:

• *How can I use these models to show the number 21?* (2 tens models,1 ones model)

• *How many tens are in 21?* (2) *How many ones are in 21?* (1)

Repeat with the numbers 13 and 30.

What Can I Do?

Read the question and the response. Then read and discuss the examples. Ask:

• *What number has 4 tens and 2 ones?* (42) *2 tens and 4 ones?* (24) *1 ten and 6 ones?* (16) *6 tens and 1 one?* (61)

• *What is the greatest number you can make that has only two digits?* (99)

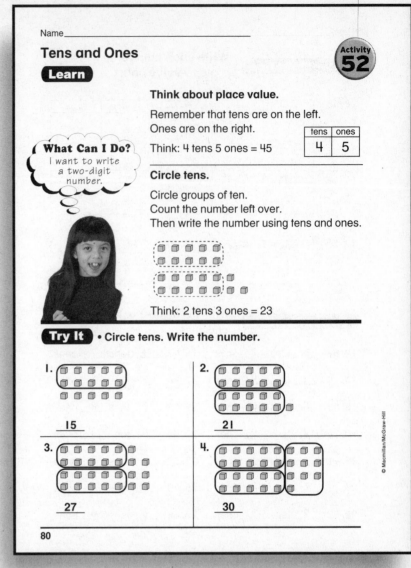

Name_____

Tens and Ones

Learn

Think about place value.

Remember that tens are on the left.
Ones are on the right.

Think: 4 tens 5 ones = 45

tens	ones
4	5

What Can I Do?
I want to write a two-digit number.

Circle tens.

Circle groups of ten.
Count the number left over.
Then write the number using tens and ones.

Think: 2 tens 3 ones = 23

Try It • Circle tens. Write the number.

1.

15

2.

21

3.

27

4.

30

80

© Macmillan/McGraw-Hill

WHAT IF THE STUDENT CAN'T

Identify Place Value

• Draw a large place-value chart on the board. Write a variety of two-digit numbers on index cards. Have the student draw cards and write the numbers in the place-value chart. Then ask the student to identify how many tens and ones are in each number.

Count Ten Items

• Give the student a pile of 15 counters and a large rubber band. Have the student count and use the rubber band to circle 10 counters. Mix the counters and have the student try again.

Place Value

Learn

What Can I Do?
I want to know the number of tens and ones in a number.

Use a place-value chart.

Write the number 78 in a chart.

tens	ones
7	8

78 has 7 tens and 8 ones.

Use expanded notation.

78 = 70 + 8
 70 = 7 tens
 8 = 8 ones

78 = 7 tens 8 ones

Try It • Write each number in a place-value chart.

1. 45

tens	ones
4	5

2. 37

tens	ones
3	7

3. 23

tens	ones
2	3

4. 50

tens	ones
5	0

Power Practice • Write the number of tens and ones.

5. 61 __6__ tens __1__ one

6. 19 __1__ ten __9__ ones

7. 88 __8__ tens __8__ ones

8. 70 __7__ tens __0__ ones

9. 94 __9__ tens __4__ ones

10. 12 __1__ ten __2__ ones

© Macmillan/McGraw-Hill

81

WHAT IF THE STUDENT CAN'T

Read a Place-Value Chart
• Give the student tens and ones models and have them show these numbers: 15, 28, 34. Then have them use their models to write the numbers in a place-value chart.

Complete the Power Practice
• Discuss each incorrect answer. Have students show each number with tens and ones models.

USING THE LESSON

Activity 53 Lesson Goal
• Identify place value in two-digit numbers.

What the Student Needs to Know
• Read a place-value chart.

Getting Started
• Give pairs of students a handful of place-value models. Have them show the following numbers and tell how many tens and ones are in each: 34, 50, 76, 92. (3 tens 4 ones, 5 tens 0 ones, 7 tens 6 ones, 9 tens 2 ones)

What Can I Do?
Read the question and the response. Then read and discuss the examples. Ask:
• *In the number 78, what does the 8 mean?* (8 ones) *What does the 7 mean?* (7 tens)
• *How can you use expanded notation to prove that 78 is the same as 7 tens 8 ones?* (78 = 70 + 8. 70 = 7 tens. 8 = 8 ones.)

Try It
To prepare students for subtraction of two-digit numbers, suggest that they write the ones first and the tens last.

Power Practice
• Have students complete the practice items. Discuss their answers.
• Point out that 6 tens 1 one is the same as 60 + 1; 1 ten 9 ones is the same as 10 + 9, and so on.

Activity 54 Lesson Goal

- Rename ones as tens and ones.

What the Student Needs to Know

- Identify place value.
- Count ten items.

Getting Started

- Display a hundred chart. Have each student select a number to read aloud and then state the number of tens and ones in the number chosen.
- *What happens to the tens as you read down a column of the chart?* (They go up by 1 ten.)
- *What happens to the ones as you read down a column of the chart?* (They remain the same.)

What Can I Do?

Read the question and the response. Then read and discuss the examples. Ask:

- *How many tens and ones are there in 15 ones?* (1 ten, 5 ones) *23 ones?* (2 tens 3 ones) *20 ones?* (2 tens, 0 ones)
- *Does it matter which items you circle when you circle tens?* (No)

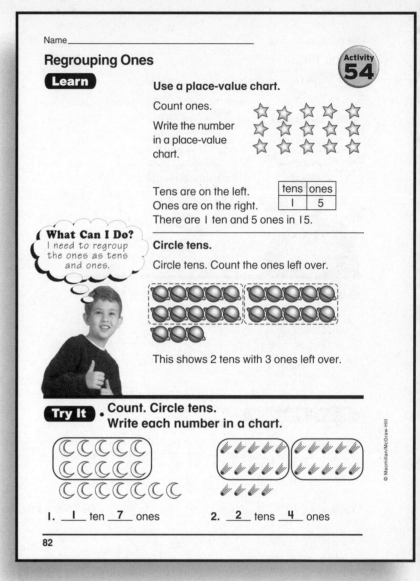

Name_____

Regrouping Ones

Learn

Activity **54**

Use a place-value chart.

Count ones.

Write the number in a place-value chart.

Tens are on the left.
Ones are on the right.
There are 1 ten and 5 ones in 15.

tens	ones
1	5

What Can I Do?
I need to regroup the ones as tens and ones.

Circle tens.

Circle tens. Count the ones left over.

This shows 2 tens with 3 ones left over.

Try It • Count. Circle tens.
Write each number in a chart.

1. __1__ ten __7__ ones

2. __2__ tens __4__ ones

82

© Macmillan/McGraw-Hill

WHAT IF THE STUDENT CAN'T

Identify Place Value

- Write two-digit numbers on the board and have the student identify the number of tens and ones in each number.
- Provide tens and ones models and have the student use them to show a variety of two-digit numbers.

Power Practice • Write each number two ways.

3. __16__ ones
   __1__ ten __6__ ones

4. __30__ ones
   __3__ tens __0__ ones

5. __22__ ones
   __2__ tens __2__ ones

6. __35__ ones
   __3__ tens __5__ ones

7. __41__ ones
   __4__ tens __1__ one

8. __19__ ones
   __1__ ten __9__ ones

9. __14__ ones
   __1__ ten __4__ ones

10. __28__ ones
    __2__ tens __8__ ones

© Macmillan/McGraw-Hill

83

Try It

Be sure students understand that they should count each group of 10, circle each group of 10, and write the number in the place-value chart.

Power Practice

- Point out that students may circle groups of ten if it helps them find the number of tens and ones.

- Have students complete the practice items. Then review each answer.

WHAT IF THE STUDENT CAN'T

Count Ten Items

- Place fifteen counters in random order. Have the student count out ten. Repeat using 12, 16, and 19 counters.

Complete the Power Practice

- Discuss each incorrect answer. Have volunteers read their answers aloud as equations; for example, "16 ones equals 1 ten, 6 ones."

Activity 55 Lesson Goal

• Rename tens and ones as ones.

What the Student Needs to Know

• Identify place value.
• Count ten items.
• Identify coins.

Getting Started

• Distribute tens and ones models to small groups of students. Have students pick one tens model and show the number of ones that are equal to 1 ten. (10 ones) Continue with 1 ten 2 ones (12 ones), 2 tens 3 ones (23 ones), 1 ten 8 ones (18 ones), and so on.

What Can I Do?

Read the question and the response. Then read and discuss the examples. Ask:

• *How many ones are there in 4 tens and 2 ones?* (42 ones) *6 tens and 8 ones?* (68 ones) *3 tens and 0 ones?* (30 ones)

• *How many pennies would you have if you traded 2 dimes and 5 pennies for pennies?* (25 pennies)

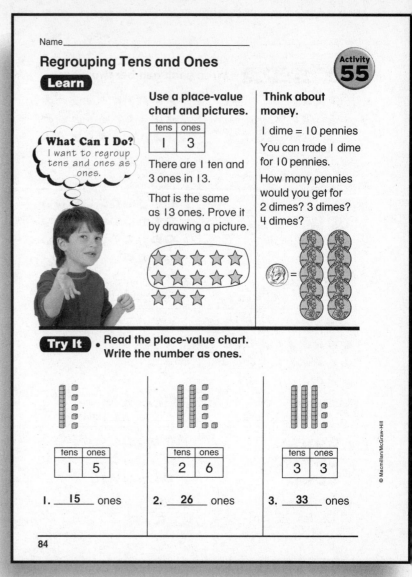

Name_____

Regrouping Tens and Ones

Learn

What Can I Do?
I want to regroup tens and ones as ones.

Use a place-value chart and pictures.

tens	ones
1	3

There are 1 ten and 3 ones in 13.

That is the same as 13 ones. Prove it by drawing a picture.

Think about money.

1 dime = 10 pennies

You can trade 1 dime for 10 pennies.

How many pennies would you get for 2 dimes? 3 dimes? 4 dimes?

Try It • Read the place-value chart. Write the number as ones.

tens	ones
1	5

1. __15__ ones

tens	ones
2	6

2. __26__ ones

tens	ones
3	3

3. __33__ ones

© Macmillan/McGraw-Hill

84

WHAT IF THE STUDENT CAN'T

Identify Place Value

• Give students a hundred chart. Have them choose five numbers at random and tell the number of tens and ones in each number.

Count Ten Items

• Give pairs of students tens and ones models. Have them take turns counting 10 ones and trading them for 1 ten.

Name_____

Power Practice • Write each number two ways.

4. __1__ ten __4__ ones

__14__ ones

5. __5__ tens __0__ ones

__50__ ones

6. __3__ tens __1__ one

__31__ ones

7. __2__ tens __2__ ones

__22__ ones

8. __4__ tens __3__ ones

__43__ ones

9. __1__ tens __8__ ones

__18__ ones

85

Try It

If students have difficulty, remind them that they may draw a picture to help them find the number of ones.

Power Practice

- Have students complete the practice items. Then review each answer. Ask:
- *Which number in Exercises 3–8 is greatest?* (50) *Which number is least?* (14)

Learn with Partners & Parents

Students can practice renaming by using dimes and pennies.

- Give students a pile of pennies and a pile of dimes. Offer suggestions such as the following:
- *Show the number of pennies you could trade for 1 dime, 2 dimes, 3 dimes.* (10, 20, 30)
- *Show the number of dimes you could trade for 10 pennies, 20 pennies, 30 pennies.* (1, 2, 3)

WHAT IF THE STUDENT CAN'T

Identify Coins

- Have students repeat the exercise entitled "Count Ten Items" using dimes and pennies instead of tens and ones models.
- Give the student a pile of play coins and have the student sort the coins into piles of pennies, nickels, dimes, and quarters. Then have the student tell what each coin is worth.

Complete the Power Practice

- Discuss each incorrect answer. Have volunteers read their answers aloud as equations; for example, "1 ten 4 ones equals 14 ones."

Activity 56 Lesson Goal

• Write numbers to 100.

What the Student Needs to Know

• Count by 10s.
• Use place-value models.
• Read a place-value chart.

Getting Started

• Give pairs of students a handful of tens blocks. Have them count the blocks by 10s to find how many they have in all.

What Can I Do?

Read the question and the response. Then read and discuss the examples. Ask:

• *How would you skip count by 10s and count on to reach the number 43?* (10, 20, 30, 40; 41, 42, 43) *the number 51?* (10, 20, 30, 40, 50; 51)

• *In the number 54, which number shows the tens?* (5) *the ones?* (4)

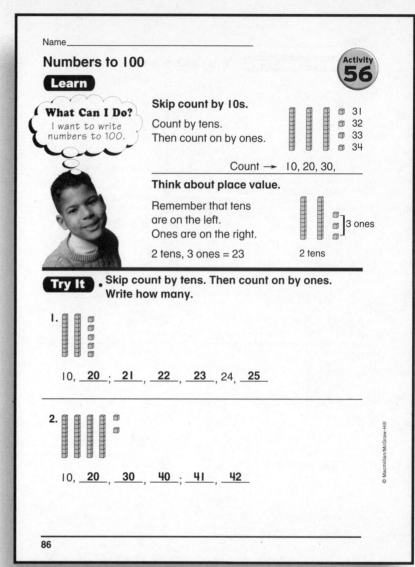

Name

Numbers to 100

Activity 56

Learn

What Can I Do?
I want to write numbers to 100.

Skip count by 10s.

Count by tens.
Then count on by ones.

31
32
33
34

Count → 10, 20, 30,

Think about place value.

Remember that tens are on the left.
Ones are on the right.

2 tens, 3 ones = 23

3 ones

2 tens

Try It • Skip count by tens. Then count on by ones. Write how many.

1.

10, __20__ , __21__ , __22__ , __23__ , 24, __25__

2.

10, __20__ , __30__ , __40__ , __41__ , __42__

86

© Macmillan/McGraw-Hill

WHAT IF THE STUDENT CAN'T

Count by 10s

• Provide a hundred chart and have the student read the numbers in the last column. Cover some of those numbers and have the student recite them again.

Use Place-Value Models

• Give the student 5 tens models and 5 ones models. Have the student show the numbers 4, 14, 24, 34, 44, and 54. Then have the student show 8, 12, 25, 31, 45, and 53.

Name_____

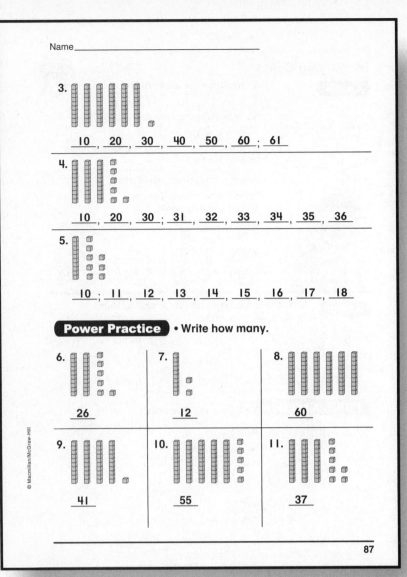

3. 10 , 20 , 30 , 40 , 50 , 60 ; 61

4. 10 , 20 , 30 ; 31 , 32 , 33 , 34 , 35 , 36

5. 10 ; 11 , 12 , 13 , 14 , 15 , 16 , 17 , 18

Power Practice • Write how many.

6. 26

7. 12

8. 60

9. 41

10. 55

11. 37

© Macmillan/McGraw-Hill

87

WHAT IF THE STUDENT CAN'T

Read a Place-Value Chart
- Have the student use some of the models from the activity above to show the numbers, and then write the numbers in a place-value chart. Ask the student to read the numbers aloud and identify the number of tens and ones.

Complete the Power Practice
- Discuss each incorrect answer. Have the student show each number with tens and ones models. Watch as he or she counts by 10s and then counts on to form the number.

Try It
- Some students might benefit from using real tens and ones models to show each number.
- Remind students to count the tens models first and then count on with the ones models to find the number.

Power Practice
- Have students complete the practice items. Discuss their answers and the strategy they used to find them.
- Point out that 2 tens 6 ones is the same as 20 + 6; 1 ten 2 ones is the same as 10 + 2, and so on.

Activity 57 Lesson Goal

- Identify coins: penny, nickel, dime, and quarter.

What the Student Needs to Know

- Recognize the meaning of *bigger* and *smaller*.
- Recognize the symbol for cents (¢).

Getting Started

Display a pile of play coins. Ask:

- *How can I find coins that are the same?* (Look for coins that are alike in size and color.)
- *How can I find how much each coin is worth?* (Look for the number on the coin.)

What Can I Do?

Read the question and the response. Then read and discuss the examples. Ask:

- *Is the biggest coin worth the most money?* (Yes) *Is the smallest coin worth the least money?* (No) *How much is it worth?* (10¢)
- *Who is pictured on the face of the penny? the nickel? the dime? the quarter?* (Abraham Lincoln, Thomas Jefferson, Franklin Roosevelt, George Washington)

Try It

Point out that students must connect the picture of the coin to its value on the left and to its name on the right.

Power Practice

- Have students complete the practice items. Discuss their answers and how they recognized each coin.

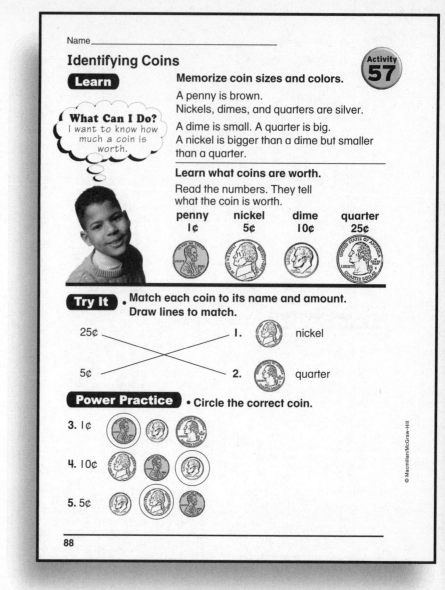

WHAT IF THE STUDENT CAN'T

Recognize the Meaning of *Bigger* and *Smaller*

- Display attribute blocks in various sizes. Have the student sort the blocks and display them in size order, from smallest to biggest.

Recognize the Symbol for Cents (¢)

- Write these amounts on the board and have students read them aloud.

  5 cents 16 cents
  25 cents 53 cents

- Have students rewrite each amount, using a cent sign in place of the word *cents*.

Complete the Power Practice

- Discuss each incorrect answer. Have students locate each coin from a pile of play coins.

Name_____

Writing Money Two Ways

Activity 58

Learn

What Can I Do?
I want to write money amounts with dollar signs or cents signs.

Read ¢ and $ symbols.

The symbol ¢ is read "cents." Read 32¢ as "thirty-two cents."

The symbol $ means "dollars." Read $1.32 as "one dollar and thirty-two cents."

Numbers **before** the decimal point are dollars. Numbers **after** the decimal point are cents. A decimal point separates dollars from cents.

dollars		dimes	pennies
$1	.	3	2

Try It • Do the numbers show the same amount? Circle *yes* or *no*.

1. $0.60 60¢ (yes) no
2. $2.50 25¢ yes (no)

3. $0.43 34¢ yes (no)
4. $0.95 95¢ (yes) no

Power Practice • Circle the two that show the same amount.

5. $1.24 (24¢) ($0.24)
6. (68¢) ($0.68) $6.80

7. (53¢) $5.53 ($0.53)
8. ($0.35) (35¢) $3.05

9. $1.66 (66¢) ($0.66)
10. $99.00 ($0.99) (99¢)

89

© Macmillan/McGraw-Hill

WHAT IF THE STUDENT CAN'T

Recognize *Dollar* ($) and Cent (¢) Signs
- Write these dollars-and-cents amounts on the board and have students read them aloud:

  $1.00 $2.40 $5.93
- Have students rewrite these phrases, using a cent sign in place of the word *cents*.

  15 cents   38 cents   99 cents

Read a Place-Value Chart
- Write these numbers in a place-value chart: 123, 410, 708, 999. Have the student identify the number of hundreds, tens, and ones in each number and write the three-digit number.

Complete the Power Practice
- Discuss each incorrect answer. Have the student read each amount aloud.

Activity 58 Lesson Goal
- Use dollar and cent signs.

What the Student Needs to Know
- Recognize *dollar* ($) and *cent* (¢) signs.
- Read a place-value chart.

Getting Started
- Display a play dollar, a play dime, and a play penny. Write these amounts on the board and have students identify the play money that matches each one: $0.01, $0.10, $1.00.

What Can I Do?
Read the question and the response. Then read and discuss the examples. Ask:
- *How many pennies are equal to 1 dime?* (10) *How many pennies are equal to 1 dollar?* (100)
- *Write these amounts on the board and have students read them aloud: $0.42, $4.20, $0.39, $3.90.* (forty-two cents, four dollars and twenty cents, thirty-nine cents, three dollars and ninety cents)

Try It
Students might read each pair of amounts aloud to see whether they are equivalent.

Power Practice
- Have students complete the exercises. Discuss their answers.
- Ask: *How can place value help you figure out which two amounts are the same?* (Knowing that the decimal point divides dollars from cents helps you read the amounts.)

Activity 59 Lesson Goal
- Identify equivalent groups of coins.

What the Student Needs to Know
- Recognize coins.
- Skip count by 5s and 10s.
- Identify equivalencies.

Getting Started
Display a play penny, nickel, dime, and quarter. Ask:

- *Which one is worth the most?* (the quarter)
- *Which one is worth the least?* (the penny)

Have students state the value of each coin. (1¢, 5¢, 10¢, 25¢)

What Can I Do?
Read the question and the response. Then read and discuss the examples. Ask:

- *What does it mean if a coin is "worth more" than another coin?* (It has a greater value; you can buy more with it.)
- *What would the value of 3 dimes be?* (30¢) *5 dimes?* (50¢)
- *What would the value of 3 nickels be?* (15¢) *5 nickels?* (25¢)
- *What are some different ways you could use coins to make 25¢?* (1 quarter, 2 dimes and 1 nickel, 1 dime and 3 nickels, 5 nickels)

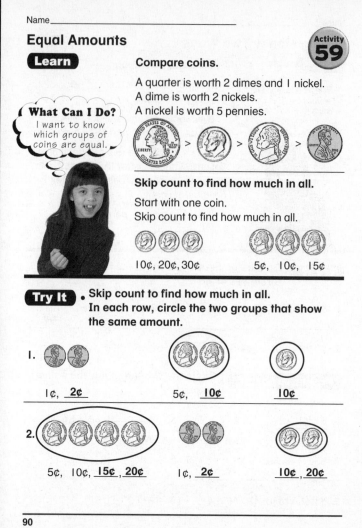

Equal Amounts

Learn

What Can I Do? I want to know which groups of coins are equal.

Compare coins.

A quarter is worth 2 dimes and 1 nickel.
A dime is worth 2 nickels.
A nickel is worth 5 pennies.

Skip count to find how much in all.

Start with one coin.
Skip count to find how much in all.

10¢, 20¢, 30¢   5¢, 10¢, 15¢

Try It • Skip count to find how much in all. In each row, circle the two groups that show the same amount.

1. 1¢, **2¢**   5¢, **10¢**   **10¢**

2. 5¢, 10¢, **15¢**, **20¢**   1¢, **2¢**   **10¢**, **20¢**

90

© Macmillan/McGraw-Hill

WHAT IF THE STUDENT CAN'T

Recognize Coins
- Display a play penny, nickel, dime, and quarter. Have the student arrange them from least value to greatest value.
- Display a play penny, nickel, dime, and quarter. Remove one and have the student tell which coin is missing and what its value is.

Skip Count by 5s and 10s
- Give the student a pile of 5 play nickels and a pile of 5 play dimes. Have them use skip counting to find the total value of each pile.
- Give the student a hundred chart and have the student use it to count by 5s and 10s to 100.

Name _____

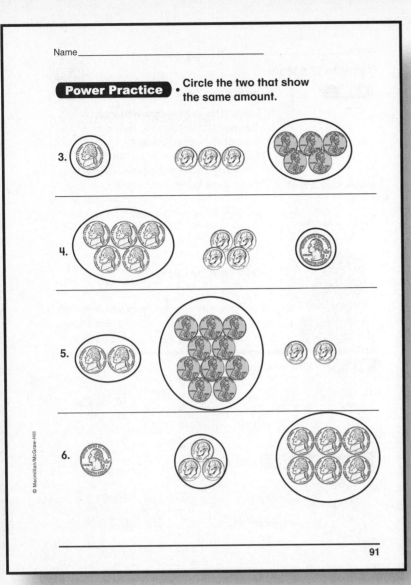

3.

4.

5.

6.

© Macmillan/McGraw-Hill

91

Try It
Remind students that in order to know what number to skip count by, they must identify the value of the coins pictured. A nickel, for example, indicates that they must skip count by 5s.

Power Practice
• Have students complete the practice items. Discuss their answers.
• Have volunteers write the value of the equivalent groups of coins using a cent sign. (5¢, 25¢, 10¢, 30¢)
• *How else might you show 10¢?* (1 nickel, 5 pennies; 1 dime.)

Learn with Partners & Parents
Use a pile of mixed coins to practice forming equivalent groups.
• First have students sort the coins into groups of the same kinds of coins.
• Then ask them to use the coins to show at least two ways to make 10¢, 20¢, 25¢, 40¢, and 50¢.

WHAT IF THE STUDENT CAN'T

Identify Equivalencies
• Write these facts and sums on the board and have students match the equivalencies.

  2 + 2   5 + 5   10 + 10
   10   20   4

• Repeat with similar examples.

Complete the Power Practice
• Discuss each incorrect answer. Have students identify the value of each group of coins pictured.

Measurement and Geometry Skill Builder   **T91**

USING THE LESSON

Activity 60 Lesson Goal
- Tell time to the hour.

What the Student Needs to Know
- Identify *hour* and *minute* hands.

Getting Started
Set a play clock for 9:00. Ask:

- *Where is the big hand?* (on the 12) *Where is the small hand?* (on the 9) *What time is it?* (9 o'clock)

Repeat with other times to the hour.

What Can I Do?
Read the question and the response. Then read and discuss the examples. Ask:

- *Which hand shows the hours?* (the small hand)
- *Which hand shows the minutes?* (the big hand)
- *What are two ways to write the same time?* (the number followed by o'clock and with 2 dots after the number)

Try It
Point out to students that when time is written with two dots in the middle (:), the hour comes before the dots, and the minutes come after the dots. In these exercises, the dots are provided.

Power Practice
- Explain that for these exercises, students should write both the time using the dots and numbers and "o'clock."
- Have students complete the practice items. Then review each answer.

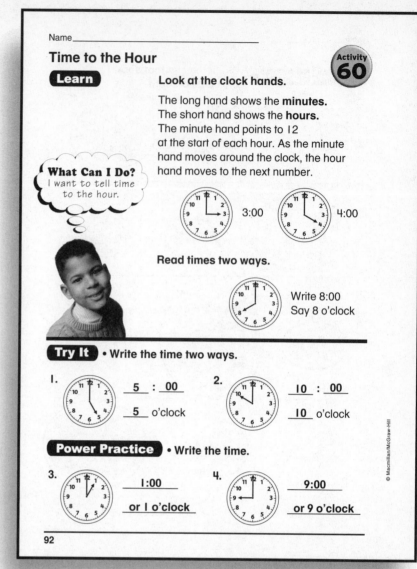

WHAT IF THE STUDENT CAN'T

Identify *Hour* and *Minute* Hands

- Give the student a play clock. Ask the student to set the hour hand to 10 and the minute hand to 12 and tell the time. Continue with other times.

Ask questions like this:

- *If the big hand is on the 12 and the small hand is on the 5, what time is it?* (5 o'clock)

Complete the Power Practice

- Have the student read the time shown on the clock aloud before writing it using a colon.
- Remind students that the hour comes before the dots, and the minutes come after the dots.

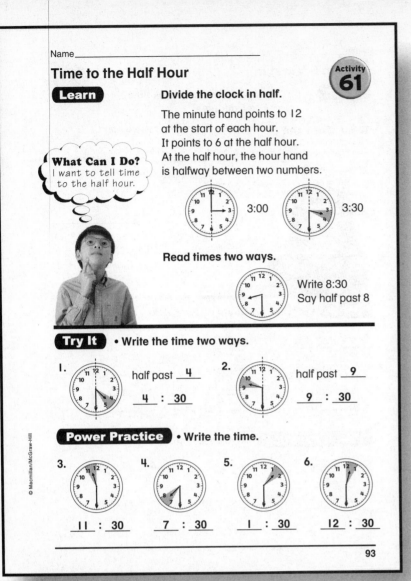

Name_____

Time to the Half Hour

Learn

What Can I Do?
I want to tell time to the half hour.

Divide the clock in half.

The minute hand points to 12 at the start of each hour.
It points to 6 at the half hour.
At the half hour, the hour hand is halfway between two numbers.

3:00   3:30

Read times two ways.

Write 8:30
Say half past 8

Try It • Write the time two ways.

1. half past __4__
   __4__ : __30__

2. half past __9__
   __9__ : __30__

Power Practice • Write the time.

3. __11__ : __30__

4. __7__ : __30__

5. __1__ : __30__

6. __12__ : __30__

© Macmillan/McGraw-Hill

93

WHAT IF THE STUDENT CAN'T

Identify *Hour* and *Minute* Hands

- Give the student a play clock. Have the student set the hour hand to 8 and the minute hand to 12 and tell the time. Continue with other times to the hour and half hour.

Recognize One-Half

- Give the student a paper plate and a crayon or marker. Ask the student to draw a line on the plate to divide it in half.

Read Times

- Use digital form to write times to the hour and half hour on index cards. Have the student pick a card and read the time aloud, and show the time on the play clock. Repeat.

Complete the Power Practice

- Have the student read the time shown aloud before writing it using a colon.
- Remind students that when a clock shows half past, the hour hand is between numbers. The number that names the hour is the lesser number.

Activity 61 Lesson Goal

- Tell time to the half hour.

What the Student Needs to Know

- Identify *hour* and *minute* hands.
- Recognize one-half.
- Read times.

Getting Started

Set a play clock at 2:00. Ask:

- *What time is it?* (2 o'clock)

Move the minute hand clockwise to 6 and the hour hand between 2 and 3. Ask:

- *Where is the minute hand?* (on 6) *Where is the hour hand?* (between 2 and 3) *What time is it now?* (2:30)

What Can I Do?

Read the question and the response. Then read and discuss the examples. Ask:

- *How many minutes go by between 3 o'clock and 3:30?* (30)
- *Why do we call 8:30 "half past eight"?* (It is halfway between 8 and 9 or half past 8 o'clock.)

Try It

Remind students that the hour comes before the dots and the minutes come after the dots. In these exercises, the dots are provided.

Power Practice

- Have students complete the practice items.

Learn with Partners & Parents

Have students play *Clock Concentration.*

- Use digital form to write times to the hour and half hour on index cards. On another set of cards write those same times using "o'clock" or "half past."
- Players mix up all the cards and place them facedown.
- Players take turns finding pairs of matching times.

Measurement and Geometry Skill Builder **T93**

Activity 62 Lesson Goal

- Tell time to 5-minute intervals.

What the Student Needs to Know

- Tell time on the hour.
- Count by 5s from 0–60.

Getting Started

Give each student a play clock. Write 3:00 on the board. Ask:

- *What time is this?* (3 o'clock) *Which hand on the clock shows the hour?* (the small hand) *Which hand on the clock shows the number of minutes?* (the big hand)

- *How can you make your clocks show 3:00?* (Put the minute hand on the 12 and the hour hand on the 3.) *Show 3:00 on your clocks.*

- Then have children count by fives from 0–60.

What Can I Do?

Read the question and the response. Then read and discuss the examples. Ask:

- *What do these numbers on the outside of these clocks show?* (the number of minutes in an hour) *The minute hand is pointing to the 1. How many minutes does that mean?* (5)

- Point out that we write a 0 and a 5 to show 5 minutes after an hour.

- *On the second clock, where is the minute hand?* (on the 2) *Count to find how many minutes that is.* (0–5–10)

Try It

Have students complete the matching.

Power Practice

Have students complete the practice items. Then review each answer.

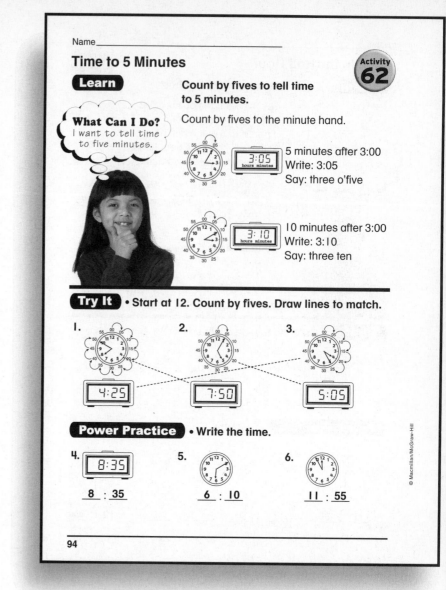

Learn

What Can I Do? I want to tell time to five minutes.

Count by fives to tell time to 5 minutes.

Count by fives to the minute hand.

3:05 — 5 minutes after 3:00
Write: 3:05
Say: three o'five

3:10 — 10 minutes after 3:00
Write: 3:10
Say: three ten

Try It • Start at 12. Count by fives. Draw lines to match.

1.   2.   3.

4:25   7:50   5:05

Power Practice • Write the time.

4. 8:35   __8__ : __35__

5. __6__ : __10__

6. __11__ : __55__

© Macmillan/McGraw-Hill

94

Count by 5s from 0–60

- Provide the student with a pile of counters. Have the student make groups of 5.

- Ask the student to shade the numbers on a 0–100 chart.

- Then have the student read the numbers he or she shaded in order.

- Have the student describe any patterns he or she sees or hears.

Complete the Power Practice

- Discuss each incorrect answer. Have the student use a play clock to set each time to the hour and then count by fives as he or she moves the minute hand around to the time shown in the exercise.

Name_____

Calendar Clues

Mr. Lee's class has student helpers. Read the clues.
Find out who is the helper.

MARCH

Sunday	Monday	Tuesday	Wednesday	Thursday	Friday	Saturday
			1	2 Tina	3	4
5	6 Lucia	7	8 Karif	9	10	11
12	13	14	15	16	17 Miles	18
19	20 Brittany	21	22 Franco	23 Miranda	24	25
26	27	28 Betsy	29	30	31 Claire	

1. Who is the helper on the second Wednesday of the
   month? _____Karif_____

2. Who is the helper the 28ᵗʰ?
   _____Betsy_____

3. Who is the helper in the third Friday of the month?
   _____Miles_____

4. Who is the helper on the 8ᵗʰ of the month?
   _____Karif_____

5. Who is the helper on the second day of the month?
   _____Tina_____

6. How many Fridays are there? How many Sundays?
   _____5_____   _____4_____

95

Activity 63 Lesson Goal

Identify dates on a calendar
by giving their row and column
locations.

What the Student Needs to Know

- Recognize days of the week and
  months of the year.
- Ordinal numbers 1–31
  (first through thirty-first).

Getting Started

Display the calendar page for the
current month. Ask:

- *What is the first day of the
  month? What is the last day of
  the month?* (Answers will vary.)
- *How many rows are on the
  calendar page?* (Answers will
  vary.) *How many columns are on
  the calendar page?* (7)

What Can I Do?

- Read the directions aloud.

Suggest that students follow these
steps:

- Find the column.
- Move your finger down the
  column to find the row.
- Write the person's name.
- Ask interested students to name
  the column and row for Lucia's
  birthday (second column,
  second row); Franco's birthday
  (fourth column, fourth row);
  Miranda's birthday (fifth
  column, fourth row); Claire's
  birthday (sixth column, fifth
  row); and Miki's birthday (seventh column, third row).

Activity 64 Lesson Goal
- Measure length using nonstandard units.

What the Student Needs to Know
- Use a measuring tool.
- Count to ten.

Getting Started
Draw a horizontal line on the board. Ask:

- *How could I measure this line using only chalkboard erasers?* (Line up erasers from the left to the right ends of the line; then count the erasers.)

Demonstrate this technique.

What Can I Do?
Read the question and the response. Then read and discuss the examples. Ask:

- *What does it mean to "line things up" at the left edge?* (Make sure the left edges of the measurement tool and the object being measured are even.)

- *Why is it important to line things up when you measure?* (It helps you get an accurate measurement.)

Try It
Point out that a pencil that is 3 clips long will not be 3 cubes long. A pencil that is 6 cubes long will not be 6 clips long. Clips and cubes are different sizes; using them results in different measurements.

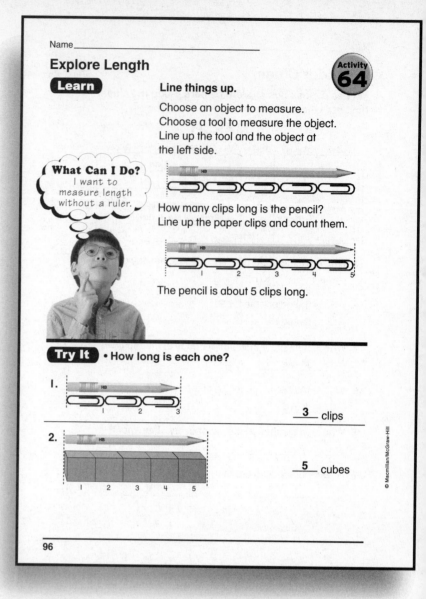

Name_____

Explore Length

Learn

Line things up.

Choose an object to measure.
Choose a tool to measure the object.
Line up the tool and the object at the left side.

What Can I Do?
I want to measure length without a ruler.

How many clips long is the pencil?
Line up the paper clips and count them.

The pencil is about 5 clips long.

Try It • How long is each one?

1. _____ **3** clips

2. _____ **5** cubes

96

© Macmillan/McGraw-Hill

Use a Measuring Tool
- Present the student with a handful of paper clips and a book. Have the student use the clips to measure the length of the book. Make alignment corrections, if necessary. Repeat with a book of a different size.

Count to Ten
- Give the student 20 counters. Ask the student to count and separate out 10 counters.

- Line up 8 paper clips and have the student count them. Repeat with 6, 9, and 5 paper clips.

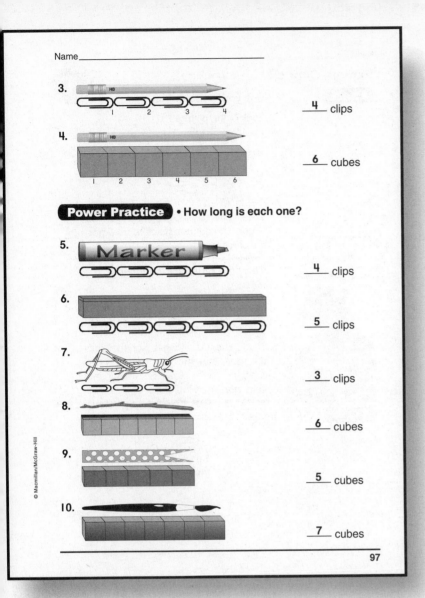

Name _____

3.

_4_ clips

4.

_6_ cubes

Power Practice • How long is each one?

5. Marker

_4_ clips

6.

_5_ clips

7.

_3_ clips

8.

_6_ cubes

9.

_5_ cubes

10.

_7_ cubes

© Macmillan/McGraw-Hill

97

Power Practice
- Point out that the measuring tools are aligned on the left side of the object being measured.
- Have students complete the practice items. Then review each answer.

Learn with Partners & Parents

Give students a handful of index cards and have them follow these Scavenger Hunt directions.

- *Find a chair. Measure the length of the seat using index cards. Write the measurement to the nearest wholecard.*

- *Find a table. Measure its length using index cards. Write the measurement to the nearest whole card.*

- *Find a window. Measure its width using index cards. Write the measurement to the nearest whole card.*

- *Tell which object was longest and which was shortest.*

WHAT IF THE STUDENT CAN'T

Complete the Power Practice

- Have the student demonstrate how he or she solved any incorrect problems. See whether the student counted incorrectly or did not understand how to use nonstandard units of measure.

Activity 65 Lesson Goal

- Identify the object that holds more or less.

What the Student Needs to Know

- Recognize the meaning of *more* and *less*.
- Recognize the meaning of *longer*, *wider*, and *deeper*.

Getting Started

Hold up a teacup and a mug or two glasses of different sizes. Ask:

- *If you were very thirsty, which one would you rather have? Why?* (the bigger one, because it holds more)
- *How can you tell that the bigger one holds more?* (It is taller or deeper; it is wider than the other one.)

Name_____

Explore Capacity

Learn

Activity **65**

Use your imagination.

Look at the pictures.
Imagine using each one.

Think: When I take a bath, I use a lot of water. When I fill a glass, I use a little water. The bathtub holds *more* water than the glass.

What Can I Do?
I want to know which one holds more.

Compare other measurements.

Think: The tub is longer than the glass. It is wider than the glass, too. It is also deeper than the glass. So, the tub must hold *more* than the glass.

Try It • Circle the one that holds *more.*

1.

2.

© Macmillan/McGraw-Hill

98

WHAT IF THE STUDENT CAN'T

Recognize the Meaning of *More* and *Less*

Ask the student questions that involve the concepts *more* and *less.*

- *Do you drink more milk than juice each day?*
- *Do you use less water to bathe than you do to brush your teeth?*

Recognize the Meaning of *Longer, Wider,* and *Deeper*

Ask the student questions like these:

- *Which is longer, your finger or your arm?*
- *Which is wider, your smile or your thumb?*
- *Which is deeper, a puddle or a pond?*

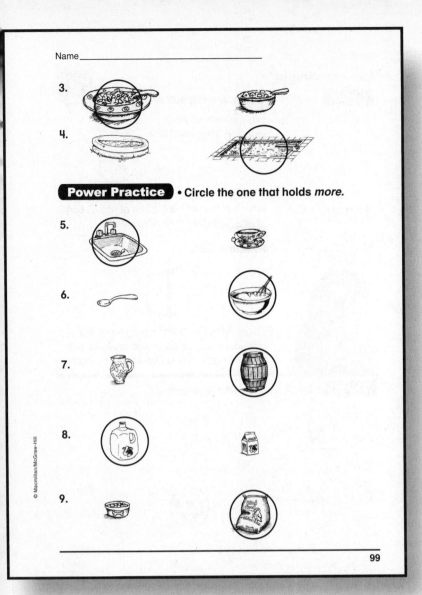

Name_____

3.

4.

Power Practice • Circle the one that holds *more*.

5.

6.

7.

8.

9.

© Macmillan/McGraw-Hill

99

WHAT IF THE STUDENT CAN'T

Complete the Power Practice
- Make sure the student is able to identify the objects in each picture.
- Discuss how each object may be used. Then ask the student to tell which one holds more.

What Can I Do?
Read the question and the response. Then read and discuss the examples. Say:

- *Use your imagination. Which would hold more, a fish tank or a lake?* (a lake)
- *Which would be longer, a fish tank or a lake?* (a lake)
- *Which would be wider, a fish tank or a lake?* (a lake)
- *Which would be deeper, a fish tank or a lake?* (a lake)

Try It
Ask students to identify the objects in each picture before they begin the exercise.

Power Practice
- Have students complete the practice items. Then review each answer.

Activity 66 Lesson Goal
- Identify the object that is heavier or lighter.

What the Student Needs to Know
- Recognize the meaning of *heavy* and *light*.
- Use a balance scale.

Getting Started
Place two equal weights on either side of a scale. Say:
- *When the scale is balanced, the weights are the same.*

Replace one weight with a heavier weight. Say:
- *When one weight is heavier, the scale tips down.*
- *What will happen if I take one weight off? (The scale will tip toward the other weight.)*

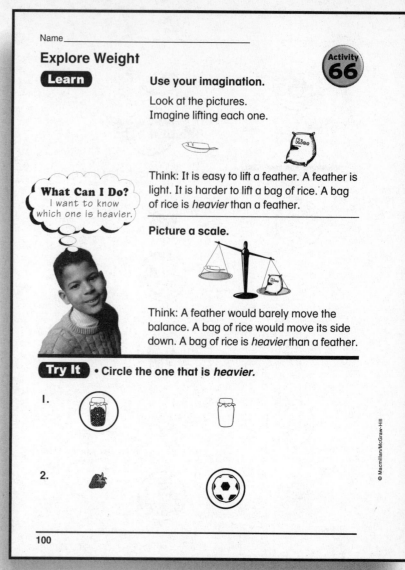

Name_____

Explore Weight

Learn

Use your imagination.

Look at the pictures.
Imagine lifting each one.

What Can I Do?
I want to know which one is heavier.

Think: It is easy to lift a feather. A feather is light. It is harder to lift a bag of rice. A bag of rice is *heavier* than a feather.

Picture a scale.

Think: A feather would barely move the balance. A bag of rice would move its side down. A bag of rice is *heavier* than a feather.

Try It • Circle the one that is *heavier.*

1.

2.

© Macmillan/McGraw-Hill

100

Recognize the Meanings of *Heavy* and *Light*
Ask the student questions like these:
- *Would you call an elephant heavy or light?* (heavy)
- *Would you call a bird heavy or light?* (light)
- *Which is heavier, a baby or an adult?* (an adult)
- *Which is lighter, a bike or a car?* (a bike)

Use a Balance Scale
- Provide a balance scale and several small objects. Have the student practice guessing which objects will move the scale most and placing them on the scale to test each guess.

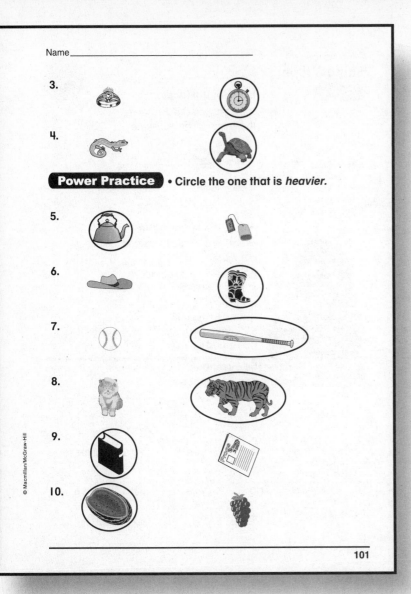

Name_____

3.

4.

Power Practice • Circle the one that is *heavier.*

5.

6.

7.

8.

9.

10.

101

Read the question and the response. Then read and discuss the examples. Say:

• *Use your imagination. Which would be heavier, an empty bucket or a bucket full of sand?* (a bucket full of sand)

• *Which would be heavier, a dry swimsuit or a wet swimsuit?* (a wet swimsuit)

Try It

Make sure students can identify the objects in each picture before they begin the exercise.

Power Practice

• Have students complete the practice items. Then review each answer.

WHAT IF THE STUDENT CAN'T

Complete the Power Practice

• Make sure the student is able to identify the objects for each pair.

• Have the student close his or her eyes and imagine lifting each item in a pair; for example, a teapot and a teabag. Which is heavier? How does the student know?

Activity 67 Lesson Goal

- Identify three-dimensional figures with the same shape.

What the Student Needs to Know

- Recognize two-dimensional shapes.
- Recognize attributes of shapes.

Getting Started

Display an attribute block triangle and a triangular prism. Ask:

- *How are these shapes different?* (One is flat, and the other is not.)
- *How are these shapes similar?* (They have three sides; the prism has faces that have three corners like those on the triangle.)

What Can I Do?

Read the question and the response. Then read and discuss the examples. Ask:

- *What flat faces appear on a cylinder?* (2 circles)
- *Which other shape has a flat face that is a circle?* (a cone)
- *Which shapes can roll?* (a cylinder, a cone, a sphere)

Name_____

Same Shape

Learn

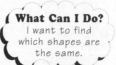

What Can I Do?
I want to find which shapes are the same.

Look for flat faces.

If the shapes are the same, the faces will be the same.

2 flat circles   6 flat squares   2 flat circles

Ask yourself questions.

Describe a shape by asking questions like these:

- Does it have a flat face?
- Does it have sharp edges?
- Can it roll?
- Can it stand up?
- If I turned it around, how would it look?
- If I stood it on end, how would it look?

Try It · **Answer the questions.**
Circle the same shapes.

1. Does it have flat faces? How many?	no	yes;6	yes;1	yes;6
2. Does it have corners?	no	yes	no	yes
3. Can it roll?	yes	no	yes	no

© Macmillan/McGraw-Hill

102

WHAT IF THE STUDENT CAN'T

Recognize Two-Dimensional Shapes

- Distribute attribute blocks and have the student sort them into piles of triangles, rectangles, squares, and circles. Ask the student to tell how each kind of block differs from the others.

Recognize Attributes of Shapes

Distribute attribute blocks. Have the student sort them into the following groups:

- all the blocks that have straight edges
- all the blocks that are round
- all the blocks that have more than three sides

Name_____

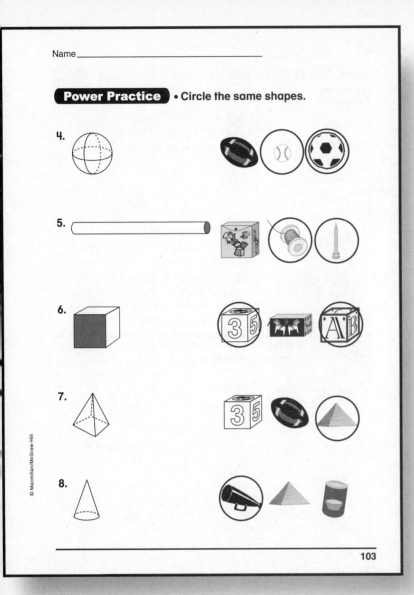

4.

5.

6.

7.

8.

103

© Macmillan/McGraw-Hill

You may wish to use a wooden model to demonstrate how to count the faces of a rectangular prism. Remind students that once they have answered all the questions, they should circle the shapes that are the same.

Power Practice

• Tell students to refer to the list of questions on page 94 as they complete this exercise.

• Have students complete the practice items. Then review each answer.

Learn with Partners & Parents

Have students go on a *Shape Hunt* in the classroom or at home to find objects that have these shapes:

• sphere
• rectangular prism
• cone
• cylinder

Have students record the items they find and share their lists with the class.

WHAT IF THE STUDENT CAN'T

Complete the Power Practice

• Make sure the student can identify the pictured objects.

• Point out that each shape matches two of the pictured objects.

• Have the student explain what attributes the objects he or she circled have in common with the given shape.

Activity 68 Lesson Goal

- Identify the shape of a given face of a three-dimensional figure.

What the Student Needs to Know

- Trace around a solid shape.
- Recognize two-dimensional shapes.
- Recognize attributes of shapes.

Getting Started

- Display a small box. Then take it apart and display it as a flat surface. Have students point to the faces and identify them as rectangles or squares. Then refold the box to recreate the original figure.

What Can I Do?

Read the question and the response. Then read and discuss the examples. Display a triangular pyramid (all four faces triangles) and a cube and ask:

- *How are the faces of these shapes different?* (The faces of one are triangles; the faces of the other are squares.)

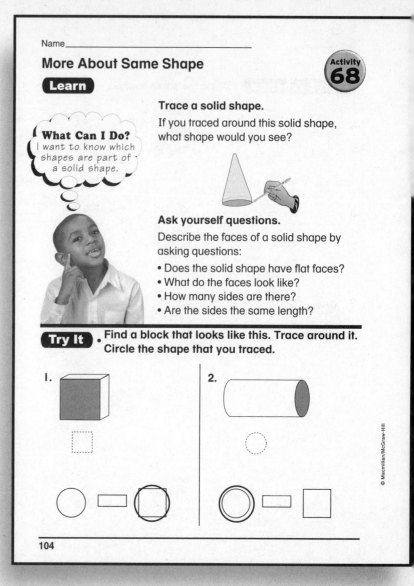

Name_____

More About Same Shape

Activity **68**

Learn

What Can I Do?
I want to know which shapes are part of a solid shape.

Trace a solid shape.

If you traced around this solid shape, what shape would you see?

Ask yourself questions.

Describe the faces of a solid shape by asking questions:

- Does the solid shape have flat faces?
- What do the faces look like?
- How many sides are there?
- Are the sides the same length?

Try It • Find a block that looks like this. Trace around it. Circle the shape that you traced.

1.

2.

© Macmillan/McGraw-Hill

104

WHAT IF THE STUDENT CAN'T

Trace Around a Solid Shape

- Begin by having the student trace around attribute blocks. Once he or she is comfortable, provide solid figures. Demonstrate how to hold the figure still while you trace around the bottom of it.

Recognize Two-Dimensional Shapes

- Distribute a variety of attribute blocks and ask the student to find 2 rectangles, 3 squares, 1 circle, and 4 triangles.

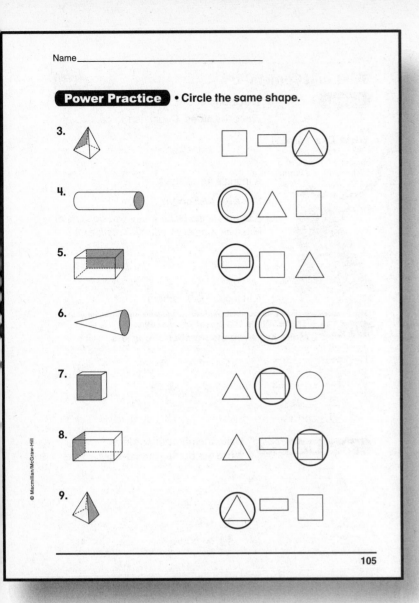

Name_____

Power Practice • Circle the same shape.

3.

4.

5.

6.

7.

8.

9.

© Macmillan/McGraw-Hill

105

Try It

Provide cubes and cylinders for students to trace. Remind them to hold the figure still and trace around the bottom—the part that rests on the paper.

Power Practice

• Explain that instead of tracing the face on each solid figure, the artist has shaded the face. Students are to find the shape that matches the shaded face.

• Have students complete the practice items. Then review each answer.

WHAT IF THE STUDENT CAN'T

Recognize Attributes of Shapes

Distribute a variety of attribute blocks. Have the student sort them into the following groups:

• all the blocks that have three sides

• all the blocks that are round

• all the blocks that have sides the same length

Complete the Power Practice

• Have the student use solid figures to identify each solid figure that is pictured.

• Have the student name the shape of each of the three choices given for each exercise.

• Ask the student to match the shape to the face of the solid figure.

Measurement and Geometry Skill Builder **T105**

Activity 69 Lesson Goal

• Identify the number of sides and corners in a two-dimensional shape.

What the Student Needs to Know

• Trace around a shape.
• Recognize and count *corners* and *sides* of a shape.

Getting Started

Draw a rectangle on the board. Ask:

• *Does this shape have sides? How can I find out the number of sides?* (count them)

• Demonstrate numbering the sides in clockwise order. Count as you write the numbers.

• Draw a square on the board and have a volunteer number the sides. Repeat with a triangle.

What Can I Do?

Read the question and the response. Then read and discuss the examples. Ask:

• *What is true about a triangle's sides and corners?* (There are the same number of sides as corners.)

• *Why might it be useful to make Xs on corners before counting?* (to make sure you count all the corners)

Try It

Remind students to trace around the object, number the sides, and make Xs on the corners before recording the answers.

Power Practice

• Tell students they may use either strategy to complete Exercises 3–5.

• You may wish to identify Exercise 3 as a parallelogram and Exercise 5 as a pentagon.

• Have students complete the practice items. Then review each answer.

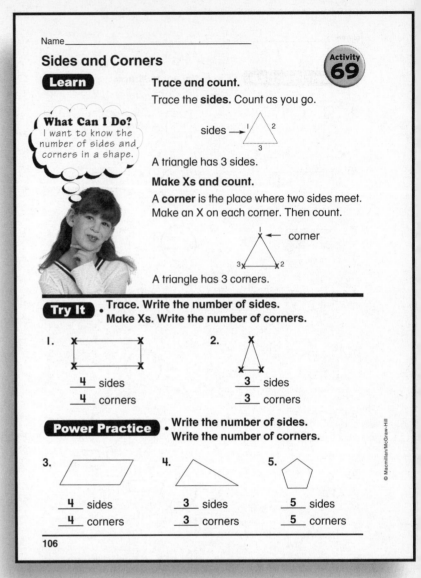

WHAT IF THE STUDENT CAN'T

Trace Around a Shape

• Have students practice tracing the letters of the alphabet on handwriting worksheets.

• Provide a variety of dotted shapes. Have a student demonstrate how to trace the shape without lifting the pencil.

Recognize and Count *Corners* and *Sides* of a Shape

• Draw a shape on the board and number its corners clockwise. Have the student count the corners and the sides. Draw another shape on the board. This time, have the student number the corners.

• Remind him or her to move around the shape in the same direction until all corners have been numbered. Then ask the student to count the sides.

Complete the Power Practice

• Have students count in front of you so you can make sure they are not omitting sides or corners as they count.

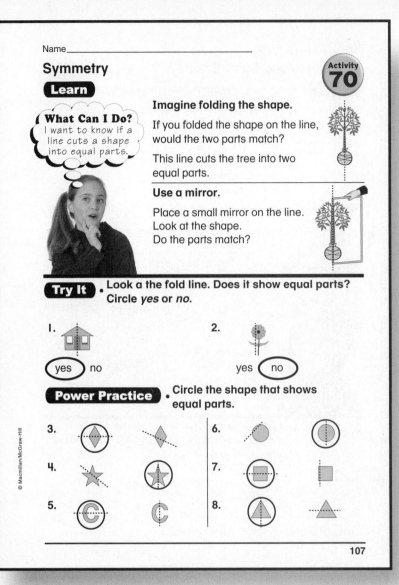

Name _____

Symmetry

Learn

What Can I Do?
I want to know if a line cuts a shape into equal parts.

Imagine folding the shape.

If you folded the shape on the line, would the two parts match?

This line cuts the tree into two equal parts.

Use a mirror.

Place a small mirror on the line. Look at the shape. Do the parts match?

Try It • Look at the fold line. Does it show equal parts? Circle *yes* or *no*.

1. (yes) no

2. yes (no)

Power Practice • Circle the shape that shows equal parts.

3.
4.
5.
6.
7.
8.

© Macmillan/McGraw-Hill

107

Activity 70 Lesson Goal
• Identify lines of symmetry.

What the Student Needs to Know
• Identify matching parts.
• Recognize the meaning of *equal parts*.

Getting Started
Fold a piece of paper and cut out a heart shape. Open the paper again. Say:
• *This heart is made up of two equal parts.*

Fold the paper again and cut out a bow tie shape. Open the paper. Say:
• *This bow is made up of two equal parts.*

What Can I Do?
Read the question and the response. Then read and discuss the examples.
• Have a volunteer come to the board to draw a shape that could not be folded into two matching parts.
• Have another volunteer draw a shape that could be folded into two matching parts.
• Discuss the differences between the two shapes.

Try It
Remind students that equal parts need not face the same way. However, when the shape is folded, the parts must match.

Power Practice
• Have students complete the practice items. Then review each answer.

WHAT IF THE STUDENT CAN'T

Identify Matching Parts
• Fold a piece of construction paper and cut out a variety of shapes. Then cut the shapes apart on the fold. Mix up the pieces and have the student find the matching parts to make each whole shape.

Identify the Meaning of *Equal Parts*
• Cut out three equal-sized circles. Cut one in halves, one in fourths, and one in sixths. Have the student identify the number of equal parts in each circle.

• Cut out three equal-sized squares. Cut one in half vertically, one in half diagonally, and one in two unequal parts. Have the student identify the squares with equal parts.

Complete the Power Practice
• Discuss each incorrect answer. Have students trace the shape on tracing paper, cut it out, and fold it to test the symmetry.

Measurement and Geometry Skill Builder **T107**

Activity 71 Lesson Goal

- Identify congruent figures.

What the Student Needs to Know

- Recognize *turns.*
- Trace around a shape.

Getting Started

Cut out a large cardboard triangle. On the board, trace around the triangle with colored chalk. Then turn it and trace it again. Ask:

- *How do you know that these are the same shape? the same size?* (You traced the same triangle.)
- *How else could you tell that these are the same size and shape?* (Measure them; trace one shape and place it over the other.)

What Can I Do?

Read the question and the response. Then read and discuss the examples. Ask:

- *Can two figures be the same shape but not the same size?* (yes) *the same size but not the same shape?* (yes)
- *When might you need to know whether two figures are the same size and shape?* (when you are building or making something)

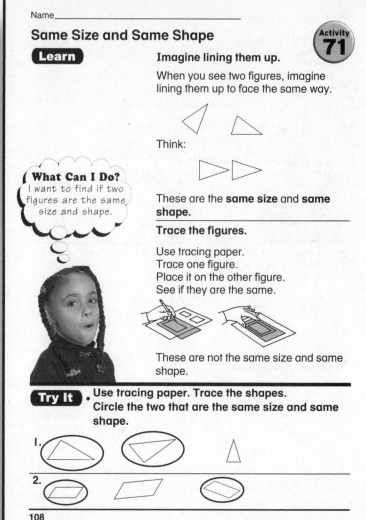

Name_____

Same Size and Same Shape

Activity
71

Learn

Imagine lining them up.

When you see two figures, imagine lining them up to face the same way.

Think:

These are the **same size** and **same shape.**

Trace the figures.

Use tracing paper.
Trace one figure.
Place it on the other figure.
See if they are the same.

These are not the same size and same shape.

What Can I Do?
I want to find if two figures are the same size and shape.

Try It • **Use tracing paper. Trace the shapes. Circle the two that are the same size and same shape.**

1.

2.

108

© Macmillan/McGraw-Hill

WHAT IF THE STUDENT CAN'T

Recognize *Turns*

- Fold a piece of construction paper in quarters and draw a shape. Have the student cut out the shape and then paste all four shapes in different configurations on another sheet of paper.

- Place an attribute block on an index card and trace around it. Turn the block 90° and trace it again on another card. Repeat with other blocks. Mix up the cards and have the student identify the matching shapes.

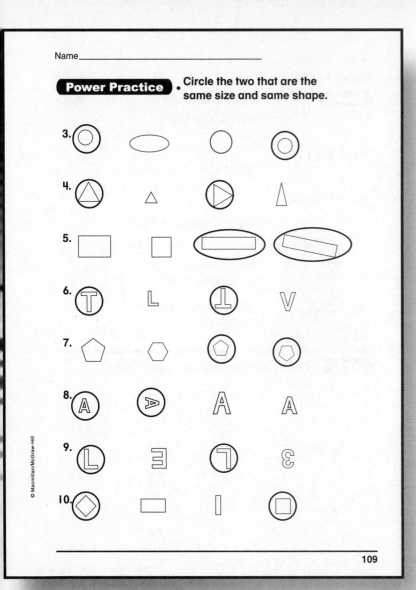

Name_____

Power Practice • Circle the two that are the same size and same shape.

3.

4.

5.

6.

7.

8.

9.

10.

© Macmillan/McGraw-Hill

109

Try It

- Provide tracing paper. If necessary, demonstrate how to use it.

- Remind students to circle the two that are the same size and shape after they trace and compare.

Power Practice

- Students may use tracing paper if they wish.

- Have students complete the practice items. Then discuss their answers.

WHAT IF THE STUDENT CAN'T

Trace Around a Shape

- Provide attribute blocks. Have the student practice tracing each shape. Then have the student use scissors to cut around the shape he or she traced.

Complete the Power Practice

- Review all the choices, having the student identify each figure in relation to the first figure. For example, for Exercise 3, the student might say, "Circle, not a circle, bigger circle, same size and shape circle." For Exercise 4, he or she might say, "Triangle, smaller triangle, same size and shape triangle, different shaped triangle."

Activity 72 Lesson Goal
- Identify equal parts of a figure.

What the Student Needs to Know
- Count parts of a shape.
- Recognize the meaning of *equal parts*.

Getting Started
Fold a piece of paper in half and then in half again. Open it. Ask:
- *How many parts did I make?* (4)

Fold the paper again and hold it up. Ask:
- *How can you tell that the parts are equal?* (They match when they are placed on top of each other.)

What Can I Do?
Read the question and the response. Then read and discuss the examples. Ask:
- *What is the difference between equal parts and parts that are not equal?* (Equal parts are the same size and shape. Parts that are not equal are not the same size and shape.)
- Draw squares on the chalkboard. Have volunteers draw lines to divide the squares into equal parts. Discuss different ways of making equal parts.

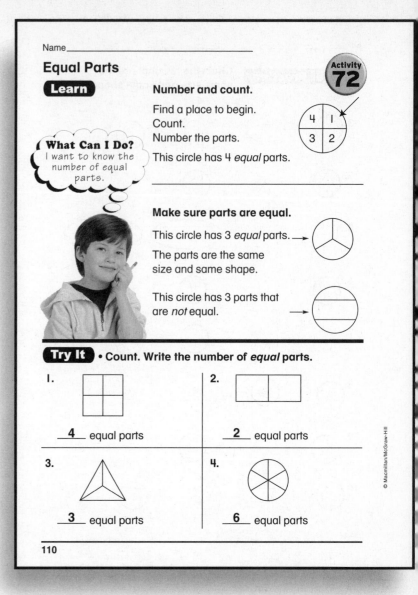

Name _____

Equal Parts

> **Learn**

> **What Can I Do?**
> I want to know the number of equal parts.

Number and count.
Find a place to begin.
Count.
Number the parts.
This circle has 4 *equal* parts.

Make sure parts are equal.
This circle has 3 *equal* parts.
The parts are the same size and same shape.

This circle has 3 parts that are *not* equal.

> **Try It** • Count. Write the number of *equal* parts.

1.   __4__ equal parts

2.   __2__ equal parts

3.   __3__ equal parts

4.   __6__ equal parts

110

© Macmillan/McGraw-Hill

WHAT IF THE STUDENT CAN'T

Count Parts of a Shape
- Draw several shapes on the board and divide them into two, four, and six equal parts. Number the parts and have the student count them. Then ask the student to number the parts of other shapes that you draw on the board. Remind the student to move around or across the shape in the same direction until all parts have been numbered.

Recognize the Meaning of *Equal Parts*
- Cut out a cardboard circle with a diameter equal to the length of a coffee stirrer or a similar object. Provide coffee stirrers and have the student use them to show how to divide the circle into 2 equal parts, 4 equal parts, and 6 equal parts.
- Cut out three equal-sized rectangles. Cut one in half vertically, one in half horizontally, and one in two unequal parts. Have the student identify the rectangles with equal parts.

Power Practice • Write the number of equal parts.

5.

__2__ equal parts

6.

__3__ equal parts

7.

__6__ equal parts

8.

__2__ equal parts

9.

__4__ equal parts

10.

__3__ equal parts

11.

__2__ equal parts

12.

__6__ equal parts

13.

__4__ equal parts

14.

__3__ equal parts

111

Try It

Remind students that they are to count the parts, numbering them as they go, before writing the total number of equal parts.

Power Practice

• Have students complete the practice items. Then review each answer.

• Discuss how students know that the parts shown are equal. (They are the same size and shape.)

WHAT IF THE STUDENT CAN'T

Complete the Power Practice

• Discuss each incorrect answer. Have the student number the parts of the shape before counting them aloud.

Activity 73 Lesson Goal
- Identify the likelihood of an event.

What the Student Needs to Know
- Recognize the meaning of *possible* and *impossible*.
- Recognize coins.

Getting Started
Place a red crayon and a blue crayon in a paper bag. Ask:

- *If you put your hand in the bag, could you pick out a red crayon?* (yes) *We say that it is "possible" to pick a red crayon.*

- *If you put your hand in, could you pick out a yellow crayon?* (no) *Why not?* (There are no yellow crayons in the bag.) *We say that it is "impossible" to pick a yellow crayon.*

What Can I Do?
Read the question and the response. Then read and discuss the examples. Ask:

- *Suppose there were 5 nickels instead of 5 pennies. Which pick would be certain?* (picking a nickel)

- *Which picks would be impossible?* (Possible answer: picking a penny, dime, or quarter)

- *Would any picks be probable?* (no)

Name_____

Certain, Possible, Impossible

Learn

Possible or impossible?

Look at these coins.
Is it possible to pick a quarter?
Is it possible to pick a nickel?

Think: There are no quarters.
So, picking a quarter is **impossible**. It could **not** happen.

There are also no nickels.
So, picking a nickel is **impossible** too.

Decide between certain and possible.

What Can I Do?
I want to know if something could happen or could not happen.

If you pick one coin, what could it be?

Think: All the coins are pennies.
So, picking a penny is **certain**. It **will** happen.

If you pick one coin, what could it be?

Think: Some coins are pennies. So picking a penny could happen.

Some coins are dimes. So picking a dime could happen.
Picking a penny and picking a dime are both **possible**. They could both happen.

112

© Macmillan/McGraw-Hill

WHAT IF THE STUDENT CAN'T

Recognize the Meaning of *Possible* and *Impossible*
Have the student identify the following occurrences as being possible or impossible.

- A squirrel eats a nut.
- A squirrel flies a plane.
- A cloud floats overhead.
- A cloud speaks aloud.

Ask the student to give other examples of possible and impossible events.

Recognize Coins
- Display a play penny, nickel, dime, and quarter. Remove one of the coins and have the student tell which coin is missing and what its value is.

Name_____

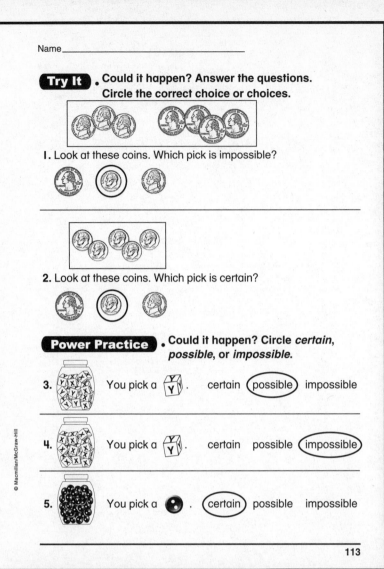

Try It . Could it happen? Answer the questions.
Circle the correct choice or choices.

1. Look at these coins. Which pick is impossible?

2. Look at these coins. Which pick is certain?

Power Practice . Could it happen? Circle *certain*,
possible, or *impossible*.

3. You pick a [Y/Y].   certain (possible) impossible

4. You pick a [Y/Y].   certain possible (impossible)

5. You pick a ●.   (certain) possible impossible

© Macmillan/McGraw-Hill

113

WHAT IF THE STUDENT CAN'T

Complete the Power Practice
- For each item, have the student identify the possible choices, the pick shown, and then explain why that pick is certain, probable, or impossible. If necessary, act out each exercise using manipulatives.

Try It
- Point out that students may circle more than one coin in each group.
- If you wish, demonstrate each exercise, using 3 play nickels, 4 play quarters, 5 play dimes, and a paper bag.

Power Practice
- Have students complete the practice items. Then discuss their answers. Have students explain their reasoning.
- If you wish, demonstrate each exercise, using play money, alphabet blocks, and buttons.

Learn with Partners & Parents
Give students hands-on experience with probability with this sock-matching activity.
- Put 3 white socks and 3 blue socks in a bag (or any other color). Have the student decide whether picking a white sock is certain, probable, or impossible. (probable)
- Repeat with 2 white socks and 4 blue socks (probable), 6 white socks (certain), and 6 blue socks (impossible).

Skill Builder
Blackline Masters

Most and Fewest

Learn

What Can I Do?
I want to know which group has the fewest.

Count and compare numbers.

Count the □s, △s, and ○s.

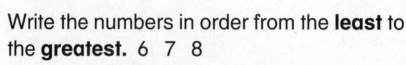

Write the numbers in order from the **least** to the **greatest.** 6 7 8

The group of □ has the **most.**

The group of △ has the **fewest.**

Try It • **Count and compare numbers.**

1. △ △ △ △
    □ □ □ □
    ○ ○ ○ ○ ○ ○

The group of _____ has fewest.

2. △ △ △ △ △ △ △ △
    □ □ □ □ □ □
    ○ ○ ○ ○ ○ ○ ○ ○

The group of _____ has fewest.

Power Practice • **Circle the group that has the fewest.**

3.

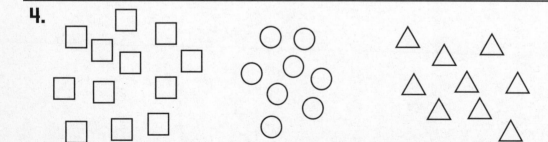

4.

2

Name_____

Identify Reasonable Estimates

Learn

Use number sense.

Do you think there are fewer than 50 fish?

Do you think there are more than 10 fish?

What Can I Do?
I want to estimate how many.

It looks like there are more than 10 but fewer than 50. A good estimate is 20 or 30 fish.

Group tens to estimate.

You can estimate how many by grouping tens. There are nearly 3 tens, or 30 fish.

Try It • Circle the best estimate.

1. 2   20   200

Power Practice • Circle the best estimate.

2. 10   30   100

3. 10   30   50

Number Line

Learn

What Can I Do?
I want to read a number line.

Count forward.

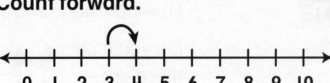

0 1 2 3 4 5 6 7 8 9 10

4 is 1 **more** than 3.

Count backward.

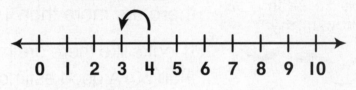

0 1 2 3 4 5 6 7 8 9 10

3 is 1 **less** than 4.

Try It • Write the missing number.

1.

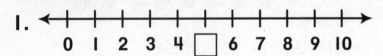

0 1 2 3 4 ☐ 6 7 8 9 10

Power Practice • Write the number that is 1 <u>less</u>.
Write the number that is 1 <u>more</u>.

	1 Less	Number	1 More
2.	_____	5	_____
3.	_____	8	_____
4.	_____	2	_____
5.	_____	4	_____

	1 Less	Number	1 More
6.	_____	1	_____
7.	_____	3	_____
8.	_____	7	_____
9.	_____	6	_____

Compare Numbers

Learn

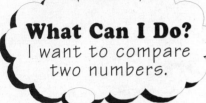

What Can I Do?
I want to compare two numbers.

Use a number line.

These numbers increase, or go up, by one.

Numbers on the right are greater.
Numbers on the left are less.

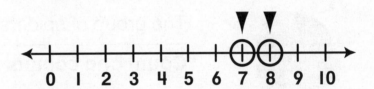

8 is greater than 7.
7 is less than 8.

Try It • **Circle all the numbers greater than 5.**
Mark an X on all the numbers less than 5.

1.

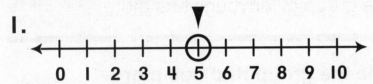

Power Practice • **Use the number line.**
Circle the greater number.

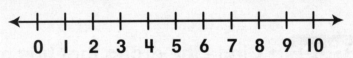

2. 4   5   **3.** 8   9   **4.** 6   5

5. 7   3   **6.** 2   6   **7.** 10   4

8. 1   3   **9.** 8   4   **10.** 0   1

More and Fewer

Learn

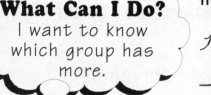

What Can I Do?
I want to know which group has more.

Use one-to-one matching.

Match. The group with items left over has more.

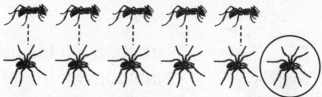

The group of spiders has <u>more</u>.

Count and compare numbers.

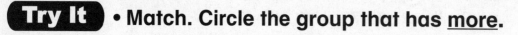

Count and compare: 7 > 5.

The group of ladybugs has <u>more.</u>

Try It • **Match. Circle the group that has <u>more</u>.**

1.

Power Practice • Circle the group that has <u>more</u>.

2.

3.

Greater Than, Less Than

Learn

What Can I Do?

I want to compare two numbers using >, <, or =.

Understand the symbols.

The symbol > means **greater than.**
The open side of the symbol is next to the greater number.

　　　5 > 3 means 5 **is greater than** 3.

The symbol < means **less than.**
The symbol points to the smaller number.

　　　3 < 5 means 3 **is less than** 5.

Use a number line.

Greater numbers are always on the right.
Lesser numbers are always on the left.

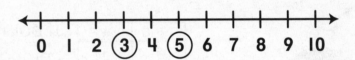

Think: 5 is to the right of 3, so 5 > 3.

Try It • **Use the number line. Compare.
Write >, <, or =.**

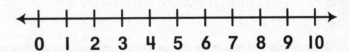

1. 6 ◯ 7　　　　**2.** 3 ◯ 3　　　　**3.** 8 ◯ 10

Power Practice • **Compare. Write >, <, or =.**

4. 12 ◯ 10　　　　　　**5.** 5 ◯ 5

6. 6 ◯ 16　　　　　　**7.** 15 ◯ 16

Name_____

Compare Numbers

Learn

Use a number line.

These numbers go up by one.
Numbers on the right are greater.
Numbers on the left are less.

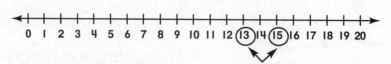

0 1 2 3 4 5 6 7 8 9 10 11 12 ⑬ 14 ⑮ 16 17 18 19 20

15 is greater than 13.   13 is less than 15.

What Can I Do?
I want to compare
two numbers.

Look at place value.

Compare the digits in the tens place.
Which digit is greater?

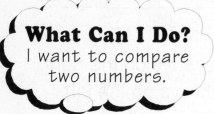

tens	ones
1	3
1	5

If both are the same, then
compare the digits in the
ones place.
Which digit is greater?

Think: 5 ones are greater than 3 ones.
15 is greater than 13.

Try It . **Use the number line.**
Circle the number that is <u>greater.</u>

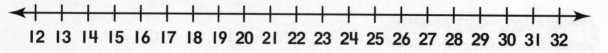

12 13 14 15 16 17 18 19 20 21 22 23 24 25 26 27 28 29 30 31 32

1. 12   21   **2.** 32   31   **3.** 24   18

4. 30   29   **5.** 19   29   **6.** 17   22

Power Practice • Circle the number that is greater.

7. 45   54

8. 33   23

9. 56   66

10. 69   70

11. 97   88

12. 17   16

13. 19   29

14. 80   79

15. 48   47

16. 47   57

17. 73   83

18. 82   28

19. 44   55

20. 50   5

21. 26   28

22. 59   58

23. 63   36

24. 43   49

25. 69   71

26. 51   31

27. 13   25

28. 28   46

29. 10   22

30. 9   90

Name_____

Compare Whole Numbers

Learn   Use a number line.

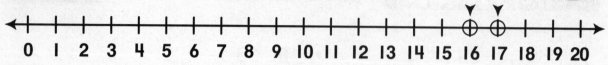

0 1 2 3 4 5 6 7 8 9 10 11 12 13 14 15 16 17 18 19 20

What Can I Do?
I want to compare
two numbers.

Each number increases by ones.
The number on the **right** is **greater.** →
← The number on the **left** is **less.**

17 is greater than 16. 16 is less than 17.

Look at place value.

tens	ones
1	6
1	7

Look at the tens digits.
Compare. Which digit is
greater?

If the tens digits are the same, look at the
ones digits. Compare. Which digit is greater?

Think: 7 ones is greater than 6 ones.
17 is greater than 16.

Try It . Use the place-value charts.
Circle the number that is <u>greater</u>.

1.

tens	ones
3	5
3	9

2.

tens	ones
2	1
1	2

3.

tens	ones
8	3
7	3

4.

tens	ones
6	7
6	8

Power Practice • Circle the number that is <u>greater</u>.

5. 68 86

6. 24 23

7. 19 91

8. 39 40

9. 27 25

10. 61 60

11. 13 11

12. 55 45

13. 98 89

14. 67 77

15. 56 50

16. 75 57

17. 22 33

18. 90 9

19. 86 68

20. 49 48

Compare Numbers

Learn

What Can I Do?
I want to compare
two numbers.

Use a number line.

These numbers increase or go up by one.

→

Numbers on the right are greater.

←

Numbers on the left are less.

0 1 2 3 4 5 6 7 8 9 10 11 12 13 14 15 16 17 18 19 20

19 is <u>greater than</u> 9. So 19 > 9.

9 is <u>less than</u> 19. So 9 < 19.

Look at place value.

Compare the digits in the tens place.
Which digit is greater?

↓

tens	ones
3	5
3	4

↑

If both digits are the same, compare the digits in the ones place.
Which digit is greater?

Think: 5 ones is greater than 4 ones. So, 35 is greater than 34.

Try It • Use the place-value charts.
Circle the number that is *greater.*

1.
tens	ones
2	5
5	2

2.
tens	ones
3	1
3	2

3.
tens	ones
7	3
5	3

4.
tens	ones
8	7
8	8

Power Practice • Compare. Write >, <, or =.

5. 38 ◯ 83

6. 44 ◯ 43

7. 19 ◯ 91

8. 89 ◯ 90

9. 27 ◯ 25

10. 31 ◯ 30

11. 11 ◯ 11

12. 65 ◯ 55

13. 69 ◯ 70

14. 97 ◯ 97

15. 78 ◯ 79

16. 65 ◯ 56

17. 53 ◯ 33

18. 30 ◯ 3

19. 66 ◯ 68

20. 100 ◯ 10

Order Numbers

Learn

> **What Can I Do?**
> I want to put numbers in order.

Use a hundred chart.

The numbers are in order from **least** to **greatest**.

1	2	3	4	5	6	7	8	9	10
11	12	13	14	15	16	17	18	19	20
21	22	23	24	25	26	27	28	29	30
31	32	33	34	35	36	37	38	39	40
41	42	43	44	45	46	47	48	49	50
51	52	53	54	55	56	57	58	59	60
61	62	63	64	65	66	67	68	69	70
71	72	73	74	75	76	77	78	79	80
81	82	83	84	85	86	87	88	89	90
91	92	93	94	95	96	97	98	99	100

Think: 36 is just <u>before</u> 37.

38 is just <u>after</u> 37.

37 is <u>between</u> 36 and 38.

Count on or back.

Start with one number, such as 78.
Count on 1. One more is 79.
79 is just <u>after</u> 78.

Start with the same number, 78.
Count back 1. One less is 77.
77 is just <u>before</u> 78.
78 is <u>between</u> 77 and 79.

Name_____

Try It • Use the hundred chart. Write the number that comes just <u>before</u>, just <u>after</u>, or <u>between</u>.

1. just <u>after</u> 44 _____

2. <u>between</u> 85 and 87 _____

3. just <u>before</u> 69 _____

4. just <u>after</u> 31 _____

5. <u>between</u> 49 and 51 _____

6. just <u>before</u> 27 _____

1	2	3	4	5	6	7	8	9	10
11	12	13	14	15	16	17	18	19	20
21	22	23	24	25	26	27	28	29	30
31	32	33	34	35	36	37	38	39	40
41	42	43	44	45	46	47	48	49	50
51	52	53	54	55	56	57	58	59	60
61	62	63	64	65	66	67	68	69	70
71	72	73	74	75	76	77	78	79	80
81	82	83	84	85	86	87	88	89	90
91	92	93	94	95	96	97	98	99	100

Power Practice • Write the number that comes just <u>before</u>, just <u>after</u>, or <u>between</u>.

7. just after 17 _____   **8.** between 55 and 57 _____

9. just before 96 _____   **10.** just after 64 _____

11. between 76 and 78 _____   **12.** just before 21 _____

13. just after 8 _____   **14.** between 93 and 95 _____

15. just before 2 _____   **16.** just after 72 _____

17. between 81 and 83 _____   **18.** just before 100 _____

19. just after 19 _____   **20.** between 19 and 21 _____

21. just before 40 _____   **22.** just after 86 _____

© Macmillan/McGraw-Hill

15

Parts of a Group

Learn

What Can I Do?
I want to know how many objects are in one part of a group.

Find the parts.

This group has different parts.

2 buttons are large and white.
3 buttons are small and black.
1 button is fancy and gray.

There are 3 different kinds of buttons.
There are 3 parts of the group.

Count, circle, and count.

Count how many in all.
Circle the ones that belong together.
Count the objects in each circle.

Try It • **Count, circle, and count. Write how many.**

1. How many in all? _____   **2.** How many ? _____

Power Practice • **Write how many.**

Z X W Z Y X Z Z X Z Y Z

3. How many in all? _____   **4.** How many Xs? _____

5. How many Zs? _____   **6.** How many Ws? _____

Equal Groups

Learn

Activity
12

Number and count.

First, number the groups.

Count. There are 4 groups.

Then count the number in each group. There are 3 in each group.

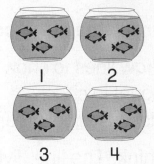

What Can I Do?
I want to know how many groups there are and how many are in each group.

Make sure groups are equal.

In this picture, there are 3 equal groups.

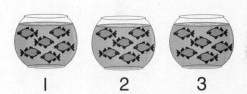

This picture shows 3 groups that are <u>not</u> equal.

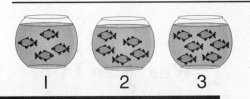

Try It • **Number and count. Write the number of groups. Write how many are in each group.**

1.

_____ groups

_____ in each group

2.

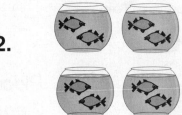

_____ groups

_____ in each group

Name_____

More About Equal Groups

Learn

Draw lines and count.

Draw lines to show **equal** groups.
Count to check.
Make 2 equal groups of stars.

Think: The line divides the stars into 2 groups.
There are 8 stars in each group.
The 2 groups are equal.

Make 2 equal groups
of balloons.

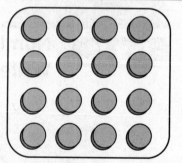

What Can I Do?
I want to divide
a group into
smaller equal
groups.

Use counters.

Count out the same
number of counters.

Place the counters in
2 **equal** groups.

Name_____

Try It • **Use counters. Then draw lines to show the number of <u>equal</u> groups.**

1.

Make 3 equal groups.

2.

Make 4 equal groups.

Power Practice • **Draw lines to show the number of <u>equal</u> groups.**

3.

Make 2 equal groups.

There are ____ in each group.

4.

Make 3 equal groups.

There are ____ in each group.

5.

Make 6 equal groups.

There are ____ in each group.

6.

Make 5 equal groups.

There are ____ in each group.

Ordinal Numbers

Activity
14

Learn

What Can I Do?
I want to use numbers to put things in order.

Use numbers to order.

Use the top numbers to count things.
Use the bottom numbers to put things in order.

one	two	three	four	five	six	seven	eight	nine	ten
first	second	third	fourth	fifth	sixth	seventh	eighth	ninth	tenth

Count from 1 to 10. Then count the order from first to tenth.

Try It • **Draw lines to match.**

1. two   fifth

2. five   seventh

3. seven   second

4. one   ninth

5. nine   first

6. four   eighth

7. eight   fourth

Name_____

8. Color the **third** duckling yellow.

9. Color the **tenth** duckling orange.

10. Color the **sixth** duckling red.

11. Color the **first** duckling brown.

12. Color the **eighth** duckling green.

13. Color the **second** duckling blue.

Write the word that tells the order.

14. The _____ fish has stripes.

15. The _____ fish has spots.

16. The _____ fish is the biggest fish of all.

17. The _____ fish is the smallest fish of all.

18. The _____ fish is white.

first	second	third	fourth	fifth
1st	2nd	3rd	4th	5th
sixth	seventh	eighth	ninth	tenth
6th	7th	8th	9th	10th

Number Chart

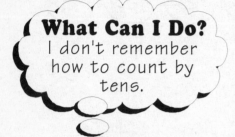

Learn

Find patterns in a hundreds chart.

Here are the first three rows of a hundreds chart.

1	2	3	4	5	6	7	8	9	10
11	12	13	14	15	16	17	18	19	20
21	22	23	24	25	26	27	28	29	30

What Can I Do?
I don't remember how to count by tens.

A hundreds chart shows the order of numbers.
It shows number patterns, too.
How can the chart help you count by 10s?
How can it help you count by 5s?
How can you tell which numbers are **greater?**
How can you tell which numbers are **less?**

Try It • **Fill in the missing numbers.**

1.

1	2	3	4	5	6	7	8	9	10
11	12	13	14		16	17	18	19	
21	22	23	24		26	27	28	29	
31	32	33	34		36	37	38	39	
41	42	43	44		46	47	48	49	
51	52	53	54		56	57	58	59	
61	62	63	64		66	67	68	69	

Power Practice • Fill in the missing numbers.

2.

1	2	3	4	5	6	7	8	9	10
11		13		15		17		19	20
21		23		25		27		29	30
31		33		35		37		39	40
41		43		45		47		49	50
51		53		55		57		59	60

3.

1	2	3	4		6	7	8	9	
11	12	13	14		16	17	18	19	
			24		26	27	28	29	
31	32	33	34		36	37		39	
41	42	43	44		46	47		49	
51		53	54	55	56	57	58	59	60
61				65	66				70
71			74			77		79	
81		83	84	85				89	90
91	92	93		95	96		98		100

Skip Counting by 2s

Learn

Use a hundred chart.

Here are the first 4 rows of a hundreds chart.
Start with 2 and count every other number.

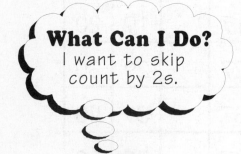

What Can I Do?

I want to skip count by 2s.

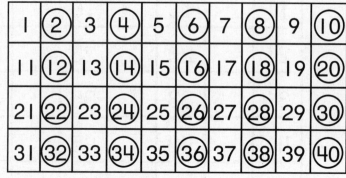

Use number patterns.

Look at the ones digits.

2 4 6 8 10 1<u>2</u> 1<u>4</u> 1<u>6</u> 1<u>8</u> 2<u>0</u>

Use the pattern "2, 4, 6, 8, 0" to decide
what comes next.

Try It • **Fill in the missing numbers.**

1.

1	2	3	4	5	6	7	8	9	10
11	12	13	14	15	16	17	18	19	
21		23		25		27		29	
31		33		35		37		39	
41		43		45		47		49	50

Power Practice • **Write each missing number.**

2. 2, 4, ____, 8, 10, ____

3. 32, ____, 36, 38, 40, ____

4. 80, 82, ____, ____, 88, 90

5. 66, 68, ____, 72, ____, 76

Skip Count by 5s and 10s

Activity **17**

Learn

What Can I Do?
I want to skip count by 5s and 10s.

Use number patterns.

Look at the ones digits.

<u>5</u> 1<u>0</u> 1<u>5</u> 2<u>0</u> 2<u>5</u> 3<u>0</u>

Counting by 5s.

Use the pattern to decide what number comes next.

10 20 30 40 50 60

Counting by 10s.

Try It • Fill in the missing numbers.

1.

1	2	3	4	5	6	7	8	9	
11	12	13	14		16	17	18	19	
21	22	23	24		26	27	28	29	
31	32	33	34		36	37	38	39	40

Power Practice • Write each missing number.

2. 25, 30, _____, 40, 45, _____

3. 40, _____, 60, 70, 80, _____

4. 50, 55, _____, _____, 70, 75

5. 20, 30, _____, 50, _____, 70

Counting On

Learn

What Can I Do?
I want to count on to find how many in all.

Use a number line.

Each number increases or goes up by one.
Move to the right to count on one.

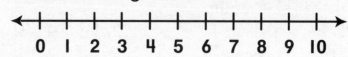

0 1 2 3 4 5 6 7 8 9 10

4 and 1 more is 5. 1 more is 6.

Draw a picture.

Draw the number you have.
Draw 1 more. Count. 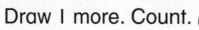 5
Draw 1 more. Count.  6

Try It • **Use the number line.**
Find 1 more.

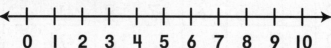

0 1 2 3 4 5 6 7 8 9 10

1. 3 and 1 more = _____   **2.** 6 and 1 more = _____

3. 9 and 1 more = _____   **4.** 8 and 1 more = _____

Power Practice • **Write each missing number.**

5. Start with 5. 1 more makes _____. 1 more makes _____.

6. Start with 3. 1 more makes _____. 1 more makes _____.

7. Start with 7. 1 more makes _____. 1 more makes _____.

1 more makes _____. 1 more makes _____.

Before, After, Between

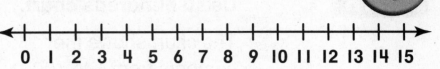

Learn

```
◄─┼──┼──┼──┼──┼──┼──┼──┼──┼──┼──┼──┼──┼──┼──┼──┼─►
  0  1  2  3  4  5  6  7  8  9  10 11 12 13 14 15
```

What Can I Do?
I want to find the number between two numbers.

Use a number line.

Think:
12 is just **after** 11.
12 is just **before** 13.
12 is **between** 11 and 13.

The numbers go in order from **least to greatest.**

11, 12, 13

Try It • Use the number line. Write the number.

```
◄─┼──┼──┼──┼──┼──┼──┼──┼──┼──┼──┼──┼──┼──┼──┼──┼──┼──┼──┼──┼──┼─►
  0  1  2  3  4  5  6  7  8  9  10 11 12 13 14 15 16 17 18 19 20
```

1. just **after** 6 _____

2. just **before** 10 _____

3. **between** 15 and 17 _____

4. **between** 11 and 13 _____

Power Practice • Write the number.

5. just **after** 14 _____

6. just **before** 18 _____

7. just **after** 34 _____

8. just **before** 59 _____

9. **between** 76 and 78 _____

10. **between** 69 and 71 _____

Skip Count by 5s

Learn

Use a hundreds chart.

The chart shows the numbers from 1 to 100. Look at the pattern for skip counting by 5s.

Look at the ones digits.

<u>5</u>, 1<u>0</u>, 1<u>5</u>, 2<u>0</u>, 2<u>5</u>, 3<u>0</u>

What Can I Do?
I want to skip count by 5s.

1	2	3	4	5	6	7	8	9	10
11	12	13	14	15	16	17	18	19	20
21	22	23	24	25	26	27	28	29	30
31	32	33	34	35	36	37	38	39	40
41	42	43	44	45	46	47	48	49	50
51	22	53	54	55	56	57	58	59	60
61	62	63	64	65	66	67	68	69	70
71	72	73	74	75	76	77	78	79	80
81	82	83	84	85	86	87	88	89	90
91	92	93	94	95	96	97	98	99	100

Try It • Fill in the missing numbers.

1.

21	22	23	24		26	27	28	29	
31	32	33	34		36	37	38	39	40
41	42	43	44		46	47	48	49	

Power Practice • Write each missing number.

2. 15, 20, _____, 30, 35, _____

3. 30, _____, 40, 45, 50, _____

4. 10, 15, _____, _____, 30, 35

Round to the Nearest Ten

Learn

What Can I Do?

I want to round a number to the nearest ten.

Use a number line.

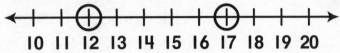

10 11 12 13 14 15 16 17 18 19 20

12 is between 10 and 20. It is closer to 10. So, 12 rounds down to 10.

17 is between 10 and 20. It is closer to 20. So 17 rounds up to 20.

Use the ones digit.

If the ones digit is less than 5, round down. Round 14 down to 10.

If the ones digit is 5 or greater, round up. Round 15 up to 20.

Try It • Use the number line.
Round to the nearest <u>ten</u>.

1. 31 _____

30 31 32 33 34 35 36 37 38 39 40

2. 58 _____

50 51 52 53 54 55 56 57 58 59 60

Power Practice • Look at the ones digit. Round each number to the nearest <u>ten</u>.

3. 73 _____   4. 19 _____   5. 25 _____

6. 54 _____   7. 36 _____   8. 88 _____

9. 42 _____   10. 65 _____   11. 7 _____

Round to the Nearest Ten

Activity 22

Learn

Use a number line.

The number 18 is between 10 and 20. It is closer to 20. So 18 rounds up to 20.

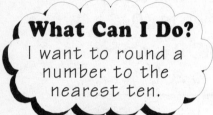

What Can I Do?

I want to round a number to the nearest ten.

The number 32 is between 30 and 40. It is closer to 30. So 32 rounds down to 30.

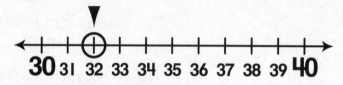

Use the ones digit.

> If the ones digit is less than 5, round down. If it is 5 or greater, round up.

Round 64 down to 60. Round 65 up to 70.

Try It • **Use the number line. Round to the nearest <u>ten</u>.**

1. 51 _____

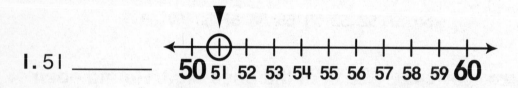

2. 17 _____

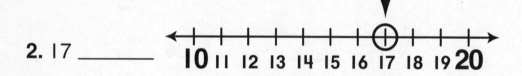

3. 34 _____

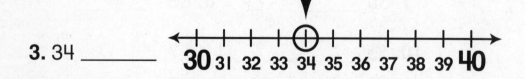

Power Practice • Look at the ones digit. Round each number to the nearest <u>ten</u>.

4. 81 _____

5. 24 _____

6. 38 _____

7. 62 _____

8. 33 _____

9. 74 _____

10. 45 _____

11. 13 _____

12. 9 _____

13. 78 _____

14. 65 _____

15. 44 _____

16. 26 _____

17. 77 _____

18. 88 _____

Name_____

Round to the Nearest Hundred

Learn

Use a number line.

The number 222 is between 200 and 300.
It is closer to 200.

So 222 <u>rounds down</u> to 200.

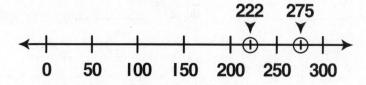

The number 275 is between 200 and 300.
It is closer to 300.

So 275 <u>rounds up</u> to 300.

Use the digit in the tens place.

Look at the tens digit.

| If it is less than 5, round down. |
| If it is 5 or greater, round up. |

Round 1**4**9 down to 100.
Round 1**5**0 up to 200.

> **What Can I Do?**
> I want to round a number to the nearest hundred.

Try It . **Use the number line.**
Round to the nearest <u>hundred</u>.

1. 130 _____

<---+----+----+----+----+----+----+----+----+----+--->
100 110 120 130 140 150 160 170 180 190 **200**

2. 580 _____

<---+----+----+----+----+----+----+----+----+----+--->
500 510 520 530 540 550 560 570 580 590 **600**

3. 320 _____

<---+----+----+----+----+----+----+----+----+----+--->
300 310 320 330 340 350 360 370 380 390 **400**

4. 258 _____

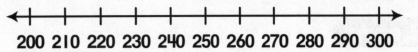
200 210 220 230 240 250 260 270 280 290 300

5. 441 _____

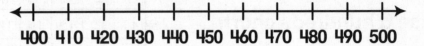
400 410 420 430 440 450 460 470 480 490 500

6. 348 _____

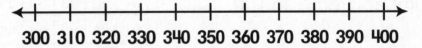
300 310 320 330 340 350 360 370 380 390 400

7. 527 _____

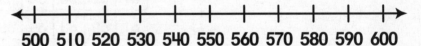
500 510 520 530 540 550 560 570 580 590 600

Power Practice • Round each number to the nearest <u>hundred</u>.

8. 730 _____   **9.** 195 _____

10. 253 _____   **11.** 543 _____

12. 236 _____   **13.** 858 _____

14. 142 _____   **15.** 659 _____

16. 75 _____   **17.** 360 _____

18. 715 _____   **19.** 907 _____

20. 455 _____   **21.** 346 _____

22. 188 _____   **23.** 220 _____

Skip Counting

Learn

Use a hundreds chart.

A hundreds chart shows all the numbers from 1 to 100.

1	2	3	4	5	6	7	8	9	10
11	12	13	14	15	16	17	18	19	20
21	22	23	24	25	26	27	28	29	30
31	32	33	34	35	36	37	38	39	40
41	42	43	44	45	46	47	48	49	50
51	52	53	54	55	56	57	58	59	60
61	62	63	64	65	66	67	68	69	70
71	72	73	74	75	76	77	78	79	80
81	82	83	84	85	86	87	88	89	90
91	92	93	94	95	96	97	98	99	100

Start at 2. Stop at every other number.

Start at 3. Stop at every 3rd number.

Start at 4. Stop at every 4th number.

Start at 5. Stop at every 5th number.

1	2	3	4	5	6	7	8	9	10

1	2	3	4	5	6	7	8	9	10

1	2	3	4	5	6	7	8	9	10

1	2	3	4	5	6	7	8	9	10

What Can I Do?

I want to skip count by 2s, 3s, 4s, or 5s.

Use number patterns.

Look at the ones digits when you count:

by 2s: 2 4 6 8 10 12 14 16 18 20

by 4s: 4 8 12 16 20 24 28 32 36 40

by 5s: 5 10 15 20 25 30 35 40 45 50

by 3s: 3 6 9 12 15 18 21 24 27

Name _____

1.

1	2	3	4	5	6	7	8	9	
11	12	13	14		16	17	18	19	20
21	22	23	24		26	27	28	29	
31	32	33	34		36	37	38	39	40

2.

71	72	73	74	75	76	77	78	79	80
	82	83		85	86		88	89	
91	92		94	95	96	97	98	99	100

Power Practice • Write the missing numbers in each skip counting pattern.

3. 60, _____, 70, 75, 80, _____, _____, _____

4. 21, 24, _____, _____, 33, 36, _____, _____

5. 64, 68, _____, 76, _____, 84, 88, _____, _____

6. 40, 44, _____, 52, _____, 60, _____, _____, 72, 76

7. 30, 35, _____, _____, 50, 55, _____, _____, 70

8. 86, 88, _____, _____, _____, 96, 98, _____

Number Patterns

Learn

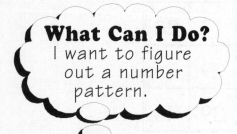

What Can I Do?
I want to figure out a number pattern.

Read the pattern aloud.

Reading aloud helps you "hear" the pattern.
Try reading these numbers aloud.
What number comes next?

44, 45, 46, 47, 48, ___?___

23, 33, 43, 53, 63, ___?___

Find the rule.

Read this pattern:

34, 44, 54, 64, 74, ___?___

Think: 44 is 10 more than 34.
54 is 10 more than 44.
64 is 10 more than 54.
The rule is Add ten.

Read this pattern:

36, 37, 38, 39, 40, ___?___

Think: 37 is 1 more than 36.
38 is 1 more than 37.
39 is 1 more than 38.
The rule is Add one.

Name_____

Try It • **Find the rule. Circle it.**

1. 11, 21, 31, 41, 51   Add one   Add ten

2. 68, 69, 70, 71, 72   Add one   Add ten

3. 97, 98, 99, 100, 101   Add one   Add ten

4. 46, 56, 66, 76, 86   Add one   Add ten

5. 19, 29, 39, 49, 59   Add one   Add ten

Power Practice • **Write the missing numbers in each counting pattern.**

6. 20, 30, _____, 50, 60, _____, _____, 90

7. 43, _____, 45, 46, 47, _____, 48, 49, _____, _____, 53

8. 15, 25, _____, _____, 55, 65, _____, _____, 95

9. 26, 27, _____, 29, _____, 31, 32, _____, 34, _____

10. 33, 43, _____, 63, 73, _____, _____

11. 48, _____, 50, 51, 52, _____, 53, _____, _____, 56

12. 42, 52, _____, _____, 82, 92

13. 17, 27, _____, _____, 57, _____, 77

Name_____

Add and Subtract One

Learn

What Can I Do?
I want to add and subtract one.

Use a number line.

Count on one to **add** 1.
Count **back** one to subtract 1.

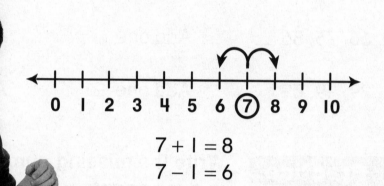

$$7 + 1 = 8$$
$$7 - 1 = 6$$

Try It • Use the number line. Add or subtract.

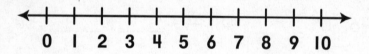

1. $4 + 1 =$ _____

2. $4 - 1 =$ _____

3. $5 + 1 =$ _____

4. $5 - 1 =$ _____

Power Practice • Add or subtract.

5. $6 + 1 =$ _____

6. $6 - 1 =$ _____

7. $9 + 1 =$ _____

8. $9 - 1 =$ _____

9. $8 + 1 =$ _____

10. $8 - 1 =$ _____

Addition Facts to 12

Learn

What Can I Do?
I want to know an addition fact. Here are three ways.

1. Draw a picture.

A picture can help you add.

$5 + 6 = ?$
$5 + 6 = 11$

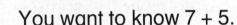

2. Use doubles.

$4 + 4 = 8$ $5 + 5 = 10$ $6 + 6 = 12$

3. Use facts you know.

You want to know $7 + 5$.
You know $7 + 3 = 10$.
Think: 5 is 2 more than 3.
$7 + 5$ must be 2 more than $7 + 3$.
So, $7 + 5 = 12$.

Try It • Add.

1. $9 + 3 =$ _____

2. $7 + 2 =$ _____

3. $8 + 4 =$ _____

Power Practice • Add.

4. $8 + 3 =$ _____

5. $6 + 4 =$ _____

6. $8 + 1 =$ _____

7. $3 + 9 =$ _____

8. $5 + 5 =$ _____

9. $6 + 5 =$ _____

10. $\begin{array}{r} 9 \\ +2 \\ \hline \end{array}$

11. $\begin{array}{r} 7 \\ +3 \\ \hline \end{array}$

12. $\begin{array}{r} 6 \\ +6 \\ \hline \end{array}$

13. $\begin{array}{r} 6 \\ +3 \\ \hline \end{array}$

14. $\begin{array}{r} 7 \\ +4 \\ \hline \end{array}$

Addition

Learn

What Can I Do?
I want to add across or down.

Draw a picture.

A picture can help you add. The numbers are the same across and down.

$2 + 3 = ?$

$$\begin{array}{r} 2 \\ + 3 \\ \hline \end{array}$$

Both say: "Two plus three."
Both have the same sum.

$2 + 3 = 5$

↑
sum

$$\begin{array}{r} 2 \\ + 3 \\ \hline 5 \end{array}$$

Try It • **Use the pictures. Add across or down.**

1. $2 + 7 =$ _____

2. $\begin{array}{r} 2 \\ + 7 \\ \hline \end{array}$

3. $3 + 4 =$ _____

4. $\begin{array}{r} 3 \\ + 4 \\ \hline \end{array}$

5. $6 + 3 =$ _____

6. $\begin{array}{r} 6 \\ + 3 \\ \hline \end{array}$

Power Practice • **Add. If you need to, draw a picture.**

7. $2 + 6 =$ _____

8. $\begin{array}{r} 2 \\ + 6 \\ \hline \end{array}$

9. $7 + 4 =$ _____

10. $\begin{array}{r} 7 \\ + 4 \\ \hline \end{array}$

11. $3 + 8 =$ _____

12. $\begin{array}{r} 3 \\ + 8 \\ \hline \end{array}$

13. $5 + 3 =$ _____

14. $\begin{array}{r} 5 \\ + 3 \\ \hline \end{array}$

Addition Facts to 8

Learn

What Can I Do?
I want to find sums to 8. Here are two ways.

Count on.

Start with the **greater number.**
Count on to find the sum.

4 + 2 = ?

Think: 4 and 1 is 5, and 1 more is 6.

Draw a picture.

Use a picture to help you add.

4 + 2 = ?

Draw 4 circles and 2 more circles.

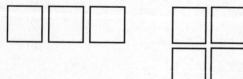

Count all the circles to find the sum.

Try It • **Add.**

1. 3 + 4 = _____

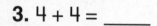

2.   5
    + 3

3. 4 + 4 = _____

4.   2
    + 4

Power Practice • Add. Count on or
draw a picture.

5. $3 + 3 =$ _____

6. $1 + 5 =$ _____

7. $2 + 3 =$ _____

8. $4 + 3 =$ _____

9. $\begin{array}{r} 5 \\ + 2 \\ \hline \end{array}$

10. $\begin{array}{r} 3 \\ + 5 \\ \hline \end{array}$

11. $\begin{array}{r} 2 \\ + 6 \\ \hline \end{array}$

12. $\begin{array}{r} 6 \\ + 1 \\ \hline \end{array}$

13. $\begin{array}{r} 6 \\ + 2 \\ \hline \end{array}$

14. $\begin{array}{r} 2 \\ + 5 \\ \hline \end{array}$

Addition and Subtraction
Facts to 12

Learn

Draw a picture.

A picture can help you add or subtract.

$4 + 6 = ?$

What Can I Do?
I forgot an addition or subtraction fact!

The **plus sign** means add. $4 + 6 = 10$

$\begin{array}{r} 11 \\ -3 \\ \hline 8 \end{array}$

The **minus sign** means subtract. $11 - 3 = 8$

Use facts you know.

You forgot $12 - 5$. You know $10 - 5 = 5$.
Think: 12 is 2 more than 10.
$12 - 5$ must be 2 more than $10 - 5$.
So, $12 - 5 = 7$.

Try It • Watch the signs. Add or subtract.

1. $2 + 9 = $ ____

2. $\begin{array}{r} 12 \\ -8 \\ \hline \end{array}$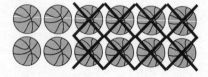

3. $9 - 7 = $ ____

4. $\begin{array}{r} 3 \\ +7 \\ \hline \end{array}$

Power Practice • Add or subtract. Draw a picture or use facts you know.

5. $2 + 7 =$ _____

6. $\begin{array}{r} 5 \\ + 6 \\ \hline \end{array}$

7. $11 - 4 =$ _____

8. $\begin{array}{r} 8 \\ + 4 \\ \hline \end{array}$

9. $10 - 9 =$ _____

10. $\begin{array}{r} 9 \\ - 4 \\ \hline \end{array}$

11. $5 + 7 =$ _____

12. $\begin{array}{r} 11 \\ - 6 \\ \hline \end{array}$

13. $6 + 4 =$ _____

14. $\begin{array}{r} 12 \\ - 8 \\ \hline \end{array}$

Write a Number Sentence

Learn

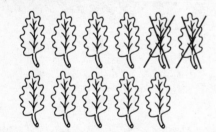

What Can I Do?
I want to write a number sentence to match a picture.

Choose the operation.

Look at the picture. Decide whether to add or subtract. Choose + or −.

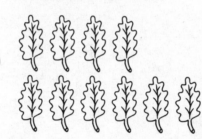

Think: A group of 4 is joining a group of 6. I can add to find how many in all.

$$4 + 6 = 10$$

Use the picture.

Count to find how many in all. Count to find how many are taken away.

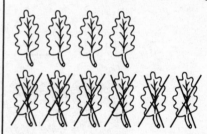

Think: There are 10 in all. 6 are crossed out. I can subtract to find how many are left.

$$10 - 6 = 4$$

Try It • Write a number sentence to match each picture.

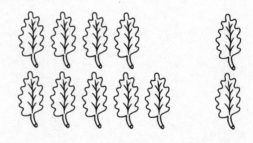

1. ___ ◯ ___ ◯ ___

2. ___ ◯ ___ ◯ ___

Power Practice • Write a number sentence to match each picture.

3. ____ ◯ ____ ◯ ____

4. ____ ◯ ____ ◯ ____

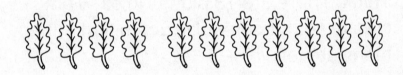

5. ____ ◯ ____ ◯ ____

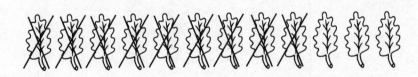

6. ____ ◯ ____ ◯ ____

Write a Number Sentence

Learn

Choose the operation.

What Can I Do?
I want to write a number sentence to match a picture.

Look at the picture. Decide whether to add or subtract. Choose + or − for your number sentence.

Think: The model planes are all the same. I can **add** to find how many in all. 7 + 6 = 13

Think: There are 13 planes in all. 6 are crossed out. I can **subtract** to find out how many are left. 13 − 6 = 7

Use numbers from the picture.

Think: I can count to find how many in all. One group has 6. One group has 7.
6 + 7 = 13

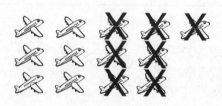

Think: I can count how many in all. I can count the number being subtracted. There are 13 in all. Seven are being subtracted. 13 − 7 = 6

Try It • Write a number sentence for each picture.

1.

___ ◯ ___ ◯ ___

2.

___ ◯ ___ ◯ ___

Power Practice • Write a number sentence for each picture.

3.

___ ◯ ___ ◯ ___

4.

___ ◯ ___ ◯ ___

5.

___ ◯ ___ ◯ ___

6.

___ ◯ ___ ◯ ___

7.

___ ◯ ___ ◯ ___

8.

___ ◯ ___ ◯ ___

Subtraction Facts to 8

Learn

Count back.

Start with the **greater number.**
Count back to find the difference.

$7 - 2 = ?$

Think: 7 and 1 less is 6, and 1 less is 5.

What Can I Do?
I want to subtract.
Here are two ways.

Draw a picture.

Use a picture to help you subtract.

$7 - 2 = ?$

Draw 4 circles. Cross out 1 circle.

Count the circles that are left to find the difference.

Try It • **Subtract.**

1. $2 - 1 =$ _____

2. $\begin{array}{r} 6 \\ -3 \\ \hline \end{array}$

3. $7 - 3 =$ _____

4. $\begin{array}{r} 8 \\ -6 \\ \hline \end{array}$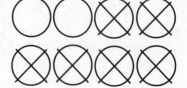

Name_____

Power Practice • **Subtract. Count back or use a picture.**

5. 8 − 2 = _____

6. 5 − 3 = _____

7. 8 − 6 = _____

8. 7 − 4 = _____

9.
   6
 − 2

10.
   3
 − 2

11.
   8
 − 5

12.
   4
 − 3

© Macmillan/McGraw-Hill

Name_____

Add or Subtract

Learn

Use word clues.

How many in all? means **add.**
How many more? means **subtract.**

How many balls in all? $4 + 2 = 6$

How many more soccerballs
than baseballs? $4 - 2 = 2$

What Can I Do?
How do I know
whether to add or
subtract?

Act it out.

Use counters. Act out the problem.

How many in all?   How many more?

Think: I can put
the groups together
and count.

Think: I can see
which group has
more and count to
find how many more.

Try It . **Look for clue words.
Write + or −. Then add or subtract.**

1.

How many more baseballs
than soccerballs?

5 ◯ 3 = ____

2.

How many in all?

6 ◯ 4 = ____

Power Practice

Write + or –.
Then add or subtract.

3.

How many in all?

7 ◯ 2 = _____

4.

How many in all?

8 ◯ 5 = _____

5.

How many more planes than boats?

6 ◯ 4 = _____

6.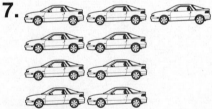

How many in all?

5 ◯ 5 = _____

7.

How many more cars than planes?

9 ◯ 4 = _____

8.

How many more cats than dogs?

11 ◯ 6 = _____

9.

How many in all?

8 ◯ 3 = _____

10.

How many more planes than cars?

8 ◯ 7 = _____

Add Tens

Learn

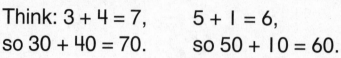

What Can I Do?
I want to
add tens.

Use addition facts.

Think: $3 + 4 = 7$, $5 + 1 = 6$,
so $30 + 40 = 70$.   so $50 + 10 = 60$.

Draw a picture.

Picture tens blocks.
Add them.

Think: $4 + 2 = 6$,
so 4 tens $+ 2$ tens $= 6$ tens
6 tens $= 60$

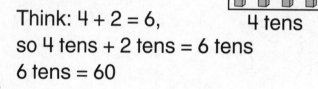

4 tens + 2 tens

Try It • Add.

1. $3 + 5 =$ _____ ,   so $30 + 50 =$ _____ .

2. $8 + 1 =$ _____ ,   so $80 + 10 =$ _____ .

3. $2 + 7 =$ _____ ,   so $20 + 70 =$ _____ .

4. $3 + 2 =$ _____ ,   so $30 + 20 =$ _____ .

Power Practice • Add.

| 5. 20 $+40$ | 6. 30 $+10$ | 7. 10 $+70$ | 8. 50 $+40$ | 9. 60 $+20$ | 10. 40 $+40$ |

Subtract Tens

Learn

What Can I Do?
I want to subtract tens.

Use subtraction facts.

Think: $9 - 4 = 5$, so
$90 - 40 = 50$

$6 - 3 = 3$, so
$60 - 30 = 30$

Draw a picture.

Picture tens blocks.
Subtract them.

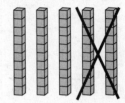

Think: $5 - 2 = 3$, so
5 tens $-$ 2 tens $=$ 3 tens
3 tens $= 30$

Try It • Subtract.

1. $6 - 5 =$ _____, so $60 - 50 =$ _____

2. $7 - 2 =$ _____, so $70 - 20 =$ _____

3. $4 - 1 =$ _____, so $40 - 10 =$ _____

4. $8 - 4 =$ _____, so $80 - 40 =$ _____

Power Practice • Subtract.

5. $\begin{array}{r} 40 \\ -30 \\ \hline \end{array}$
6. $\begin{array}{r} 30 \\ -10 \\ \hline \end{array}$
7. $\begin{array}{r} 60 \\ -40 \\ \hline \end{array}$
8. $\begin{array}{r} 50 \\ -30 \\ \hline \end{array}$
9. $\begin{array}{r} 70 \\ -40 \\ \hline \end{array}$
10. $\begin{array}{r} 90 \\ -50 \\ \hline \end{array}$

Addition Facts to 20

Learn

What Can I Do?
I want to add
facts to 20.

Use doubles.

Think about doubles.

$2 + 2 = 4$ $6 + 6 = 12$

$3 + 3 = 6$ $7 + 7 = 14$

$4 + 4 = 8$ $8 + 8 = 16$

$5 + 5 = 10$ $9 + 9 = 18$

Think: $6 + 7$ is like $6 + 6 + 1$.
$6 + 7 = 13$

$6 + 5$ is like $6 + 6 - 1$.
$6 + 5 = 11$

$$\begin{array}{r} 6 \\ + 7 \\ \hline \end{array}$$

Try It • **Add.**

1. $5 + 5 =$ _____ $5 + 6 =$ _____ $5 + 4 =$ _____

2. $8 + 8 =$ _____ $8 + 7 =$ _____ $8 + 9 =$ _____

3. $7 + 7 =$ _____ $7 + 6 =$ _____ $7 + 8 =$ _____

4. $9 + 9 =$ _____ $10 + 9 =$ _____ $9 + 8 =$ _____

Power Practice • **Add.**

5.
$$\begin{array}{cc} 2 \\ + 8 \\ \hline \end{array} \qquad \begin{array}{cc} 3 \\ + 9 \\ \hline \end{array} \qquad \begin{array}{cc} 9 \\ + 7 \\ \hline \end{array} \qquad \begin{array}{cc} 7 \\ + 5 \\ \hline \end{array} \qquad \begin{array}{cc} 6 \\ + 9 \\ \hline \end{array} \qquad \begin{array}{cc} 8 \\ + 6 \\ \hline \end{array}$$

Name_____

Addition Facts to 20

Activity 38

Learn

Use doubles.

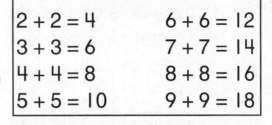

Think about doubles.

2 + 2 = 4	6 + 6 = 12
3 + 3 = 6	7 + 7 = 14
4 + 4 = 8	8 + 8 = 16
5 + 5 = 10	9 + 9 = 18

Think: 5 + 6 is like $\boxed{5 + 5}$ + 1
          10 + 1
5 + 6 = 11

5 + 5 is like $\boxed{5 + 5}$ − 1
          10 − 1
5 + 4 = 9

Use turnaround facts.

If you know one fact, then you really know two facts.

Think: 4 + 5 = 9, so 5 + 4 = 9
          8 + 6 = 14, so 6 + 8 = 14

What Can I Do?
I want to add facts to 20.

Try It • Add.

1. 5 + 5 = _____   5 + 4 = _____   5 + 6 = _____

2. 7 + 7 = _____   7 + 6 = _____   7 + 8 = _____

3. 9 + 9 = _____   9 + 10 = _____   9 + 8 = _____

4. 8 + 8 = _____   8 + 7 = _____   8 + 9 = _____

Power Practice • Add.

5. 7   6. 5   7. 3   8. 5   9. 4   10. 2
   +6   +6   +4   +4   +3   +3

© Macmillan/McGraw-Hill

Related Facts

Learn

What Can I Do?
I often forget that numbers may be added in any order.

Draw a picture.

Draw 4 dots and 6 dots. Flip the picture in any order.

Think: The numbers are the same, so the sums must be the same.

$$4 + 6 = 6 + 4$$

$$\begin{array}{cc} 4 & 6 \\ +6 & +4 \end{array} =$$

Try It • **Draw a picture. Then add.**

1. $6 + 8 =$ _____ $8 + 6 =$ _____

2. $7 + 4 =$ _____ $4 + 7 =$ _____

Power Practice • Add.

3. $5 + 8 =$ _____

$8 + 5 =$ _____

4. $7 + 6 =$ _____

$6 + 7 =$ _____

5. $9 + 7 =$ _____

$7 + 9 =$ _____

6. $4 + 9 =$ _____

$9 + 4 =$ _____

7. $3 + 6 =$ _____

$6 + 3 =$ _____

8. $8 + 4 =$ _____

$4 + 8 =$ _____

9. $3 + 9 =$ _____

$9 + 3 =$ _____

10. $7 + 8 =$ _____

$8 + 7 =$ _____

11. $6 + 8 =$ _____

$8 + 6 =$ _____

12. $5 + 7 =$ _____

$7 + 5 =$ _____

Subtraction Facts to 20

Learn

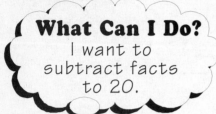

What Can I Do?
I want to subtract facts to 20.

Use doubles.

Think about doubles:
$5 + 5 = 10$ and $10 - 5 = 5$.

You can use doubles to find $11 - 6$.

Think: 11 is 1 more than 10.
$11 - 5$ is 1 more than $10 - 5$.
So, $11 - 5 = 6$.

Try It • **Subtract.**

1. $16 - 8 =$ _____

$17 - 8 =$ _____

2. $14 - 7 =$ _____

$15 - 7 =$ _____

3. $8 - 4 =$ _____

$9 - 4 =$ _____

4. $12 - 6 =$ _____

$13 - 6 =$ _____

Power Practice • **Subtract.**

5. 12 -8

6. 13 -9

7. 16 -7

8. 13 -5

9. 14 -8

10. 17 -9

Subtraction Facts to 20

Learn

Use doubles.

Think about doubles.

$2 + 2 = 4$	$4 - 2 = 2$
$3 + 3 = 6$	$6 - 3 = 3$
$4 + 4 = 8$	$8 - 4 = 4$
$5 + 5 = 10$	$10 - 5 = 5$
$6 + 6 = 12$	$12 - 6 = 6$
$7 + 7 = 14$	$14 - 7 = 7$
$8 + 8 = 16$	$16 - 8 = 8$
$9 + 9 = 18$	$18 - 9 = 9$

Think: $13 - 6$ is one more than $12 - 6$.
$13 - 6 = 7$

Use fact families.

If you know one fact, then
you may know other facts.

Think: $15 - 8 = 7$, so $15 - 7 = 8$
$9 - 3 = 6$, so $9 - 6 = 3$

What Can I Do?
I want to
subtract facts
to 20.

Try It • Subtract.

1. $14 - 7 =$ _____ ,   so $15 - 7 =$ _____

2. $10 - 5 =$ _____ ,   so $11 - 5 =$ _____

3. $6 - 3 =$ _____ ,   so $7 - 3 =$ _____

Power Practice • Subtract.

4. $11 - 8 =$ _____   **5.** $14 - 9 =$ _____   **6.** $17 - 8 =$ _____

Fact Families

 Learn

Write number sentences.

Begin with an addition fact. Then put the same numbers together in different addition and subtraction sentences.

What Can I Do?
I can't remember all four facts in a fact family.

$7 + 8 = 15$ $8 + 7 = 15$

$15 - 8 = 7$ $15 - 7 = 8$

Addition sentences and subtraction sentences that use the same numbers are called a **fact family**.

Try It • Complete each fact family.

I. $6 + 8 = $ _____

$8 + 6 = $ _____

$14 - 8 = $ _____

$14 - 6 = $ _____

2. $7 + 3 = $ _____

$3 + 7 = $ _____

$10 - 7 = $ _____

$10 - 3 = $ _____

3. $8 + 5 = $ _____

___ + _ = _____

$13 - 8 = $ _____

___ - _ = _____

Name _____

4. 7 + 6 = _____

_____ + _____ = _____

13 – 7 = _____

_____ – _____ = _____

5. 8 + 9 = _____

_____ + _____ = _____

17 – 8 = _____

_____ – _____ = _____

6. 6 + 4 = _____

_____ + _____ = _____

_____ – _____ = _____

_____ – _____ = _____

7. 5 + 9 = _____

_____ + _____ = _____

_____ – _____ = _____

_____ – _____ = _____

8. 5 + 5 = _____

_____ – _____ = _____

9. 9 + 9 = _____

_____ – _____ = _____

Use the numbers. Write the fact family.

10. 5, 6, 11

_____

_____

_____

_____

11. 7, 9, 16

_____

_____

_____

_____

Name_____

Adding Three or More Numbers

Learn

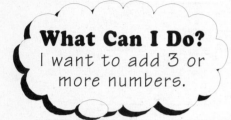

What Can I Do?
I want to add 3 or
more numbers.

Look for 10.

Look for numbers that add up to 10. |
Add those numbers first. 3
Then add the other numbers 4 ⎤10
+ 7 ⎦

Think: 3 + 7 = 10. Add 1 + 4 = 5. Then add
10 + 5 = 15.

Add in stages.

Add the first two numbers. 4 ⎤6
Then add the third number. 2 ⎦
Then add the fourth number. 1
Check by adding the numbers + 6
in a different direction.

Think: 4 + 2 = 6. Add 6 + 1 = 7, then
7 + 6 = 13.
6 + 1 + 2 + 4 = 13

Try It • **Look for 10. Add.**

1. 5
   4 ⎤
   6 ⎦
   + 2

2. 5
   2 ⎤
   1 ⎦
   + 8

3. 1 + 9 + 7 = _____

4. 5 + 4 + 5 + 4 = _____

Power Practice • Add.

5.
```
   6
   4
   3
 + 7
```

6.
```
   2
   2
   9
 + 8
```

7.
```
   5
   7
 + 5
```

8.
```
   4
   5
   1
 + 6
```

9.
```
   3
   7
 + 7
```

10.
```
   4
   4
   4
 + 8
```

11. 3 + 6 + 1 = _____

12. 4 + 7 + 3 = _____

13. 9 + 1 + 4 + 3 = _____

14. 5 + 5 + 6 + 2 = _____

15. 2 + 3 + 4 + 5 + 6 + 7 = _____

16. 8 + 2 + 7 + 3 = _____

17. 1 + 5 + 3 + 7 + 5 = _____

18. 6 + 2 + 8 + 4 = _____

19. 1 + 3 + 3 + 4 + 6 = _____

20. 4 + 5 + 1 + 6 = _____

Add Two-Digit Numbers

Learn

Decide whether to regroup.

```
  26            26
+ 43          + 47
```

Think: I can add 6 ones and 3 ones without regrouping.

I can't add 6 ones and 7 ones without regrouping.

No Regrouping

Regroup 13 ones as 1 ten 3 ones.

```
  26            ¹
+ 43            26
  69          + 47
                73
```

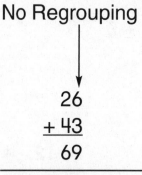

What Can I Do?
I want to add two-digit numbers.

Add the other way to check.

Check addition by adding in the other direction.

```
  26  ⤬  43        26  ⤬  ¹47
+ 43     + 26    + 47     + 26
  69       69      73       73
```

Try It . Circle *Regroup* or *No Regrouping*. Then add.

1.   55   Regroup
   + 34
             No Regrouping

2.   62   Regroup
   + 19
             No Regrouping

3.　28　　Regroup
　　　+17
　　　　　　　No Regrouping

4.　31　　Regroup
　　　+27
　　　　　　　No Regrouping

5.　24　　Regroup
　　　+48
　　　　　　　No Regrouping

6.　16　　Regroup
　　　+27
　　　　　　　No Regrouping

Power Practice • **Add. Check by adding in the other direction.**

7.　32
　　　+8

8.　40
　　　+22

9.　57
　　　+27

10.　33
　　　+29

11.　64
　　　+31

12.　65
　　　+6

13.　42
　　　+52

14.　35
　　　+45

15.　86
　　　+12

16.　14
　　　+68

17.　21
　　　+67

18.　47
　　　+39

19.　13
　　　+18

20.　53
　　　+8

21.　46
　　　+19

Subtract Two-Digit Numbers

Activity 45

Learn

Decide whether to regroup.

$$
\begin{array}{r} 55 \\ -33 \\ \hline \end{array} \qquad \begin{array}{r} 55 \\ -38 \\ \hline \end{array}
$$

Think: I can subtract 3 ones from 5 ones without regrouping.

I can't subtract 8 ones from 5 ones without regrouping.

No Regrouping

Regroup 1 ten 5 ones as 15 ones.

$$
\begin{array}{r} 55 \\ -33 \\ \hline 22 \end{array} \qquad \begin{array}{r} ^{4\ 15} \\ \cancel{55} \\ -38 \\ \hline 17 \end{array}
$$

What Can I Do?
I want to subtract two-digit numbers.

Add to check.

Check your subtraction by adding.

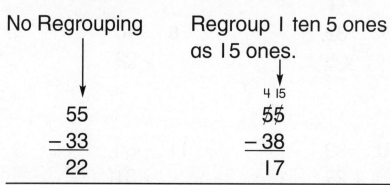

$$
\begin{array}{r} 55 \\ -33 \\ \hline 22 \end{array} \quad \begin{array}{r} 22 \\ +33 \\ \hline 55 \end{array} \qquad \begin{array}{r} 55 \\ -38 \\ \hline 17 \end{array} \quad \begin{array}{r} ^1 \\ 17 \\ +38 \\ \hline 55 \end{array}
$$

Try It . Circle *Regroup* or *No Regrouping*.
Then subtract.

1. $\begin{array}{r} 64 \\ -14 \\ \hline \end{array}$ Regroup

   No Regrouping

2. $\begin{array}{r} 47 \\ -19 \\ \hline \end{array}$ Regroup

   No Regrouping

3.　50
　　　−25

Regroup

No Regrouping

4.　42
　　　−31

Regroup

No Regrouping

5.　83
　　　−14

Regroup

No Regrouping

6.　37
　　　−29

Regroup

No Regrouping

Power Practice • Subtract. Check by adding.

7.　92
　　　− 6

8.　45
　　　− 32

9.　56
　　　− 17

10.　82
　　　− 48

11.　56
　　　− 21

12.　98
　　　− 57

13.　72
　　　− 58

14.　85
　　　− 29

15.　36
　　　− 18

16.　66
　　　− 65

17.　74
　　　− 26

18.　48
　　　− 29

19.　63
　　　− 35

20.　47
　　　− 28

21.　59
　　　− 21

Subtract Two-Digit Numbers

Learn

Decide whether to regroup.

$$\begin{array}{r} 66 \\ -44 \\ \hline \end{array} \qquad \begin{array}{r} 66 \\ -47 \\ \hline \end{array}$$

What Can I Do?
I want to subtract two-digit numbers.

Think: I can subtract 4 ones from 6 ones without regrouping.

I can't subtract 7 ones from 6 ones without regrouping.

No Regrouping

Regroup 1 ten 6 ones as 16 ones.

$$\begin{array}{r} 66 \\ -44 \\ \hline 22 \end{array}$$

$$\begin{array}{r} \overset{5\ 16}{\cancel{66}} \\ -47 \\ \hline 19 \end{array}$$

Add to check.

Check your subtraction by adding.

$$\begin{array}{r} 66 \\ -44 \\ \hline 22 \end{array} \quad \begin{array}{r} 22 \\ +44 \\ \hline 66 \end{array} \qquad \begin{array}{r} 66 \\ -47 \\ \hline 19 \end{array} \quad \begin{array}{r} 19 \\ +47 \\ \hline 66 \end{array}$$

Try It . **Circle *Regroup* or *No Regrouping*. Then subtract.**

1. $\begin{array}{r} 45 \\ -24 \\ \hline \end{array}$

   Regroup

   No Regrouping

2. $\begin{array}{r} 80 \\ -45 \\ \hline \end{array}$

   Regroup

   No Regrouping

3. $\begin{array}{r} 62 \\ -17 \\ \hline \end{array}$

   Regroup

   No Regrouping

Power Practice • Subtract.
Check by adding.

4. 22
    − 8

5. 83
    − 12

6. 76
    − 27

7. 43
    − 25

8. 94
    − 33

9. 67
    − 7

10. 32
     − 18

11. 65
     − 25

12. 46
     − 17

13. 94
     − 65

14. 54
     − 20

15. 58
     − 39

16. 23
     − 15

17. 67
     − 28

18. 55
     − 51

19. 86
     − 44

20. 57
     − 29

21. 34
     − 14

22. 62
     − 19

23. 74
     − 37

24. 49
     − 23

Place Value: Tens and Ones

Learn

What Can I Do?
I want to write numbers in tens and ones.

Use a place-value chart.

Write the number.

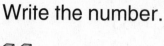 6 ones = _____

tens	ones
	6

6 ones is the same as 6.
So, 6 ones = 6.

 4 tens = _____

tens	ones
4	0

4 tens is the same as 40.
So, 4 tens = 40.

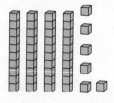 4 tens 6 ones = _____

tens	ones
4	6

Try It • Fill in each place-value chart.

Write the number.

1.

tens	ones

5 tens = _____

2.

tens	ones

3 tens 4 ones = _____

Write each number.

3. 3 tens = _____

4. 7 ones = _____

5. 7 tens 8 ones = _____

6. 4 tens 1 one = _____

Power Practice • Write each number.

7. 2 tens = _____

8. 1 ten 9 ones = _____

9. 8 tens = _____

10. 4 ones = _____

11. 1 ten 1 one = _____

12. 6 tens 5 ones = _____

13. 7 tens = _____

14. 2 tens 3 ones = _____

15. 5 ones = _____

16. 9 tens = _____

17. 8 tens 7 ones = _____

18. 4 tens 4 ones = _____

Tens and Ones

Learn

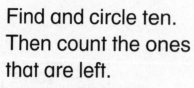

What Can I Do?
I want to write a two-digit number.

Circle ten.

Find and circle ten.
Then count the ones
that are left.

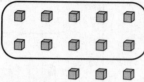

1 ten   3 ones
The number is 13.

Try It • Circle ten. Write each number.

1. _____

2. _____

Power Practice • Circle ten. Write each number.

3. _____

4. _____

5. _____

6. _____

Name_____

Greater Than, Less Than

Learn

Use a number line.

Numbers on the **right** are greater. →
← Numbers on the **left** are less.

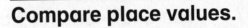

0 1 2 3 4 5 6 7 8 9 10 11 12 13 14 15 16 17 18 19 20

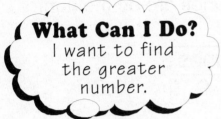

What Can I Do?
I want to find the greater number.

Think: 14 is to the left of 16.
So, 14 is less than 16.

Compare place values.

Look at the tens place. Which digit is greater?
If both are the same look at the ones place.
Which digit is greater?
6 is greater than 4.
So, 16 is greater than 14.

tens	ones
1	4
1	6

Try It • **Use the number line.**
Circle the *greater* number.

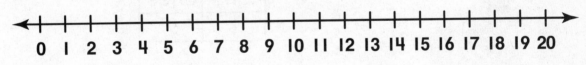

0 1 2 3 4 5 6 7 8 9 10 11 12 13 14 15 16 17 18 19 20

1. 12   2   **2.** 15   17

Power Practice • **Circle the number that is *greater*.**

3. 71   17   **4.** 12   21   **5.** 33   22

Circle the number that is *less*.

6. 68   67   **7.** 50   51   **8.** 39   40

Place-Value Chart

Learn

Use a place-value chart.

This place-value chart shows tens and ones.
Tens are on the left. Ones are on the right.

tens	ones
1	9

What Can I Do?
I want to write a number as tens and ones.

There is 1 ten and 9 ones in 19.

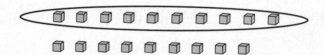

This shows 1 ten with 9 ones.

tens	ones
1	9

Try It • Write each number in a place-value chart.

1. 15

tens	ones

2. 17

tens	ones

3. 20

tens	ones

4. 12

tens	ones

Power Practice • Write each number.

5. _____
tens	ones
	6

6. _____
tens	ones
1	3

7. _____
tens	ones
1	1

8. _____
tens	ones
	2

9. _____
tens	ones
1	8

10. _____
tens	ones
1	6

11. _____
tens	ones
1	0

12. _____
tens	ones
1	4

13. _____
tens	ones
2	0

14. _____
tens	ones
1	2

15. _____
tens	ones
	9

16. _____
tens	ones
	5

Name_____

Place Value

Learn

What Can I Do?
I want to know the number of tens and ones in a number.

Use a place-value chart.

Write the number 34 in a place-value chart.

tens	ones
3	4

34 has 3 tens and 4 ones.

Understanding place value.

The ones digit is on the right. The tens digit is to the left of the ones digit.

The 4 tells how many **ones** are in 3<u>4</u>.
The 3 tells how many **tens** are in <u>3</u>4.

Try It • Write each number in a place-value chart.

1. 78

tens	ones

2. 39

tens	ones

3. 14

tens	ones

4. 60

tens	ones

• **Draw lines to match.**

5. 3 tens 8 ones   18

6. 8 tens 1 one   38

7. 1 ten 8 ones   81

Power Practice • Write each number in a place-value chart.

8. 15

tens	ones

9. 63

tens	ones

10. 75

tens	ones

11. 96

tens	ones

12. 53

tens	ones

13. 87

tens	ones

Power Practice • Write the number of tens and ones.

14. 82 _____ tens _____ ones

15. 47 _____ tens _____ ones

16. 24 _____ tens _____ ones

17. 90 _____ tens _____ ones

18. 55 _____ tens _____ ones

19. 78 _____ tens _____ ones

20. 29 _____ tens _____ ones

21. 44 _____ tens _____ ones

22. 11 _____ tens _____ ones

23. 57 _____ tens _____ ones

24. 72 _____ tens _____ ones

25. 40 _____ tens _____ ones

26. 93 _____ tens _____ ones

27. 68 _____ tens _____ ones

Name_____

Tens and Ones

Learn

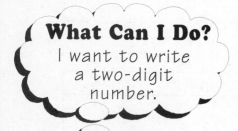

What Can I Do?
I want to write a two-digit number.

Think about place value.

Remember that tens are on the left.
Ones are on the right.

Think: 4 tens 5 ones = 45

tens	ones
4	5

Circle tens.

Circle groups of ten.
Count the number left over.
Then write the number using tens and ones.

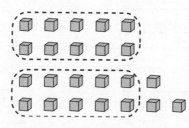

Think: 2 tens 3 ones = 23

Try It • Circle tens. Write the number.

1.

_____

2.

_____

3.

_____

4.

_____

80

© Macmillan/McGraw-Hill

Place Value

Learn

What Can I Do?
I want to know the number of tens and ones in a number.

Use a place-value chart.

Write the number 78 in a chart.

tens	ones
7	8

78 has 7 tens and 8 ones.

Use expanded notation.

78 = 70 + 8
    70 = 7 tens
     8 = 8 ones

78 = 7 tens 8 ones

Try It • **Write each number in a place-value chart.**

1. 45

tens	ones

2. 37

tens	ones

3. 23

tens	ones

4. 50

tens	ones

Power Practice • **Write the number of tens and ones.**

5. 61 _____ tens _____ one

6. 19 _____ ten _____ ones

7. 88 _____ tens _____ ones

8. 70 _____ tens _____ ones

9. 94 _____ tens _____ ones

10. 12 _____ ten _____ ones

Regrouping Ones

Learn

Use a place-value chart.

Count ones.

Write the number in a place-value chart.

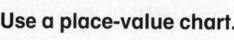

Tens are on the left.
Ones are on the right.
There are 1 ten and 5 ones in 15.

tens	ones
1	5

What Can I Do?
I need to regroup the ones as tens and ones.

Circle tens.

Circle tens. Count the ones left over.

This shows 2 tens with 3 ones left over.

Try It • **Count. Circle tens.**
Write each number in a chart.

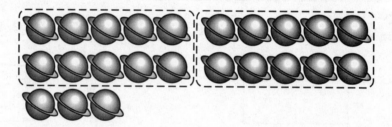

1. ____ ten ____ ones

2. ____ tens ____ ones

Name_____

Power Practice • Write each number two ways.

3. _____ ones
_____ ten _____ ones

4. _____ ones
_____ tens _____ ones

5. _____ ones
_____ tens _____ ones

6. _____ ones
_____ tens _____ ones

7. _____ ones
_____ tens _____ one

8. _____ ones
_____ ten _____ ones

9. _____ ones
_____ ten _____ ones

10. _____ ones
_____ tens _____ ones

Regrouping Tens and Ones

Learn

What Can I Do?
I want to regroup tens and ones as ones.

Use a place-value chart and pictures.

tens	ones
1	3

There are 1 ten and 3 ones in 13.

That is the same as 13 ones. Prove it by drawing a picture.

Think about money.

1 dime = 10 pennies

You can trade 1 dime for 10 pennies.

How many pennies would you get for 2 dimes? 3 dimes? 4 dimes?

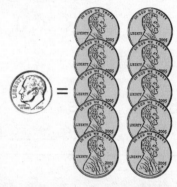

Try It • Read the place-value chart.
Write the number as ones.

tens	ones
1	5

1. _____ ones

tens	ones
2	6

2. _____ ones

tens	ones
3	3

3. _____ ones

Power Practice • Write each number two ways.

4. ____ ten ____ ones

____ ones

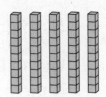

5. ____ tens ____ ones

____ ones

6. ____ tens ____ one

____ ones

7. ____ tens ____ ones

____ ones

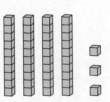

8. ____ tens ____ ones

____ ones

9. ____ tens ____ ones

____ ones

Numbers to 100

Learn

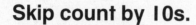

What Can I Do?
I want to write
numbers to 100.

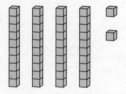

Skip count by 10s.

Count by tens.
Then count on by ones.

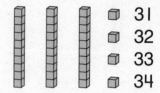

31
32
33
34

Count → 10, 20, 30,

Think about place value.

Remember that tens
are on the left.
Ones are on the right.

2 tens, 3 ones = 23

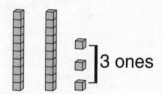

3 ones

2 tens

Try It • **Skip count by tens. Then count on by ones.
Write how many.**

1.

10, _____; _____, _____, _____, 24, _____

2.

10, _____, _____, _____; _____, _____

3.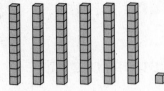

_____ , _____ , _____ , _____ , _____ , _____ ; _____

4.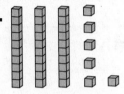

_____ , _____ , _____ ; _____ , _____ , _____ , _____ , _____ , _____

5.

_____ ; _____ , _____ , _____ , _____ , _____ , _____ , _____ , _____

Power Practice • **Write how many.**

6.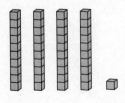

_____

7.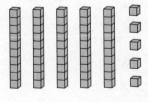

_____

8.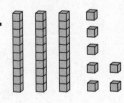

_____

9.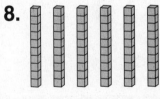

_____

10.

_____

11.

_____

Identifying Coins

Learn

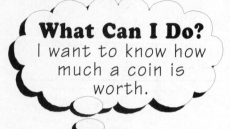

What Can I Do?
I want to know how much a coin is worth.

Memorize coin sizes and colors.

A penny is brown.
Nickels, dimes, and quarters are silver.

A dime is small. A quarter is big.
A nickel is bigger than a dime but smaller than a quarter.

Learn what coins are worth.

Read the numbers. They tell what the coin is worth.

penny	nickel	dime	quarter
1¢	5¢	10¢	25¢

Try It • **Match each coin to its name and amount. Draw lines to match.**

25¢

1.   nickel

5¢

2.   quarter

Power Practice • **Circle the correct coin.**

3. 1¢

4. 10¢

5. 5¢

Name_____

Writing Money Two Ways

Learn

What Can I Do?
I want to write money amounts with dollar signs or cents signs.

Read ¢ and $ symbols.

The symbol ¢ is read "cents." Read 32¢ as "thirty-two cents."

The symbol $ means "dollars." Read $1.32 as "one dollar and thirty-two cents."

Numbers **before** the decimal point are dollars. Numbers **after** the decimal point are cents. A decimal point separates dollars from cents.

dollars		dimes	pennies
$1	.	3	2

Try It • **Do the numbers show the same amount? Circle *yes* or *no*.**

1. $0.60   60¢   yes   no   2. $2.50   25¢   yes   no

3. $0.43   34¢   yes   no   4. $0.95   95¢   yes   no

Power Practice • **Circle the two that show the same amount.**

5. $1.24   24¢ $0.24   6. 68¢ $0.68 $6.80

7. 53¢ $5.53 $0.53   8. $0.35   35¢ $3.05

9. $1.66   66¢ $0.66   10. $99.00 $0.99   99¢

Name_____

Equal Amounts

Learn

What Can I Do?

I want to know which groups of coins are equal.

Compare coins.

A quarter is worth 2 dimes and 1 nickel.
A dime is worth 2 nickels.
A nickel is worth 5 pennies.

Skip count to find how much in all.

Start with one coin.
Skip count to find how much in all.

10¢, 20¢, 30¢   5¢, 10¢, 15¢

Try It • Skip count to find how much in all.
In each row, circle the two groups that show the same amount.

1.

1¢, _____   5¢, _____   _____

2.

5¢, 10¢, _____,_____   1¢, _____   _____,_____

Power Practice • Circle the two that show the same amount.

3.

4.

5.

6.

Time to the Hour

Learn

Look at the clock hands.

The long hand shows the **minutes**.
The short hand shows the **hours**.
The minute hand points to 12
at the start of each hour. As the minute
hand moves around the clock, the hour
hand moves to the next number.

What Can I Do?
I want to tell time
to the hour.

3:00   4:00

Read times two ways.

Write 8:00
Say 8 o'clock

Try It • **Write the time two ways.**

1.

____ : ____

____ o'clock

2.

____ : ____

____ o'clock

Power Practice • **Write the time.**

3.

_____

_____

4.
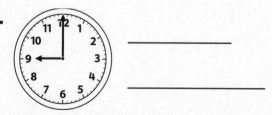

_____

_____

Time to the Half Hour

Learn

Divide the clock in half.

What Can I Do?
I want to tell time
to the half hour.

The minute hand points to 12
at the start of each hour.
It points to 6 at the half hour.
At the half hour, the hour hand
is halfway between two numbers.

 3:00

 3:30

Read times two ways.

Write 8:30
Say half past 8

Try It • **Write the time two ways.**

1. half past _____

_____ : _____

2. half past _____

_____ : _____

Power Practice • **Write the time.**

3.

_____ : _____

4.

_____ : _____

5.

_____ : _____

6.

_____ : _____

Time to 5 Minutes

Learn

What Can I Do?
I want to tell time to five minutes.

Count by fives to tell time to 5 minutes.

Count by fives to the minute hand.

5 minutes after 3:00
Write: 3:05
Say: three o'five

10 minutes after 3:00
Write: 3:10
Say: three ten

Try It • Start at 12. Count by fives. Draw lines to match.

1.

2.

3.

Power Practice • Write the time.

4.

___ : ___

5.

___ : ___

6.

___ : ___

Name_____

Calendar Clues

**Mr. Lee's class has student helpers. Read the clues.
Find out who is the helper.**

MARCH

Sunday	Monday	Tuesday	Wednesday	Thursday	Friday	Saturday
			1	2 Tina	3	4
5	6 Lucia	7	8 Karif	9	10	11
12	13	14	15	16	17 Miles	18
19	20 Brittany	21	22 Franco	23 Miranda	24	25
26	27	28 Betsy	29	30	31 Claire	

1. Who is the helper on the second Wednesday of the

   month? _____

2. Who is the helper the 28th?

   _____

3. Who is the helper in the third Friday of the month?

   _____

4. Who is the helper on the 8th of the month?

   _____

5. Who is the helper on the second day of the month?

   _____

6. How many Fridays are there? How many Sundays?

   _____   _____

Explore Length

Learn

Line things up.

Choose an object to measure.
Choose a tool to measure the object.
Line up the tool and the object at
the left side.

How many clips long is the pencil?
Line up the paper clips and count them.

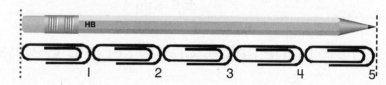

The pencil is about 5 clips long.

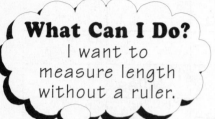

What Can I Do?
I want to
measure length
without a ruler.

Try It • **How long is each one?**

1.

_____ clips

2.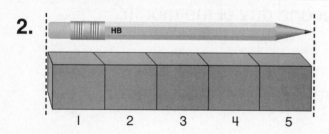

_____ cubes

3.

__ clips

4.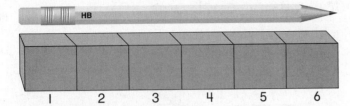

__ cubes

Power Practice • How long is each one?

5.

__ clips

6.

__ clips

7.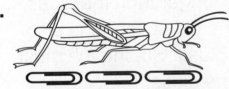

__ clips

8.

__ cubes

9.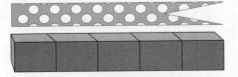

__ cubes

10.

__ cubes

Name_____

Explore Capacity

 Learn

Activity
65

Use your imagination.

Look at the pictures.
Imagine using each one.

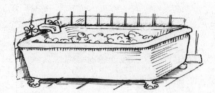

Think: When I take a bath, I use a lot of water. When I fill a glass, I use a little water. The bathtub holds *more* water than the glass.

What Can I Do?
I want to know which one holds more.

Compare other measurements.

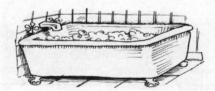

Think: The tub is longer than the glass. It is wider than the glass, too. It is also deeper than the glass. So, the tub must hold *more* than the glass.

Try It • **Circle the one that holds *more*.**

1.

2.

© Macmillan/McGraw-Hill

98

Name _____

3.

4.

Power Practice • Circle the one that holds *more.*

5.

6.

7.

8.

9.

Explore Weight

Learn

Use your imagination.

Look at the pictures.
Imagine lifting each one.

Think: It is easy to lift a feather. A feather is light. It is harder to lift a bag of rice. A bag of rice is *heavier* than a feather.

What Can I Do?
I want to know which one is heavier.

Picture a scale.

Think: A feather would barely move the balance. A bag of rice would move its side down. A bag of rice is *heavier* than a feather.

Try It • Circle the one that is *heavier.*

1.

2.

3.

4.

Power Practice • Circle the one that is *heavier.*

5.

6.

7.

8.

9.

10.

Name_____

Same Shape

Learn

Look for flat faces.

If the shapes are the same, the faces will be the same.

2 flat circles | 6 flat squares | 2 flat circles

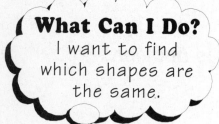

What Can I Do?
I want to find which shapes are the same.

Ask yourself questions.

Describe a shape by asking questions like these:

• Does it have a flat face?
• Does it have sharp edges?
• Can it roll?
• Can it stand up?
• If I turned it around, how would it look?
• If I stood it on end, how would it look?

Try It • Answer the questions.
Circle the same shapes.

1. Does it have flat faces? How many?				
2. Does it have corners?				
3. Can it roll?				

© Macmillan/McGraw-Hill

102

Power Practice • Circle the same shapes.

4.

5.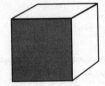

6.

7.

8.

Name_____

More About Same Shape

Learn

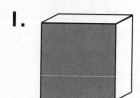

What Can I Do?
I want to know which shapes are part of a solid shape.

Trace a solid shape.

If you traced around this solid shape, what shape would you see?

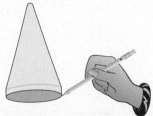

Ask yourself questions.

Describe the faces of a solid shape by asking questions:

- Does the solid shape have flat faces?
- What do the faces look like?
- How many sides are there?
- Are the sides the same length?

Try It • Find a block that looks like this. Trace around it. Circle the shape that you traced.

1.

2.

Name_____

Power Practice • Circle the same shape.

3.

4.

5.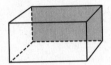

6.

7.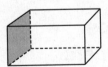

8.

9.

© Macmillan/McGraw-Hill

Sides and Corners

Learn

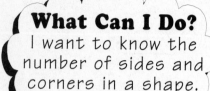

What Can I Do?
I want to know the number of sides and corners in a shape.

Trace and count.

Trace the **sides.** Count as you go.

sides →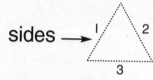

A triangle has 3 sides.

Make Xs and count.

A **corner** is the place where two sides meet. Make an X on each corner. Then count.

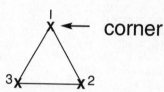

A triangle has 3 corners.

Try It • Trace. Write the number of sides.
Make Xs. Write the number of corners.

1.

_____ sides

_____ corners

2.

_____ sides

_____ corners

Power Practice • Write the number of sides.
Write the number of corners.

3.

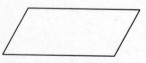

_____ sides

_____ corners

4.

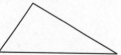

_____ sides

_____ corners

5.

_____ sides

_____ corners

Symmetry

Learn

What Can I Do?
I want to know if a line cuts a shape into equal parts.

Imagine folding the shape.

If you folded the shape on the line, would the two parts match?

This line cuts the tree into two equal parts.

Use a mirror.

Place a small mirror on the line.
Look at the shape.
Do the parts match?

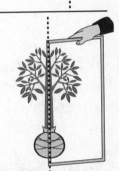

Try It

• Look a the fold line. Does it show equal parts? Circle *yes* or *no*.

1.

yes   no

2.

yes   no

Power Practice

• Circle the shape that shows equal parts.

3.

4.

5.

6.

7.

8.

Same Size and Same Shape

Learn

Imagine lining them up.

When you see two figures, imagine lining them up to face the same way.

Think:

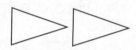

These are the **same size** and **same shape**.

___

Trace the figures.

Use tracing paper.
Trace one figure.
Place it on the other figure.
See if they are the same.

These are not the same size and same shape.

What Can I Do?

I want to find if two figures are the same size and shape.

___

Try It . **Use tracing paper. Trace the shapes.**
Circle the two that are the same size and same shape.

1.

2.

Power Practice • Circle the two that are the same size and same shape.

3.

4.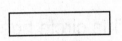

5.

6.

7.

8.

9.

10.

Name_____

Equal Parts

Learn

What Can I Do?
I want to know the number of equal parts.

Number and count.

Find a place to begin.
Count.
Number the parts.

This circle has 4 *equal* parts.

Make sure parts are equal.

This circle has 3 *equal* parts. →

The parts are the same size and same shape.

This circle has 3 parts that are *not* equal.

→

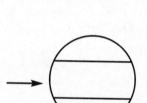

Try It • Count. Write the number of *equal* parts.

1.

_____ equal parts

2.

_____ equal parts

3.

_____ equal parts

4.

_____ equal parts

© Macmillan/McGraw-Hill

110

Name_____

Power Practice • Write the number of equal parts.

5.

_____ equal parts

6.
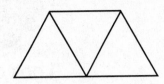
_____ equal parts

7.

_____ equal parts

8.

_____ equal parts

9.
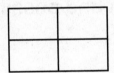
_____ equal parts

10.

_____ equal parts

11.

_____ equal parts

12.

_____ equal parts

13.

_____ equal parts

14.
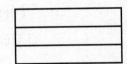
_____ equal parts

Certain, Possible, Impossible

Learn

Possible or impossible?

Look at these coins.
Is it possible to pick a quarter?
Is it possible to pick a nickel?

Think: There are no quarters.
So, picking a quarter is **impossible.** It could **not** happen.

There are also no nickels.
So, picking a nickel is **impossible** too.

Decide between certain and possible.

If you pick one coin, what could it be?

Think: All the coins are pennies.
So, picking a penny is **certain. It will** happen.

What Can I Do?
I want to know if something could happen or could not happen.

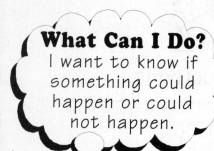

If you pick one coin, what could it be?

Think: Some coins are pennies. So picking a penny could happen.

Some coins are dimes. So picking a dime could happen.
Picking a penny and picking a dime are both **possible.** They could both happen.

Try It . **Could it happen? Answer the questions.**
Circle the correct choice or choices.

1. Look at these coins. Which pick is impossible?

2. Look at these coins. Which pick is certain?

Power Practice . **Could it happen? Circle** *certain,*
possible, **or** *impossible.*

3.  You pick a .   certain   possible   impossible

4.  You pick a .   certain   possible   impossible

5. 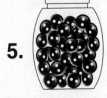 You pick a .   certain   possible   impossible